They Wrote the Boo

Thirteen Women Mystery Writers T

Also edited by Helen Windrath

The Women's Press Book of New Myth and Magic (1993)

Reader, I Murdered Him, Too: Crime Stories (1995)

Feast! Women Write About Food (1996) with Laurie Critchley

Something to Savour: Food for Thought from Women Writers (1996) with Laurie Critchley

The Female Odyssey: Visions for the 21st Century (1999) with Charlotte Cole

They Wrote the Book

Thirteen Women Mystery Writers Tell All

Helen Windrath, Editor

Spinsters Ink
Duluth, Minnesota, USA

First published by The Women's Press Ltd., 1999
A member of the Namara Group
34 Great Sutton Street, London EC1V 0LQ

32 E. First St., #330
Duluth, MN 55802-2002 USA

Cover photograph by Lola Troy Fiur, LTF Studios
Cover design by Sara Sinnard and Erin Scott, Sarin Creative

Production: Camila Aguilar, Liz Brissett, Helen Dooley, Joan Drury, Tracy Gilsvik, Marian Hunstiger, Claire Kirch, Kim Riordan, Amy Strasheim, Liz Tufte, Nancy Walker

Library of Congress Cataloging-in-Publication Data
They wrote the book : thirteen mystery writers tell all / Helen Windrath, editor.
p. cm.
ISBN 1-883523-35-4 (alk. paper)
1. Detective and mystery stories—Authorship. 2. Women and literature—Great Britain. 3. Women and literature—United States. I. Windrath, Helen.
PN3448.D4 T44 2000
808.3'872—dc21 00-024188

Printed in Canada

Printed on recycled paper

Contents

Introduction

As an aficionado of crime fiction, I have long been fascinated by the genre, voraciously reading each new mystery by my favourite authors as soon as it hits the book shops. And as a consequence I've often toyed with the idea of writing a novel myself, an idea I suspect that crosses the minds of many a crime fiction fan! So when the suggestion of editing a collection of essays on the subject of crime writing was put to me, I leapt at the chance. The Women's Press has a strong track record in publishing outstanding crime fiction by women, so a non-fiction book by leading writers in the genre seemed a natural and logical extension of that work. The book I had in mind was not a nuts-and-bolts writers' handbook. Rather, I was hoping for a more personal exploration of the issues the genre raises for writers through a discussion of different aspects of the craft. And I wanted to put together a book that would appeal not only to the would-be writer, but equally to the avid reader, keen for an insight into how their favourite writers work. So, I approached a number of authors, asking them if they would like to contribute a piece to the book, and was delighted by the response. They took up my brief with gusto!

In *They Wrote the Book* you will find advice and hints on everything from undertaking research to creating credible characters, from pace to plot, with plenty of insightful and helpful personal stories and anecdotes along the way. With a genre as tightly constructed as crime fiction, it is not always possible to separate the different strands, so there is, inevitably, some overlap between the pieces. But as the authors gathered here share what are sometimes quite different approaches to their work, they reveal, above all else, that there is no one "right way" to write crime fiction. There may be certain ground rules and conventions and ways of working that are often effective, but ultimately each writer has found her own path—what works best for her.

Women's crime writing deservedly has a huge and loyal following, given the tremendous impact these authors have had on the genre. I hope that *They Wrote the Book* will be a useful addition to the library of aspirant authors, helping them to find their own "path," as well as providing a fascinating picture of writers at work for all who read and admire the exciting and entertaining crime stories these women create.

Finally, I want to thank Laurie Critchley for her work in the early stages of this book, but most of all, I would like to express my appreciation of the contributors for their wonderful pieces, their support, and enthusiasm.

Helen Windrath

Penny Sumner

Beginning at the Beginning

Mary Wings and Barbara Wilson did it for me—*She Came Too Late, Murder in the Collective* (titles, in more than one sense, to die for). Although I can't honestly claim they were the first because in my teens I'd had brief, albeit passionate, flirtations with both Agatha Christie and Dorothy L. Sayers. During the last summer holiday following school, I lay on my home beach at Surfer's Paradise, Queensland, conscientiously working on my tan and succumbing to the charms of *Death on the Nile, Murder on the Orient Express, Gaudy Night* . . .

But after that last summer spent with Agatha and Dorothy, there was little opportunity to indulge in crime. Crime novels didn't feature on any of my undergraduate reading lists and, by the time I'd finished my first degree, and made my way to England to embark on a long postgraduate haul, I'd given up reading novels for pleasure. Eventually, however, I finished being a student and remembered that I'd started out with the intention of becoming a writer. Aged thirty, it was probably time to start.

A first novel is a first love affair, nothing will be this intense again. I'm back in Australia for three months after an absence of six years. I've cleared the table *(Rule One For Becoming a Writer: clear the table)* and shut the door *(Rule Two: shut the door)*. Two months ago I roughly planned *The Island* which, set in north Queensland, isn't so much a crime novel as a political thriller. Now I drop the first sheet of paper into the heavy Royal typewriter . . .

Before going on, however, I feel I should confess that the idea of becoming a writer wasn't originally mine at all; it came from my library teacher, Audrey Oldfield. One lunchtime she said, out of the blue, "Why don't you write a novel?" I couldn't stop my eyes from rolling. "Not for publication," she peered at the book she was shelving, "for the discipline. To show yourself you can begin at the beginning and end at the end."

At eleven years of age I thought this suggestion completely mad, but also rather wonderful. Now I know it to be one of the best pieces of advice a writer can have. *(Rule Three: begin at the beginning and end at the end.)* The week before I left for high school she reminded me about the novel idea, solemnly adding that if I was going to write there was something else I'd need to remember: to keep the seat of my pants on the seat of the chair. She was right about that as well *(Rule Four)*.

So here I am, twenty years later. Because the days are hot, the mornings are the best time to work so I get up at five and start with a cup of coffee. On one particular morning, I take the coffee and my notes and amble across to the beach. Sitting on the warm sand, I open the black ring binder and admire what I have so far. Every word has been painstakingly polished, every comma and full stop lovingly contemplated. I've read and reread each sentence aloud, adjusting the balance, the weight, the rhythm. With the result that, in three weeks, I have produced two paragraphs.

Two paragraphs.

This morning the enormity of this hits me. Because maybe what these two polished paragraphs mean is that I'm not going to be able to do it, begin at the beginning and end at the end. Maybe two paragraphs in three weeks means I'm not going to be able to write after all.

When I tell people about the two paragraphs, they usually assume I'm exaggerating. I'm not. I spent three weeks writing two, remarkably short paragraphs. Sitting there on the sand, I faced the fact that at this rate I would never finish anything, and that what I had to start thinking about, for the first draft at least, was quantity versus quality. Instead of weighing every word, I'd forge ahead. Five pages a day. Longhand. And if I had problems churning out the five pages, I'd write down whatever came into my head, anything so that my quota of pages was done.

Not only that, but I wouldn't revise. All I'd do was read the pages at night and scribble comments in red for the next draft: there'd be no redrafting till the end. And I would (wouldn't I?) get to the end.

I'm always amazed when someone tells me they once wrote a novel, then gave up altogether when it wasn't accepted. Sometimes they give up after the first rejection! *(Rule Five: learn how to survive rejection.)* At the same time you need to be aware that most first novels don't make it into print (it's claimed less than one percent do), and this is often because they're wildly over-ambitious, both in content and structure. *(Rule Six: keep it simple to start with.)*

I'm not exactly sure how long *The Island* took to write (I wish now I'd kept a diary). At a guess, it must have been around eighteen months, going through four to five drafts. I do know how long I kept sending it out to publishers because I forced myself to file, rather than bin, the rejections: somehow I managed to keep it out there for four long years, doing the rounds of about ten publishing houses. Some of the responses were kind: We really did think it was very attractive work. Unfortunately . . . Others had me weeping buckets. The one agent I contacted read my book then rang with some free advice: *Craft!* You must understand that a writer must have *craft!* (I have no idea why I didn't try more than one agent.)

So far my description of getting started has been fairly general, certainly not specific to crime writing. And in fact, I don't believe there's a world of difference between genre and non-genre writing. For me, the basics of a novel are: story (I like a strong one); viewpoint (first person or third? intimate or distant?); plot (under this heading, I'd include not only the shape you give to your story but also the hooks you put in to keep your reader reading); characterization and motivation (what the characters are like and why they do what they do); structure (the organization of the whole); and pace (which is largely a matter of how incidents are foregrounded or backgrounded, allowing you to speed up, or slow down, the action). All fiction writing involves these elements, genre or not. One problem with beginning your writing career with a genre novel—and you do need to be aware of this if you're starting out—is that many publishers seem to feel that once a writer chooses a genre they should then remain faithful for life. But as the barriers between genres, and between genre writing and non-genre writing, become increasingly blurred (and feminist crime is certainly partly responsible for this), perhaps more writers will be able to move easily between different forms.

Although most of my published work has been crime, the novel I'm currently working on isn't, and I think of myself as a writer, rather than a genre writer. Or, to be more specific, I think of myself as a feminist writer—and in fact it was feminism that led me to the detective novel. In Sally R. Munt's excellent study of feminism and crime writing, *Murder By the Book?* (Routledge, 1994), she observes that in the mid 1980s "a small smattering of feminist crime novels appeared, and began to proliferate into *the* feminist book to be reading." This sums it up for me. Works like Mary Wings' *She Came Too Late* and Barbara Wilson's *Sisters on the Road* were a revelation because here you had writing that was politically charged, wonderfully written, and great fun to read. It's undoubtedly true that the feminist interest in crime has much to do with righting injustice in an unjust world, but it's also true that in the first instance the pleasure offered by crime writing, for writers as well as readers, is that it's *exciting.*

Mary Wings and Barbara Wilson understood this perfectly. They also knew their genre and weren't too frightened to use it. They'd gone back to Raymond Chandler (which is where, stylistically, crime-as-we-know-it begins), liked a lot of what they'd seen, and then remoulded the *noir* tradition to their own feminist purposes.

The Island, I suddenly realized, was an attempt to write a genre novel, a political thriller, without my knowing anything about, or even being particularly interested in, that genre. *(Rule Seven: know your genre and become familiar with its conventions. Have you provided enough red herrings? Is your detective's life convincingly endangered? It's only when you know what the conventions are that you can successfully challenge them.)* I was, however, interested in crime and was now aware that there were a whole lot of feminist writers out there—Mary Wings and Barbara Wilson in the States, Val McDermid and Gillian Slovo in Britain—doing the most thrilling things with it.

My first publication was a short story in the anthology *Reader, I*

Murdered Him. A brief note on the *Guardian* Women's Page announced that the editors at The Women's Press would welcome contributions, so I dutifully cleared the desk and shut the door.

After "Caroline" was accepted (there's nothing like the discipline of a short story for improving one's craft, and a short crime story needs to be really disciplined), the time seemed right to embark on my second novel. These days I was reading as much crime as possible: past and present; American, English, Australian, French; feminist and non-feminist. *(Rule Eight: in order to write you MUST read.)* What I liked about American feminist crime was the energy and humour, the brilliance of the language, and the blatant appropriation of the *noir* tradition. On the British side, the writing was a good deal more realistic and far less violent, and I decided that what I wanted for my own work was a blend of the two. Thus Victoria Cross, my archivest-turned-sleuth (all my years of postgraduate research in the archives!) would be driven by curiosity rather than machismo and would break from the masculine tradition of the solitary, family-less sleuth in that she was a lesbian who would have a long-term partner and be involved in raising a child.

After carefully selecting an A4 notebook, I spent happy evenings jotting down ideas for Victoria's character: her family history, the books she reads, her crazy dress sense, her feelings about her lover, her friends. And carefully outlining my plot (a good plot is crucial for a crime novel; if you have trouble with this, a useful place to start is Syd Field's *Screenplay: The Foundations of Screenwriting,* Dell, 1994). Then I cleared my desk, shut the door, positioned myself firmly on the seat. And promptly panicked. It was almost a year since I'd finished *The Island,* and I couldn't recall how I'd written something that long. How had I started at the beginning and somehow ended two hundred pages later? I tried a first page but on rereading it that night, it was so rough, so unpolished. What, I agonized, if I couldn't do it, write a second novel?

It felt like starting out all over again, but *The End of April* gradually took shape. I was uncomfortably aware that I had very little idea of what real private detectives do, so I attempted to make up for this by putting in lots of local colour (Oxford was the city I knew best in England). I'd been told that publishers are keen on an ongoing character, so I designed this novel to be the first in a series and, as Victoria's relationship was to be long-term, emphasized the romance almost as much as the crime. You can understand why publishers might want you to commit to a series: readers often like to follow a character's adventures, and it enables the publisher to create a clear profile for both the sleuth and the author. But I'm not so sure that a series is always a good thing for a writer at the very beginning of her career, at a time when she probably feels the urge to experiment. You need to think about this—do you really want to go much further with the character you've created in your first novel? If you do, that's fine. But if not, you might well find yourself able to produce novel number two, but baulking at the prospect of the third. *(Rule Nine: there's not much joy in trying to write a novel you don't want to write.)*

When I'd finished *The Island,* I'd thrust it on half a dozen friends to read, and they'd all declared they loved it. How could I expect them to say anything else? When I finished *The End of April,* I gave it to just two people, both of whom were writers with an interest in the genre. Their suggetions were enormously *helpful (Rule Ten: listen to good advice),* and when I sent this manuscript off, I felt confident it would be taken.

The first rejection was short and sharp:

> We've now had a chance to consider *The End of April* and I'm afraid we don't feel able to make an offer for it. Allow me to give you a piece of advice: you shouldn't mix genres, i.e. crime and romance.

I was up enough on crime to know this piece of advice was wrong *(Rule Eleven: learn to tell the difference between good advice and bad)*, but that didn't make me any happier. In fact, this rejection hit harder than any of those I'd received for *The Island.* On the verge of a migraine, I dosed myself with a couple of stong gin and tonics, and woke up the next morning with a nervous tic under my right eye.

What was required, I told myself as I watched my dancing eye in the bathroom mirror, was an agent—now! Okay, the agent who'd read *The Island* was somewhat daunting, but what the hey. She *had* said she'd be willing to read my next book. I made a cup of tea, prepared a little speech on how hard I'd worked on improving my *craft,* and phoned the agency. Only to be informed she'd retired, leaving strict instructions that she never wanted to be sent a manuscript again.

Despair slid into desperation. Racing to the bookshelves, I grabbed the nearest novel. Then I went to my desk, threw a copy of *The End of April* into an envelope, and scrawled the address of the publisher. Half an hour later, my book was in the post again. *(Rule Twelve: try to get yourself an agent. If you aren't successful, do some sensible research on publishers before you send your manuscript anywhere. And do remember that most publishers, and agents, don't want to see your whole manuscript at first. What they usually want is a gripping synopsis accompanied by a couple of sample chapters. And, of course, an SASE for return . . .)*

The publishing company I'd chosen didn't even have a crime list, and I was soon disappointed, although a generous editor had somehow found time to look at the manuscript and scribble some words of encouragement:

> I enjoy reading detective novels and think that yours will quickly find a home on another publisher's list. I thought it was well-written and well-structured and that you played fair with the reader . . .

She suggested the name of another publisher, one with a crime list, and I sent yet another photocopy of my poor book off again.

As far as "how-I-got-published" stories go, mine certainly isn't the worst I've heard: in fact, I suspect it's pretty much par for the course. Not that that makes the experience any less depressing. We've got to the point, however, where my luck should change. This is the bit where, if there's any justice, the phone rings, and a husky voice gasps, "I've just read your novel. In fact I was up all night and couldn't put it down! I'm just hoping to God that someone else hasn't already snapped you up . . ." And, for a moment, this seems to be the direction of the script; one afternoon I get a message saying an editor's been trying to ring me, and it's urgent. She'll try me at home later tonight. So this is it, I tell myself, I'm going to get published after all. I'm calmer than I would have expected.

The call comes at six, a tired voice asking if this is Penny Sumner. Yes, I gulp, this is she. And I sent a manuscript to be read some weeks back? Uh-huh, that's right. (How come she's asking? She knows I sent a manuscript! After all, she's ringing to tell me she's gong to publish it, isn't she?)

Okay, so we know she isn't. But at the time, I couldn't think of why else she'd be on the phone. It certainly didn't cross my mind she might be calling to say there'd been a slip-up at the office . . .

You see, she's saying, the person who was responsible for sending manuscripts to readers walked out last week, and now no one's sure what was sent where. "You've bloody well *lost* my book?" is what I want to yell, but instead I just continue with the gulping noises. She wearily explains that unsolicited manuscripts are not usually considered at all, but mine will be passed on to a reader if I send another copy. "Oh thank you," I gulp: if it sounds like I'm drowning it's because I am. "I'm very, very grateful."

She assures me there's no need to be, and she's right. A week later *The End of April* has found its way back home. "I'm sorry," the note escorting it is apologetic, "but I hadn't realized your book was a crime novel. Unfortunately, we recently had to make the decision to end our crime list . . ." Enough was enough: the tic had turned into a definite squint; there were grey hairs in my fringe; I was avoiding friends and colleagues in case they asked for news. I addressed a brown jiffy bag to an American feminist publishing house and, as it was the end of term, scraped together the money for a ticket home. The time had come to sit on the beach and rethink my life. Because I was beginning to suspect that the whole novel-writing thing mightn't have been such a great idea in the first place.

Maybe I did decide not to go on, I can't remember now. All I know is that the day after I got back to Britain, the telephone rang, and this time an American woman with a wonderful Southern accent was saying she liked my book. (That's nice, I found myself thinking, now let's get to the problem.) The problem was that the manuscript was way too long for a first novel, about one hundred pages too long, in fact. (Too long? One hundred pages? Jesus!) Which was a pity, I half-heard her sigh, because if it weren't for the length she would just love to publish it. Anyway, she thought she'd ring to let me know how much she'd enjoyed reading it.

"I'll cut it."

She sounded surprised. I'd be willing to cut it that much?

No problem, managing to keep my voice steady. (One hundred pages! How can I cut one hundred pages?) It'll be no problem at all.

Funnily enough, it isn't. Sitting at a computer in a house in South London—which is where I'm spending my maternity leave—I pull out the subplot like fish on a line. It's a strangely satisfying experience this, my body ballooning outwards as my novel gets thinner. However, we're working to a tight deadline and, as it turns out, my son and the American edition of the novel appear in the same week.

Which should have been a double blessing, but he's a month early and, after a forceps delivery, spends his first week in Special Care, tube-fed, pumped full of antibiotics, and subjected to x-rays and brain scans. As he cries in pain, high-pitched wails, a midwife looks up and smiles in sympathy, "He sounds like a wee bird."

I sit watching this small, shivering bird and never give the novel a thought.

The Women's Press brought out the British edition of *The End of April*, and there was also a German translation. So, suddenly there I was, published and with a contract for the second in the series. However, my life was different now in other ways as well, and where my first two novels were written in the evenings and weekends, in trains, cafés and pubs, I needed a sabbatical before I could start work on *Crosswords*. For the third time I cleared a space, shut the door (my son, who was absolutely fine by the end of that first week, was happy with his childminder), and switched on the computer.

The beginning of *The End of April* was, I felt in retrospect, far too slow (an insightful reviewer had felt the same) so in this new novel I intended to speed things up (I'm not convinced I was successful in this attempt). I also wanted to stress the crime element rather than the romance; the problem being, however, that I still had virtually no idea of what real private detectives actually do. Luckily a friend mentioned she knew an Australian enquiry agent, living and working in London. She was completely wonderful, with the most amazing true-crime stories, and generously offered advice for this next book.

My aim was to make the novel as realistic as possible, and as Victoria searched London and Brighton for a missing person, armed only with addresses and telephone numbers from twenty-five years ago, I researched from Newcastle upon Tyne by phone—ringing public libraries, the Forensic Science Society (based in York and enormously helpful), the Telecom Museum, Telephone House, St. Catherine's House (for births, deaths, and marriages), tourist information offices. Everywhere and everyone in order to ensure the details were reasonably accurate. Victoria finally tracks the person she's after to the Brompton Oratory, so on a day trip to London I detoured and wandered the aisles with a notebook *(coloured marble, statuary, overhead the ceilings are aglow with gold stars in an azure heaven . . .)* For the rest, I made do with a *London A–Z* and guide books. Calling the Catholic cathedral in Newcastle, I quizzed the Irish duty priest on nuns "for a novel I'm writing."

Sitting in front of the computer solidly for eight hours a day, five days a week, was very different from the earlier experiences, and I didn't think I could, or should, do this for long. Awash with coffee and tea, I developed writer's bladder, convinced the twinge in my back was kidney disease. When my head throbbed from staring at the screen, I worried I had a brain tumour. Large quantities of chocolate were vitally important in getting me through each day, and on my next visit the dentist was suitably aghast. "What on earth have you been doing?" Poking something thin and sharp into two new cavities.

What had I been doing? Well, I'd cleared the table, shut the door, begun at the beginning ...

Val McDermid

Sugar and Spice and All Things Nice . . .
Character Creation and Development

Occasionally, I tutor a workshop on the creation and development of character. In fiction, that is, as opposed to in life. I make a series of points, set a couple of exercises, lead the discussion, and hope that everyone has taken something constructive away from the session. When the group works well, I often think I'm the one who benefits most, gaining valuable insight into the way I do my own work. Sometimes, however, it just leaves me more baffled than before. "How," someone asked recently, "do you know when you know something about a character?"

It was a question that provoked some serious consideration

beyond my initial and probably unhelpful response of "Well, you just do." Although we discussed it in the workshop, I found myself pondering the question for some time afterwards. After all, I have two flourishing crime series, each of which features a very individual heroine. The fact that both are successful in their role as detective implies some common ground in their personalities, yet to me they are as distinct as each of my cats from the other. What was it that allowed me to understand what makes each of them tick?

I suspect that most crime writers with successful series characters would agree that those protagonists fall into one of two broad categories—the alter ego or the imaginary friend. I know which is true of my central characters, and each of the women had a very different genesis.

When I created Lindsay Gordon, my first detective, my confidence as a writer was at its lowest ebb. After some early success with radio and stage plays, I had run into the buffers, probably because, not understanding what I had done right, I wasn't able to replicate it. As the rejection slips piled higher, my self-esteem sank lower. But I still had the burning desire to write, so I decided to go back to my first love, prose. And, on the principle of writing what you know, I decided to try a murder mystery.

I'd always read a lot of crime fiction, and I understood the bare bones of construction that underpinned the form—a corpse, a detective, a selection of suspects (or none at all), and some form of resolution at the end. With that instinctive knowledge, I felt a small surge of confidence that I might be able to make a mystery novel work. But I needed something more. To free up my creative instincts so they could be directed at the crucial areas of plot and subsidiary characters, I needed a central character that I knew like the back of my hand.

I'd been a national newspaper reporter for a few years by then, and I knew all the details of the journalistic life. I'd also done some investigative journalism, and I knew techniques from that could be transferred to investigate crime. I felt this could be useful because, to my mind, there's too much of a credibility gap if an amateur sleuth has no formal connection to the world of professional curiosity. So I made Lindsay a journalist, albeit a freelance where I was on staff. I was a Scot living in exile in England, so although I based her in Glasgow, I transplanted her for her first adventure to Derbyshire, where I lived then. And because I'm a lesbian, that's how Lindsay ended up, too. With all those common factors between us, I didn't have to think too hard about the external elements of her life, and I was free to concentrate on creating her emotional and psychological characterisitics as I went along.

I spent years with Lindsay Gordon before a single line ever appeared on the page. She was always Lindsay, but she went through a variety of surnames until I settled on the one that felt right. Over the years, I tested all sorts of possible past lives for her, imagining her history, her background, the forces that shaped her growing up gay in a small fishing village on the west coast of Scotland, and getting to know her tastes and foibles. By the time I started writing *Report For Murder,* she was like the sister I never had. Stubborn, impatient, headstrong, intelligent, loyal, fierce, funny, and sometimes flashy, with an odd mix of cynicism and idealism, she had all the appropriate qualities for my tenacious amateur sleuth. And I knew her like I knew myself, so close I never had to think twice about her actions or reactions in any given circumstance. When a zealous copy editor suggested a 2CV or a Renault 4 might be a more politically correct means of transport than Lindsay's classic MGB roadster (with chrome bumpers, of course), I knew she'd failed a crucial comprehension test!

Incidentally, although no one else was writing lesbian crime novels in Britain at that time, it never occurred to me not to make Lindsay gay. I didn't have a crusading mission either to provide dykes with role models or to proselytize the straight masses; I just wanted to write about a world I understood. In a way, coming first made it easier for me since I had no expectations to confound or live up to. The only decision I remember arising from this trail-blazing aspect to *Report For Murder* was my resolution never to describe Lindsay physically. I wanted anyone who read the text to be able to have their own fantasy Lindsay—lover, friend, alter ego, whatever—and I didn't want an image I'd imposed to stand in the way of that. She had to have distinct personality traits, but in looks she could be Everydyke, and that was a choice I made deliberately because of the paucity of fantasy figures in the popular media in the mid-1980s.

Happy though I was with Lindsay as a basic creation, I knew that wasn't enough to satisfy the expectations of contemporary series readers. In the classic age of crime fiction, series characters were frozen in aspic. It doesn't matter in which order one reads the Miss Marple novels; Jane Marple herself changes infinitesimally, if at all. Her exposure to sudden death, deceit, and corruption has no impact on her. That many in her immediate circle end up as corpses, suspects, or key witnesses never gives her pause. She never thinks to ask herself why it is that this should be the case, nor do these events alter the way she looks at herself or her world. I think a writer can no longer get away with this. As a reader, I expect development in a character who occupies centre stage in a series of books. As a writer, it's part of my job to make the reader care enough about that person to await eagerly the next installment of her life.

So I had to consider the effects that whatever happened to Lindsay would have on the woman she became. And some of the events in her life have turned out to be ordeals, serious tests that have stretched love, loyalty, and discretion to the limits. But because I spent a long time getting to know Lindsay, getting close to her and absorbing her under my own skin, I have seldom had to think twice about the practical effect of these external events on her inner life and her personality.

After three Lindsay Gordon books, however, I knew I needed a change. I'm a Gemini; I have a short attention span and if all I wrote was one series featuring a single recurring character and her support nexus, I'd go mad with boredom. So I sent Lindsay off to live in California. A sense of place is important to me when I write, and I knew I wasn't familiar enough with Californian culture or geography to set a novel there. Therefore, it seemed as good a way as any to remove the temptation of sneaking back to the safe familiarity of Lindsay and her world because, just as my friends are a diverse bunch who often have next to nothing in common, so must be the denizens of my imagination. For the sake of my sanity, I had to do something that would be a contrast, a challenge, that would stimulate me to achieve every committed writer's goal—to produce stronger, better work with each book. So, having written three lesbian feminist mystery novels that, in spite of their radical surface, are actually deeply rooted in the classic English "cosy" tradition, I decided to attempt one of the other sub-genres and have a go at the American hard-boiled private eye novel. Thus was Kate Brannigan born to stalk the mean streets of Manchester, a city where I had worked for a dozen years and had grown to love as much as Lindsay's stamping grounds in Glasgow.

There are distinct differences in writing an amateur and a professional sleuth. One is the credibility issue. It seems to me that there are only so many corpses the amateur sleuth can trip over without the reader beginning to say, "Oh puh-leeze, not another body . . ." It also means that the only real starting point for the book is a murder. Right from the word go, every character apart from Lindsay and her current lover are potential suspects because we know they're going to be tied up in an unnatural death. With a professional investigator, whether a police officer or a private eye, other sorts of crime are continuously under investigation. With Brannigan, there is a low body count and often the murder victims don't get dead until two-thirds of the way through the book. But along the way she's investigated such diverse things as counterfeit watches, child pornography, credit fraud, art theft, medical experimentation and the underbelly of the rock music industry. I live in hope that as they progress through the book, my readers never know quite how any one character will fit in by the end.

I doubt I could have written Brannigan successfully without the knowledge I gained from writing Lindsay, because I suspect the expertise involved in creating a central character so distanced from my own experience only came with practice. I knew when I started that Brannigan was going to be straight, since if I was ever going to make a living from writing, I was going to have to break into the mainstream. I also knew that breaking out with Brannigan was a way of giving Lindsay Gordon a wider audience because of the way crime fiction readers read—whenever they encounter a writer they enjoy, they immediately rush out and grab everything else that person has ever written, regardless of whether it's the kind of mystery they normally buy. Now that Brannigan has raised my profile, people who would never have considered buying a lesbian thriller have become avid fans of Lindsay. I know—men and women send me e-mail from all over the world to tell me so.

Apart from her gender and her sexual orientation, Brannigan was a blank canvas. It was like sending a lonely hearts ad into the ether of my imagination. "Writer seeks Manchester-based woman private eye. Must have a brain and a sense of humour." What I ended up doing was inventing an imaginary best friend, as small children do. It wasn't that I wanted Brannigan to eat my spinach and demand more chocolate by proxy. Rather, I needed her to be someone who could do all the things I can't do but who wasn't superwoman. I had to like her enough to want to spend six months a year for the foreseeable future in her company, but I didn't want her to be some Goody Two Shoes who gave me an inferiority complex every time I switched on the computer.

So, I went walking on the moors above my house (the place where many of my "getting to know you" sessions take place) and considered my real best friends. What was it about them that I liked and respected? Which of their weaknesses drove me crazy and which could I put up with without too much clenching of the jaw muscles? What had made them the people they were? Gradually, a woman started to take shape at the edge of my mind. Interestingly, and unlike Lindsay, right from the start I had a very clear physical image of Brannigan.

Eventually, the matching personality emerged with great clarity. A woman with whom I could spend hours on the phone, go shopping, gossip about lovers over a pizza, swap CDs and books, exchange off-the-wall e-mail. Imaginative, tenacious, smart-mouthed, bossy, brave, adaptable, technophile, devious and manipulative professionally but scrupulously honest personally, a believer in the value of friendship, a passionate advocate of justice rather than law. She is also someone who is very good at what she does. I was fed up with woman detectives who spent more time worrying about the utility bills than they did about their cases. I thought it was about time we had a feminist tradition of success.

As I had done with Lindsay, I spent a long time getting to know the character before I committed myself to words on the page. What her family background was like (working class, only child, grew up in the shadow of the car plant at Cowley), when she lost her virginity (aged 15, with her worst enemy's boyfriend, for two reasons—revenge and also so she didn't have to admit to her 20-year-old boyfriend that she wasn't a sexually experienced 18-year-old), what she drinks (vodka and grapefruit juice, preferably Stolichnaya and freshly squeezed pink), what she drives (nondescript small hatchbacks with engines that could blow off Michael Schumacher), where she lives (in the inner city in a small enclave of private housing, next door to the man she loves, their two bungalows connected by a conservatory that runs along the back because Brannigan knows that although she loves him, to share a home would cause more arguments than their relationship could survive). Some of these decisions were deliberate and had a purpose, others seemed to flow organically from my concept of the character. And, like Lindsay, Brannigan has grown and developed as a result of the things I've put her through.

Although the two women are quite distinct in my mind, there are obviously some elements of their characters that link them. They're both feminist, both lean to the left politically. They're both hard to discourage once they've got the bit between their teeth. They're both loyal to friends and lovers and probably the greatest crime to each of them is betrayal. But the strongest common link to my mind is that they share a sense of humour. That's the one thing it's impossible for any author to invent—you're always stuck with whatever it is that tickles your personal funny bone.

With central characters firmly in place, I work on the plot. Writers tend to fall into two camps—those who outline and those who fly by the seat of their pants. From what I can gather from fellow crime writers, I'm atypical, in that I'm right out there at the extreme end of the outliners. I spend years thinking about a book before I'm ready to write it, and before I write the first sentence, I hone the outline until I have a very clear idea of exactly where each chapter starts and finishes and how it gets there.

Hand in hand with that long process of working out exactly what the story is, goes the evolution of the characters who people that story. It's a cliché that if the characters don't work, the novel won't, but it didn't get to be that way by accident. Developing the rest of the team who are going into battle for or against my protagonists is a form of psychoanalysis, and it operates in a kind of biofeedback with the plot. The plot tells me what the characters need to be doing; the characters tell me the stories that made them the sort of people who might do these things.

At this stage, I never commit anything to paper. As I'm wandering around the garden or the moors, I have conversations with my characters. All my neighbours think I'm barking, but it works for me. Gradually, I get to know their past histories, their dislikes. Most of this material is ultimately irrelevant, but then, so is most of what our friends tell us over the years.

Inevitably, this brings me back to the question I started with: How do you know when you know something about a character? I suppose one answer is that "It has the ring of truth." That clear, bell-like tone comes when the picture inside the head or the words on the page chime perfectly with what we know of real people—our friends, lovers, family, workmates, neighbours. We are all observers, all reporters, all drawers of conclusions about the people we encounter in our daily lives, and they are the raw material of our fictions.

That raw material becomes transformed in the crucible of imagination into a finished creation that will be as unrecognizable to the people it is based on as baby pictures are to anyone but mothers. Freda's mannerisms are welded to Josy's speech patterns then bolted on to Jackie's attitude to make an emotionally fractured teacher, just like chromosomes in the genetic soup. Just as brothers and sisters who emerge from the same building blocks are widely different, so the character amalgams we create become discrete individuals with their own idiosyncrasies and behaviour patterns.

If there is a rule about writing it is that there are no rules. But at the back of my mind, I keep a handful of yardsticks to measure my imaginary people against. Are their motivations clear? Are their reactions consistent? Are they acting out of character, and is there a purpose in that? What is it about them that readers will relate to? Do I like them or dislike them and is that the reaction I want the reader to have? Is this person too "good;" does she/he need a few more human failings? Of course, it's easier in the early stages to apply these yardsticks to an alter-ego character like Lindsay, but few of my characters ever fall anywhere near that category, so I have had to learn to measure every significant figure in my stories to the same rigorous tests.

Once the head work is done, it's time for the practical, technical details of transferring what's in my head to the page. How do I actually reveal character to the reader? I reckon there are five basic ways to do this, and any competent writer will use all of them in varying proportions throughout their work. The first is straight description—what someone is wearing, what they look like, what they are doing. Simple and unadorned, this is often the laziest and the dullest way to introduce the reader to someone we want them to care about. But peppered with sharp observation in the hands of someone like Sara Paretsky or Raymond Chandler, it can be a wonderfully revealing tool, slicing away the superficial to reveal the deeper elements of personality. This is something that works particularly well in first-person narrative. For example, it's easy for Brannigan to be straightforwardly opinionated about a person's appearance and speech mannerisms because she's in direct communication with the reader. With Lindsay, I have to find more oblique ways to convey the same messages, so other techniques work better.

Secondly, actions speak louder than words. By showing how the person behaves and what they physically do, it's possible to illuminate their character. Do they move decisively or hesitantly? Are they slow or swift to act? Are their actions those of a foolhardy drunk or a cautious anal retentive? We constantly judge people on the most superficial actions; writers can use this to convey subtle conclusions to readers. We are never in any doubt about how we are supposed to view the hero of a Dick Francis action novel; on a different scale, we can apply those techniques to our own characters to carve out a niche for them in the reader's mind.

Thirdly, reactions to events and other individuals are often telling elements in our make-up. Is this a person who flares up when insulted or does she or he back off? Is this a person who rushes towards a road traffic accident to help, or who calls the emergency services, or who simply melts back into the night? This is often where I discover I haven't done quite as much work on a character as I think I have. In the early days of writing Brannigan, I often had to stop and think carefully about her responses, particularly because I needed to be clear that I wasn't confusing what I thought she would do with what I knew Lindsay would do. Now, six books later, Brannigan is as clear in reaction as she is in speech.

Fourthly, the reactions of others are a mirror of personality. Imagine walking into a room where we know all but one of the people present and consider how long it would take us to gain some understanding of the kind of person the stranger is simply by observing how those we know behave towards her or him. It's the same on the printed page. The reactions, particularly of our protagonist, towards other characters are often the fastest way to acquire some insight into the kind of person we're dealing with.

Finally, if the eyes are the windows of the soul, the mouth is the front door. Dialogue is one of the most powerful demonstrations of character available to the writer. Good dialogue crackles off the page not just because it resembles reality but because it's probably the quickest route to understanding what makes another person tick. Speech rhythms, vocabulary, delivery, articulacy, and coherence are all indicators of the person lurking beneath the surface. One of the things that differentiates Lindsay and Brannigan very clearly for me is that Lindsay's speech is Scottish and Brannigan's is standard English altered by a dozen years of living in Manchester. That difference lies in far more than dialect words or regional expressions—the rhythms of their speech are also quite dissimilar, and I hear those distinctions as I write their dialogue. I literally cannot read Brannigan in my natural Scottish accent any more than I can utter Lindsay's lines in my adopted northern English.

Armed with these basic techniques, which can be blended and mixed to produce a dozen more subtle ways of exploring and revealing the warts and all of any of our characters, we try to convince you, the reader, that these people have an independent life of their own, a life that goes beyond the rich fantasies that occupy a disturbingly large number of our brain cells. I know it works, because people ask me eagerly what's going to happen to Lindsay, to Brannigan, and to half a dozen other regulars in my fiction.

I wish I knew the answers.

Gillian Linscott

Hunting the Galosh

The Business of Research

Around one o'clock, lunchtime, on Wednesday 19 February 1913, a twelve-year-old girl named Cissie Savage, schoolmaster's daughter, walked through a field next to a golf course in Surrey and picked up a galosh. People born in the 1950s or later may never have seen galoshes—the rubber overshoes which the prudent wore to preserve their shoes in rainy weather. I can just remember, from childhood, an old pair kept in our scullery on the bottom shelf of the vegetable rack, so at least I knew what they looked and smelt like. That memory was another small bridge between me and my suffragette detective character, Nell Bray.

I've been writing about Nell for eight books now, from 1909 when she's just out of Holloway for throwing half a brick through the window of 10 Downing Street, to early 1919. In the book I was researching, she was about to make a fictional attempt to head off a real suffragette bombing. If you were a suffragette setting out on a damp February night to put a fire-bomb in a house belonging to the Chancellor of the Exchequer, naturally you'd want to protect your footwear. Which is why one particular galosh found its way into the Surrey Constabulary official records, Dorking Division, February 1913, reported on lined paper in the painstaking handwriting of a police officer none too confident of his own literacy. (He got the date wrong and misspelled the name of one of his own senior officers.) But then the policeman taking down the account of young Cissie was probably severely rattled because he was investigating an event unprecedented in his quiet rural career. The suffragettes' bomb had caused considerable damage to a new and unoccupied house, built as a gift to David Lloyd George next to his favourite golf course at Walton Heath by one of his rich newspaper-owning friends. The galosh in question had almost certainly been shed by one of the bombers making her getaway after planting a seven-pound tin of black gunpowder.

> The tin had been bound round with cord and had a fuse attached composed of a strip of rag inserted in the opening at the top of the tin, with the other end of the rag in a round baking tin in which was a candle in a candle stick and around the candle was shavings saturated with paraffin and also some small percussion caps. (Letter from Superintendent Henry Coleman, to the Chief Constable of Surrey, 19 February 1913.)

I didn't know about the police records when I stood outside Tadworth railway station, Surrey, on 19 February, exactly 83 years after the bomb was planted. All I knew then was the short account of the bombing I'd read in Roger Fulford's history, *Votes For Women,* making the mental note that Nell Bray would probably be in there somewhere. I was at Tadworth station because in 1913, as now, it was the nearest to Walton Heath golf course. Being there on the exact anniversary had seemed important, in the way you do get obsessive about particular details while researching, because I wanted to get the light right. If Nell had arrived there at 5:30 p.m., say, would it be light, dark, or half light? The scribble in my diary says: *5:30 p.m., still mostly light but getting dusk. Lights coming on 5:45 dusk.* Another of my notes made at the time reads: *Tadworth is small. Even now a stranger feels a bit conspicuous. Couldn't linger long by station without attracting attention.* Nell would have to walk across country to the golf course. What sort of country? Heath, copses of birch and bramble. Not easy walking in the dark. I was breaking one of my own rules by then and looking out at it from a taxi. Usually where Nell walks I walk, including, for another book, most of the way up Mont Blanc. The other question that occurred to me in the warm taxi, looking out at the frozen grass outside, was what the ground underfoot would have felt like in February 1913. I found the answer to that next day, in the Surrey Local Studies Library at Guildford. A reader in 1913 had written to his local paper, the *Surrey Advertiser,* noting that the rainfall for January had been well above average. So the going was probably heavy. I found other oddments in the paper, quite apart from the bomb incident that was the main object of my research. For instance, that a Mr. Young, who worked in the motor trade, was up in court for driving a car at more than 30 mph after dark. Nine previous convictions. Fined £5 and licence suspended for six months. So, when Nell heard the suffragette bombers' car rushing through the darkness, I was able to attribute to her with some confidence the thought that they were going very fast, "maybe as much as thirty miles an hour." (I resisted the temptation of having them meet the awful Mr. Young, travelling in the opposite direction.)

That morning at Guildford I was combining the two most useful sources for my kind of research, the local history or local studies sections of public libraries, and contemporary newspapers. For researchers, it's a fortunate fact that the librarians in charge of local history collections are almost invariably enthusiasts, reacting to the most out-of-the way queries with showers of books and documents. As for newspapers, there's a treasure house that has provided details for almost all my books and even a whole plot for one of them: the newspaper library in Colindale, North London, which contains both national and local papers and periodicals from the eighteenth century onwards.[1]

But the knowledge of the constabulary reports on what the police called the Bomb Outrage at Walton-on-the-Hill came as a piece of luck. The driver of the taxi I took at Tadworth station happened to be a friend of a leading member of the Walton-on-the-Hill and district Local History Society, and this historian knew about the reports filed in the Surrey County Record Office and only quite recently released to the public. When it comes to research, I'm superstitious. There's a researcher's luck, very like traveller's luck, that waits until you've stumbled your way on to the right track, then rewards you by putting good things along the path. Those good things are the details that you didn't realize you were looking for, but once you've found them you recognize as essential to what you're trying to do in a particular book—even though at that point you have only a dim idea of what it is.

1. The Newspaper Library, Colindale Avenue, London NW9 5HE. Tel: 0171 412 7353. It is part of the British Library, and there is no charge for using it. All you have to do is turn up with some form of identification.

At the time when I was worrying about the precise light conditions at Walton Heath and whether it was firm or soggy underfoot, I had only the vaguest idea of what my plot was going to be. When the book came to be written, the Walton Heath sequence took up only the first chapter. Still, it's the first step that's the hard one, and the police records from the Surrey Record Office were full of precious details. As well as Cissie and the galosh, they included the sound of a motor car that woke the licensee of the Chequers Inn, Ellen Emma Green, in the dark hours of the early winter morning, even the number of the suspect car, J (or possibly P) 8487. Then, from another source, I found some inside information which the police would have loved dearly at the time. Sylvia Pankhurst in her book *The Suffragette Movement,* published in 1931, writes:

> The story of a motor car passing through the village at 4 a.m., two broken hat-pins, a hairpin, and a golosh indisputably feminine, found on the site, were the only traces of the incendiaries. Emily Wilding Davison and others, all of whom escaped undiscovered.

The same Emily Wilding Davison who, less than four months later, dashed in front of the king's horse during the Derby and was fatally injured—only a few miles away cross country from the Chancellor's bombed house at Walton Heath. So I had one of the historical culprits, police reports, young Cissie's discovery of the galosh, a car, and hat-pins. What did I do with them all?

Mostly, I threw them away.

Not literally. They're all there in the bulging files that clutter my study and outhouse labelled things like "Walton Heath 1913," "Cotton Towns & Canaries," "George V Coronation," "Holloway 1911." But of the hundreds of facts stored in those files, only a few make it into the books. In my account of the Lloyd George bombing, there's no Cissie, not much of the bomb technology, only a reference to an Emily that an alert reader might pick up as referring to Wilding Davison, but no matter if not. There is a reference to a lost galosh, but only because I couldn't quite resist putting it in there somewhere, although it has nothing material to do with the plot. So what am I doing, spending time and money collecting details that I regard as essential, and then not using them?

One reason is that I am, after all, writing fiction, and that particularly controlled form of fiction: the whodunit. Facts have to be both a jumping-off point and an anchor. If you stay too firmly attached to them, you can never take off into your own story. On the other hand, if you lose touch with them completely you go bobbing about in a narrative never-land with no feeling of time and place. Once you move away from the here and now—and in writing you inevitably move away from the here and now—you're in a country where no landmarks can be taken for granted. That applies to modern crime writing just as much as to historical. In some ways, getting the balance of research right is more difficult in a contemporary book. If your character is living in 1909 or 1066 the writer and the reader both start with the knowledge that there are bridges to be built to make the period and characters come alive. But suppose, for example, that your central character works on a supermarket checkout in Wolverhampton, present day. It sounds easier, until you start thinking about it. What are the shift patterns in supermarkets? What's the trade gossip? Dress code? If it was wet and mild last winter in Wolverhampton and your plot demands snow, can you get away with it? If your character has a car, where does she or he park it, and can it be left there more than three hours without getting clamped? Details, all of them, and if you happen to get them wrong, many readers won't notice. And yet, anybody who's worked in a supermarket or parked a car in Wolverhampton will know and will stop trusting you. On the other hand, if you get bored by the research process and let yourself be vague about what your character does or where the action takes place, you've lost most of the things that make a book worth reading.

The aim is to give the reader a feeling of reality in time and place without jogging her or his elbow all the time with guidebook notes. If you're writing about ancient Athens or modern Manchester, medicine, drug-taking, computer fraud, horse racing, whatever, the assumption is that you know more about it than most of your readers. You're inviting them to make a temporary contract with you, like a guide touting for business in the square of a tourist city. "Trust me. I know this place inside out." Any guide can point out the big landmarks. What we all want in any new place is something for ourselves, something to fix on and to be both strange and familiar at the same time. That something is more likely to be a small detail than a big event. The important events or characters don't necessarily look that way at the time. When William the Conqueror arrived at Hastings, I doubt if people were standing around on the beach saying to each other, "Of course this is the end of Anglo-Saxon hegemony as we know it." More likely, it would be something on the lines of "Better get home and shut the goats in" or "I wonder if they'd miss one of those cider casks."

One reason why I enjoy writing historical crime novels is that the big events are there already, and the challenge is trying to get footholds and fingerholds on them to find out what they looked like, felt like, smelt like. The aim is to pare some of the history away and try to come near what it would have felt like in the disordered and untidy circumstances when things were actually happening. The clues to that are in the details, but you don't know what details, and you have to collect hundreds or even thousands of them to find the few that make you see something with the vividness of being there. Like what's the most boring thing about being on a supermarket checkout? How do you tell the difference between satsumas and clementines, and what happens if you can't? At what point in the process would you notice if somebody was pointing a poison-loaded syringe at you? Contemporary or historical, there will be some details in the heap you've collected that make the whole thing come alive. Take Lady Constance Lytton on Holloway. She was a leading suffragette and a marvellous observer of the details of prison life, like shoes. On arrival, when issued with prison clothes, she mentions to a wardress that the shoes don't fit. The wardress "shouted past me into the air, as if she were proclaiming an edict written by another person, 'It's-no-good-complaining-about-those.'" This shoe detail seemed to me to punch home what must be one of the horrors of prison, the shock of finding that even the smallest details of life are governed by regulations. I borrowed Constance Lytton's ill-fitting shoes for Nell—one of the occasions when fact went directly into narrative.

But the mind-set that doesn't know when to discard facts, that insists in cramming into the narrative everything from the bulging research files, is more likely to kill a sense of reality than to create it. It's instructive sometimes—as well as depressing—to look at the progress of some authors from short first book to long squillion-dollar mega-seller. (Not a process to which I've been exposed myself, so naturally I observe with total objectivity.) For the first book, the author is poor. She or he can only afford so much time and money for research, but the smell, touch, and taste of something directly experienced or vividly imagined are there. Reviewers praise the detail. Author, with large advance, travels, maybe pays a research assistant. The piles of files grow higher, the books thicker, the research multiplies. Want to know the precise colour of the chairs in the Kremlin in the 1980s? You have it. Want to know the price tag on the gun you need to shoot a charging psychopath? Sure—and the trademark of the firm you buy it from as well. It's all there, but for the reader it's the difference between being served a well-cooked meal or rammed in the guts with a loaded supermarket trolley. The thinner, earlier books may have carried less weight of research, and yet they had what mattered.

The over-indulgence in facts is a trap for any writer, whether the book is historical or present-day. Piling on details and background to make the scene live, can kill it stone dead.

Meg stepped out of the Hotel d'Angleterre and turned right in front of the Casino, reflecting how much more fashionable Biarritz had become since King Edward VII had decided to honour it with his presence every summer. With sterling standing, in the confident days of the Empire, at twenty-five French francs to the pound, she could easily have afforded the one and a half francs it would have cost to take a one-horse cab along the promenade of the smartest beach, the half-mile-long Grande Plage, but she decided instead to walk, past the baths and the Grand Hotel, enjoying the feel of the wind ruffling her light dress. How glad she was that the new fashion set by the French designer Monsieur Paul Poiret decreed clothes that flowed with the line of the body, rather than the clinched and corseted confections of Queen Victoria's reign. Some people found the change shocking, but Meg . . .

If I found I'd committed a passage like that to the word processor, I'd know there was heavy work ahead for the delete key. Okay, love, we'll allow you your GCSEs in geography, history, politics, economics, and sociology, but where's the bloody story?

The temptation to pile on the detail like layers in a compost heap can be equally dangerous if you're writing a modern novel with a specialist background. The trick—and it's a difficult one—is to get in enough detail to convince without sounding like pass-notes for exam candidates. In thrillers with nautical backgrounds, I feel cheated if characters don't at some point note the swell of the spinnaker and check the starboard backstay. I've no idea what a starboard backstay is and should not thank the author for trying to enlighten me, but I've grasped that we're afloat and the captain is competent. If she or he is still checking the rigging two pages later, then either I'm going overboard or the book is. The same applies to wardrobe notes.

What do I care who made the trainers? Just lace them up and get on with the action. And yet, maybe for another reader who wears the same sort of trainers, that will be the clinching stroke that makes the character real. It's a difficult judgement, but what you can't do is keep throwing brand names on the page in the hope that sooner or later one of them will connect.

One detail, carefully used, is worth a dozen flung haphazard into the mix. There's a detail from one of Lindsey Davis's books that sticks in my mind. Falco, her detective in ancient Rome, has been given a very large fish, a turbot, by the emperor's son as a mark of favour. But how do you cook a very large turbot in an ordinary Roman apartment? Answer, you use a shield, upside down over the fire. That little problem and its solution somehow brings everyday life in Rome closer than a great weight of information. (Typically, Lindsey Davis didn't just rely on imagination for the turbot. She tells me: I did actually cook one myself, rather a change from the normal menu in the household of a then struggling writer, which tended to be sardines on toast.)

As a writer, you need all that information that you don't use, because in your capacity of tourist guide you need to know the famous landmarks, even if your aim is to take your customers somewhere not so well-trodden. Also, it's a matter of getting the attitudes right, like those actors who assure us that you can't play Jane Austen properly without authentic Regency underwear, even though the viewers don't see it. When I was doing some research in the Royal Horticultural Society's Lindley Library on Victorian and Edwardian hothouse peach growing (for a short story that involved cyanide in a peach), I discovered the method used in grand houses for transporting ripe peaches from glasshouse to kitchen without the bloom on them being spoiled. An apprentice would be sent to fill a basket with stinging nettles. The peaches would then be laid, very carefully, on the microscopic hairs on the nettle leaves, which would cushion them more gently than cotton wool. I didn't use that fact, but the polite and ceremonious greed of those upper-class houses that it illustrated coloured the whole story.

However productive the library, there comes a point when you need to move away from books and even newspapers to the actuality of things. In one of my books, set in 1917, Nell is shown a box of Mills bombs or hand grenades, "sitting there with their red painted tops they looked obscenely like a clutch of Easter eggs." When she's given one to hold, she's so surprised by the weight that she nearly drops it. I'd been able to handle a Mills bomb and look at a box of them, courtesy of the very helpful Exhibits and Firearms Department of the Imperial War Museum. The same department showed me a First World War officer's revolver and saved me from an elementary error. In my first draft, a character had released the safety catch on such a revolver—a difficult feat since they didn't have safety catches. Perhaps one in a thousand readers would have picked up that mistake, but that reader would very reasonably conclude if I got that wrong, I was liable to get everything else wrong as well. In the same book, Nell had to steal a car. In my first draft, she just cranked the handle and was in and away. By the time I'd been talked through the starting routine by a member of the Veteran Car Club who drives a 1914 Rover, I knew I'd have to give her a much longer start on the opposition to get through a dozen complicated actions, including getting out to lift the bonnet and flood the carburettor.

Meeting the helpful expert is one of the delights of crime writing. I'm constantly astonished by the number of people who are prepared to share their knowledge and enthusiasm on almost any subject you care to name. But how do you find your expert? Briefly, back to the public library. Ask the librarian for the *Directory of British Associations* (published by CBD Research Ltd.). This invaluable book is almost invariably kept behind the counter, presumably because of its tendency to be stolen by the unprincipled. It lists almost every organization on anything in the country, with addresses and contact numbers. One page at random gives some idea of the variety: Cordage Manufacturers' Institute; Cornwall Archaeological Society; Coroners' Society; Corriedale Sheep Society; Cosmetic, Toiletry, and Perfumery Association; Costume Society; Cottage Garden Society . . . Probably a potential whodunit in every one of them. However esoteric the information you need, modern or historical, the chances are that somewhere in the pages of the *Directory of British Associations* is the person who can help you. A polite approach (stamped addressed envelope with letter, promise—to be kept—of a copy of the book in due course) will usually start the chain of contacts that leads to the one person in the country who can tell you just what you need to know.

Above all, there's no substitute for seeing things for yourself and, whenever legal and practicable, doing them. I admit I haven't scrambled over the railings of Kensington Gardens into the Bayswater Road on a dark night, but at least before making Nell do it, I went to look at the railings and check that they would be climbable. No book or expert can give you the sheer physicality of things—the doorknob or gear lever under your hand, the mud or pavement underfoot, the different look of things by electric light or candlelight, a stink hitting your nose. Of course, these things matter for any writer, but in whodunitry—where you are often asking the reader to accept some inherently unlikely events—it's even more important to ground things in convincing detail. The more fantastical the plot, the more the reality of the details matters. It's a sound rule for a whodunit writer to take any opportunities that offer themselves for things like climbing walls, going up unfamiliar stairways in the dark, getting soaked to the skin, or running on cobblestones to build up an experience bank.

One thing that brought this home to me was a passage in the book I'd set mostly on and around Mont Blanc, in which Nell has quite a long conversation with a murder suspect hanging on a rope down a crevasse. I'd sent the draft passage to a friend who's a climbing guide and when we discussed it over coffees outside a café in the main street of Chamonix, he pointed out that it's quite difficult to hear anybody when they're down a crevasse, let alone carry on a conversation. "Let's go and find a crevasse, and I'll show you." To my relief, the handiest crevasse to the main street of Chamonix turned out to be quite a shallow specimen on the snout of the Glacier des Bossons. Still, it proved his point. The scene was rewritten, with less dialogue and more in the way of shrieks and muffled shouts.

In my experience, research isn't as orderly a process as most of us like to pretend once the book is finished. Especially in its early stages, it's not so much a steady march and an efficient amassing of facts as a semi-organized hunt for you're-not-quite-sure-what, fuelled by the belief that you will recognize it when you find it. Then, when you have found it, the question is how you drag yourself away from the rainbow possibilities of research and start the hard slog of writing the book. But that's a different problem.

Jean Bedford

From Rough Idea to Final Draft

Some Thoughts on Plot

Where do plots come from? This is the question that is most asked of published writers, yet if you are genuinely a writer, or a potential writer, the answer is obvious—they come from everywhere. The world is full of plots; your own life is full of plots, as is your imagination. You may spend your entire life in a country vicarage and write *Wuthering Heights.* Story-telling is intrinsic to being human. We constantly construct stories out of our lives and the lives of people we know or have only heard of. We are incapable, as a species, of *not* telling stories. But as writers, we choose to tell the significant stories, the ones others will want to be told and the ones we need to tell. If you don't feel this *need* to tell your stories to a wider audience than your immediate circle, then you might as well stop now—you are not a writer.

Many detective writers conceive their plots from an incident they read about in the papers or hear about on the news. Gabrielle Lord based her thriller, *Fortress,* on a real incident in which a group of children and their teacher were abducted and held hostage. She combined her own imaginings about the situation, how people cope with such ordeals, with other personal preoccupations—with courage and defiance and what individuals are capable of under great stress—to make a novel. It was a story she needed to tell and that a wide audience wanted to read.

The plot idea for my first detective novel, *Worse Than Death,* came from a report I read in the paper about a woman who went to prison for years for kidnapping her daughter from her husband—a man who habitually abused the child yet had gained custody of her. It made me think about the sorts of sacrifice we are capable of making for our children, and that, married to ideas I already held about child abuse and parental power, led to a story I thought was worth telling.

In general, then, your plots may come from anything in the world around you, but they will usually illustrate something you already feel the urge to say. When you can ask yourself, "What is this story about?" and give yourself a clear and concise answer, you have a viable plot idea. Your answer may be one word—lust, power, jealousy, fear, hatred. It may be a phrase or sentence—the abuse of power; what happens when love turns to hatred; what negative childhood influences will do to someone; how people cope with loss, and so on. In any case, it will be concise. If you don't know what your story is about, it will be very difficult for your readers to make a guess. If you do know, in this sense, what your story is about, then you will have a valid focus for the necessary workings of your plot/s. It will also be useful to have thought in this way when you are asked to provide a synopsis for a publisher or, when your book is accepted, to draft a cover blurb. The actual plotting, the storyline—who does what to whom, how, when and why—is the vehicle by which you reveal what you are writing about, and this evolves from what you believe, imagine, read, observe, hear, or experience.

Before we move on to talk about making plot outlines, we should look at some general aspects of the detective plot, as some of the traditional exigencies of the genre can be useful to the beginning writer. Fortunately, there are certain accepted procedural guidelines that you can use. Of course, if you are confident enough, you can choose to ignore them as well, but as in any art, you must understand what you are rejecting and why.

The plots of most detective stories proceed in similar ways, with similar preconceptions. Even where these preconceptions have been deliberately discarded or played around with, as in some recent "postmodernist" or "experimental" or "cross-genre" examples, I would argue that they are still strongly embedded, even if negatively, in the text.

For a start, usually the most important thing has *already happened.* This may be the central incident of the plot—the main murder, or set of murders—or it may be a salient occurrence (or sequence of occurrences) in the remote or recent past which has led up to the story now being told. This important thing may be revealed at once, as in the classic private eye novel, where a client appears with a specific problem, or it may not be revealed until the very end of the novel, when strands from the past finally emerge to create a pattern, but it will always have happened essentially before your story begins.

Second, something great must be at stake—preferably life itself—for either the protagonist or another main character. It can be the life of the client or, in less traditional plots, the life of a loved one of the protagonist, but there must be real and present danger. For me, personally, the best detective novels play for the greatest stakes: they must centre on murder, and there must be at least the threat of more murder to come.

Third, there should be significant obstacles to overcome in what is essentially the detective's quest. These obstacles can take the form of red herrings and spurious but convincing alternative suspects, as in the clue-puzzle mystery; or lies and threats of physical violence, as in the more hard-boiled novels, but they must be real and convincing. The skeleton of your plot, upon which every other element depends for success, is the recounting of *how* these obstacles are overcome and the problem/mystery solved. Your job, here, is to show your readers, against all the odds, why the crimes have been, or are being, committed, and by whom.

Fourth, the mystery should be solved and justice should be done or seen to be done. This does not necessarily mean that the culprit answers to the law for his or her crime. There is a long tradition of the perpetrator escaping legal justice yet still being satisfactorily punished or made to pay. There is also a long tradition of the immediate culprit being caught, but the malaise that produced the crime continuing—corruption in high places, untouchable principals, the abuse of money and power. Even here, however, we should come away with the sense that some blow, even if a small, insignificant one, has been struck against evil. When the criminal appears to have escaped justice, he or she is usually clearly in line for some other, perhaps worse, punishment. There is a recent trend that even leaves the mystery unsolved on this level—that is, the protagonist never fully finds out what has happened and why—but resolves a deeper mystery, to do with character and motive, instead.

Some writers make elaborate plot outlines and stick to them, chapter by chapter. Robert B. Parker, the creator of the Spenser series, makes highly detailed chapter outlines—almost synopses of each chapter—before he begins his first draft. Others simply have a broad idea of what their story is about (perhaps only our one-word answer) and let what they write define what they will write next. Others use various combinations of these methods.

My own version of making a plot outline and sticking to it is to begin with a fairly general synopsis of the main plot and the various subplots. I write a short and simple account of what the central crime is and who has committed it and why. Then I write a more elaborate set of notes about the *apparent* circumstances of the crime—that is, how the situation will be presented to my detective. This will include the red herrings and any other obstacles to solving the mystery. I make a list of main characters, with their personal details—age, sex, looks, physical characteristics, relationships to each other. I try to sketch out the main changes of action and direction, which will provide the basis for chapters. I often end up discarding or ignoring a great deal of this, but I always plot (or re-plot) ahead in some detail while I am writing.

Other writers do none of this. Some see where their writing leads them and rely on rewriting to fix any glaring inconsistencies or fill any gaps. Others write very broad outlines of the major action and make up everything else as they go along. Some start with an idea and a character and not much else and see where that leads them. Agatha Christie said that she always wrote the final chapter first so she'd know who'd done it and why, then she plotted the rest of the book. I have heard of writers who put descriptions and pieces of action on file cards, then toss them in the air and let where they fall determine the sequence of their plot. There is no right or wrong way to approach writing your novel, only the way that works for you. I feel safe if I know in advance the main events; other writers are bored by knowing everything that will happen. With experience, you will find out which sort of writer you are.

How do you find the right way in to your novel? Sometimes you're lucky, and the first chapter you write remains the first chapter. More often, you will find at revision stage that the first few pages are tentative and not really working. What we know about the exigencies of the genre can help you here. The important thing has already happened. So your first necessity is to inform your protagonist (and the reader) about the immediate consequence of this important thing—that is, the crime that apparently needs to be solved. The best advice I can give you about starting a detective novel is to leap straight in. Detective novels are, almost by definition, action novels—your readers want action, and they want it now. Then they want more. Introduce your protagonist, then bring her or him immediately up against the problem that will occupy most of the plot. Again, with experience, you will be able to play around with this, but it is a good rule to follow when you are starting.

There are various possible approaches to your first draft, and you will find the one that suits you. Some of the lucky instinctive story-builders among us will only ever write one draft, and it will be the first and final one, needing no more than some peripheral tinkering at the end to make it publishable. But most of us will need to go through some process of drafting and redrafting.

Many writers grimly persevere until they have a finished draft, even when they know there are things wrong, or inconsistencies, or gaps in what they have written. Perhaps they will make notes as they go, as a guideline to rewriting; perhaps they will hope that the problems will simply go away once they have written the final sentence. They don't. Usually some degree of revison should occur during the writing of your first draft, but not so much that it impedes your writing new material.

My own approach is to take incrementally larger steps backward for each step I go forward. I rework everything I have written in my previous work session before I write anything new. This often means, as the manuscript accumulates, that I have to rework things from sessions before that as well. I keep running notes about anything or anybody that didn't arise out of my original plot outline (which is, by half way through the novel, usually a beacon of lucidity and logic desperately glimpsed from within the impenetrable muddle I seem to have achieved). These notes often lead to subplots, or at least twists of the plot, that I had not anticipated. This, in turn, necessitates going back even further to seed their beginnings, or to delete things that are no longer relevant.

I check events and characters against a timeline and a list of characters and their attributes as I write—though I still find inconsistencies in the final version, and publishers' editors find even more after that. I try to correct grammar, punctuation, and spelling and to keep an eye on words overused or repeated. During this process, I delete far more than I add, usually finding that in thoughtless moments I've over-explained or used irrelevant dialogue which leads nowhere. I try to keep several questions in mind as I check what I have written. "What is the main story (the 'truth')?" is the most important one, and "What is at stake? What is the desired outcome and how will the detective reach it? What events, information, false assumptions, wild-goose chases, will stand in the detective's way? How will the detective overcome these obstacles?" I also try to keep in mind the elements of at least one major subplot, even when new ones are springing out at me all over the place.

At final draft stage, I usually repeat the whole process for the finished story. This is an obsessive's way of writing, and I don't necessarily recommend it.

Assuming that your approach will be the more common one of completing a draft and then revising, it is still essential that you come to rewriting focused on your central intentions. Ask yourself if it is clear who did what to whom, what they did to conceal it, how your protagonist discovers the truth, and whether the culprit/s will be brought to justice (and if so, what sort of justice). "Does the story fulfil its original intention? Is it clear what it is about?" You must also ask yourself practical, craft questions. "Does the dialogue serve to move the plot along, illuminate the action, or reveal character and relationship? Or is it a filler, repeating what we already know, and irrelevant to the plot? Are your characters believable? Is their behaviour consistent?"

One supremely important question you should ask at this stage, and which may not have occurred to you during the initial plotting, is: *Is everything written here necessary?* The answer, unfortunately, will often be no. Segments of dialogue, description, sometimes complete characters and whole scenes, even your personal favourites, may have to go out the window if you are honest.

In a detective novel, perhaps more stringently than in more general fiction, every word, scene, piece of dialogue, character (however minor), and event must be absolutely necessary to the plot. Detective novels, whatever sub-genre they belong to, are essentially plot-driven, and the requirements of the plot dictate everything you write. No matter if your character makes an amusing digression that scintillates with wit and insight—if it doesn't work somehow to move the plot along, to underline it, initiate action, provide context, or illustrate motive or character, then hit the delete button.

The same with dialogue. Dialogue is not conversation, nor is it something useful to fill in gaps between scenes. It is a codified version of human speech which works in fiction to reveal character, emotion, relationship, motive, irony, action, history, previously unknown information. It should not reiterate what the reader already knows, unless to cast new light on it, nor should it be aimless talk. It should always fulfil a distinct purpose in the plot.

Description, too, should perform a function. It need not move the plot along, as such, but it should add texture, provide a context for character, or supply an appropriate (or contrasting) background to action. Sometimes descriptions of places can make those places almost characters in their own right, enhancing the reader's perceptions of the lives of the human characters in the novel. Ask yourself constantly, "Why is that there?" If you can't find an adequate answer, get rid of it.

The dramatic structure of your novel as a whole is something you should have worked out in your initial plotting. This should be checked as part of structural editing, when you read your draft for revision, but for me it is often the very last thing I look at. You may choose to look at it at any stage you like. Perhaps I leave it till last because I am so afraid there will be a problem with it. Perhaps I have left discussing it till last now because it is such an amorphous and difficult concept.

There are classical rules for dramatic structure. They are: the set-up (statement of problem), the explication and working out (obstacles to overcome), the climax two-thirds of the way through, then the resolution (solution) and after that, perhaps, the anticlimax (the winding down or the postscript). Personally, I am attracted to this approach. But it is possible to successfully change the order around, and you can dispense with the idea of one cathartic climax altogether and still achieve a book with a strong and viable structure. That's what makes it so hard to discuss structure in any general way—it's tempting to say that the structure of a novel either works or it doesn't.

Perhaps the most important thing is that *you* understand the structure you were aiming for and that you are able to look at the structure of your first draft with an uncompromising eye. Did you really intend all the action to happen in the last ten pages? Was it deliberate that the main characters went on a peaceful vacation for two chapters half way through the most exciting and suspenseful part of the plot? Did you really mean to reveal the identity of the perpetrator in Chapter 3 and for the rest of the novel to be an anticlimax? Only you can answer these questions, and only you can present a justification when a publisher's editor asks them.

This is also where you may find you need to move slabs of material around—a frustrating task, but much easier in these days of computers than the old cut-and-paste method. You may realize that your structure is too linear, that you don't want the reader just to follow along from one thing to the next, so you may want to shift some information to later, make some scenes flashbacks, or leap some altogether. Or you may realize that your scenes don't follow each other sequentially and that some transition scenes are needed, or that they have to be reorganized in a different sequence. Don't be afraid of shuffling your material around like this—it is a mechanical task and much easier than it sounds. It can also make a huge difference. You can always change it back again if it doesn't work. Don't worry too much if you have a vague feeling that this sort of reshuffling might be necessary, but you don't see quite where to do it. If your novel works on other levels, the publisher's editor will make suggestions along these lines.

Finally, keep detailed notes of where you need to make revisions. If you are lucky, and if you have methodically attacked all the problems of your first draft, then the next version may be your last. Sometimes a book may need three or four completely revised drafts before it reaches a final one. Don't despair if this happens—it's quite common. The need for revision and rewriting doesn't go away when you ignore it, it lurks and festers in the pages of a book that is not as good as it could have been.

Marcia Muller

Partners in Crime
Developing a Series Character

Like many crime writers, I came to the genre through a love of reading, and the novels that most appealed to me were those featuring private investigators. Possibly because I don't respond well to any type of authority, I was fascinated by detectives who, unhampered by regulations and procedure, would set off down the mean streets to right wrongs, strong and unafraid. I'd read about them and, as was natural for one who had always wanted to write, I'd then dream of creating my own character who would also walk those streets, strong and unafraid.

Unfortunately, almost all the fictional models at that time were male, and while I could empathize with men and understand them on an individual basis, of course I didn't know the slightest thing about actually being male. Thus the character I'd dream of creating was always a woman. It simply didn't occur to me that this was, as one traditionalist critic later commented, "something that can't and shouldn't be done."

Gender aside, I sensed a lack in many of the fictional private investigators. While reading the works of Raymond Chandler or Ross MacDonald, I would search hungrily for personal details about their heroes, for some hint of the inner man. When Philip Marlowe mentioned a love interest, I would wait for further information and be disappointed when none was forthcoming. I knew that Lew Archer once had a grandmother in Martinez, but otherwise he revealed nothing to me of his past.

By the time I'd seriously begun to consider writing a novel featuring a private investigator of my own, I'd been fortunate to discover several authors who were doing excellent characterization within the framework of the crime novel. Bill Pronzini (whom I did not know at the time, but to whom I'm now married) wrote about a detective who had no name, yet I knew intimate details about him that made him more real to me than many characters *with* names. Lillian O'Donnell had created New York City policewoman Norah Mulcahaney who, in addition to a lively professional life, had a fully developed personal life as well, the details of which provided a rich backdrop to the cases she solved. Similarly, Dorothy Uhnak's three novels about another New York City policewoman, Christie Opara, demonstrated that a tough-minded woman investigator need not lose her humanity or vulnerability; what kept me coming back to her books was not so much each one's mystery elements but an ongoing romantic tension between Opara and her boss.

When I sat down to write the first (unpublished and quite horrible) Sharon McCone novel, I was well aware of my options as far as characterizing her. On the one hand, I could create a woman who would conform to the stereotype of the hard-bitten loner with the whiskey bottle in the desk drawer. Or I could make her a camera who observed the world around her without fully reacting or interacting. Or, at the far end of the spectrum, I could create a woman who would be a fully developed individual. Given my reading tastes, the correct choice was obvious.

Sharon McCone, I decided, was to be as close to a real person as possible. And real people age, grow, change; they experience joy and sorrow, love and hatred—in short, the full range of human emotions. In addition, McCone was to live within the same framework most of us do, complete with family, friends, co-workers, and lovers; each of her cases would constitute one more major event in an ongoing biography. (One of her recent readers wrote to say that each novel in the series is like "receiving an eagerly awaited yearly letter from an absent friend," which I consider the highest of compliments.)

While predicated upon my reading tastes, this choice also had a practical basis. In writing crime fiction, the author frequently asks the reader to suspend disbelief in situations which have little chance of occurring in real life. Private investigators do not, as a rule, solve dozens of murder cases over the courses of their careers. And what few criminals they do encounter do not tend to be as clever and intelligent as their fictional counterparts. In order to make the story convincing to the reader, the character and day-to-day details of her life must be firmly grounded in reality.

My essential choice made, I realized I hadn't a clue as to how to go about creating such an individual. The task seemed daunting. I had a name: Sharon, for my college roommate; McCone, for the late John McCone, former head of the CIA (a joke, since politically Sharon is as far from any CIA employee as one can get). I also had a location, San Francisco, my adopted home city. But as for the rest . . .

Should I make my character like myself in background, lifestyle, appearance, and spirit? Certainly not! At the time I had no job, no recognizable skills, no prospects, a failing marriage, and was afraid of my own shadow. I longed to be three or four inches taller, to be fifteen to twenty pounds lighter, to be able to eat all the ice cream I wanted and never gain an ounce. And I was vehemently opposed to Sharon's background being similar to mine, lest I fall into the trap of undisciplined autobiographical writing. I was self-aware enough to realize that if anyone could fall into that sort of writing trap, it was I.

I therefore began building McCone's character by giving her a backgound as different from mine as I could make it. She is a native Californian; I am not. She comes from a large blue-collar family; I do not. She put herself through the University of California at Berkeley by working as a security guard; I was supported by my parents during my six years at the University of Michigan. And she has striking Native American features and long black hair, is enviably tall and slender, and can eat whatever she likes without gaining weight. If I myself couldn't possess such qualities, I wanted to spend time with a character who did.

At the time I was developing McCone, I was participating in an informal writers' workshop that met every week; fear of having nothing to read aloud at the sessions drove me daily to the typewriter. I chose to take the suggestion of the group leader (a published author) to work up a biographical sheet on McCone, in which I fine-tuned the other details of her life: names of parents; siblings; likes and dislikes; religious and political attitudes; talents and weaknesses; even the circumstances of her first sexual experience. (Years later, when trying to remember the first name of Sharon's mother, I would go to my files and find the sheet had vanished. I had to rename Mrs. McCone and hope that no overlooked mention of the former name had appeared in either the novels or the short stories.)

The biographical sheet completed, McCone had finally emerged as real to me. Still, it was a form that was more like a questionnaire than a work of fiction. At this point, I was forced to face the fact that the only way to fully develop a character is to write her. And write her, and write her . . .

Anyone who claims first manuscripts aren't simply learning exercises is either exceptionally gifted or completely deluded. My early efforts were stiff and wooden and—with the exception of McCone's narrative voice, which was the same from the very first—totally different from what eventually saw publication. A first novel that will never be committed to printer's ink currently resides in a dark corner of my garage; a second was reworked into parts of the fourth McCone novel, *Games to Keep the Dark Away* (1984). I was insecure as to how to go about constructing a mystery, and in spite of my resolve to let the events flow from character, I found my stories becoming very plot-driven. I manipulated secondary characters and their actions to fit the plot, kept elaborate charts showing what every person was doing at every moment during the story, wrote long accounts of the back story (the events that set the crime in motion). I wasted paper, time, and energy concocting cryptic clues, red herrings, and unnecessary complications. Even after my third manuscript was accepted for publication, I continued to fall back on stock scenes and situations: ongoing antagonism between private investigator and police; the standard body-finding scene; the obligatory talk about the case in the office of Sharon's boss.

Fortunately, through all of this, McCone came into her own as a person and also became my full partner in fictional crime. I take little credit for this; it simply happened. Writers constantly talk about how their characters "just take over," and when I hear myself doing the same, I feel vaguely embarrassed, as if I were discussing speaking in tongues. But it *does* happen, and is vitally important to any long-running series.

My theory about this phenomenon is that knowing the character intimately allows the writer to tap into her subconscious mind, which works long and hard and usually far ahead of the conscious mind. The fictional character's actions and reactions are a manifestation of this process, and often have little to do with the writer's original intention. In this area, McCone has served me well.

I first experienced her determination to be her own person while writing the second book in the series, *Ask the Cards a Question* (1982). In the first McCone novel, as well as the unpublished effort, Sharon had many analytical conversations about her cases with her boss, Hank Zahn, and they inevitably took place in his office at All Souls Legal Cooperative, the poverty law firm where she was employed. A third of the way through *Cards*, it seemed time for one of these talks, so I had her leave her office for Hank's. But, against my intentions, she detoured down the hall to the desk of the co-op's secretary, Ted (who, poor thing, had no last name), to ask him where Hank was. In bed, he replied, taking a mental-health day off. This time Sharon had the conversation at her boss's bedside—with him clad in pyjamas printed with little pigs and the initials MCP. The story behind those pyjamas that emerged offered an interesting glimpse into Hank's personality.

This incident demonstrated to me that I was in serious danger of becoming formulaic and repetitious in my story-telling and forced me to take a long look around the big Victorian house in which McCone's employer was headquartered. What I saw was a goldmine in terms of possibility; there were rooms, lots of them; there were attorneys and paralegal workers and other support staff; since some of the employees lived there communally, there was the opportunity for them to have potlucks and parties and poker games; and, as in any situation where people live and work at close quarters, there was the opportunity for conflict and resolution.

Where Hank Zahn had once been the only partner who had an identity—much less a name—I now began to flesh out others. In time, a number of them became important in McCone's life. And as they developed, they began to demand more important roles. Soon I realized that they—as well as McCone—would determine the direction that both my individual plots and the series as a whole would take.

From the foregoing, it should be apparent why the development of fully-realized characters is essential to creating a strong series. Without them, the author is simply going through an exercise in the manipulation of cardboard people aimed at a specific—and usually contrived—end. Eventually, she becomes bored with the artificiality of the story and loses all sense of identification with the characters. And if the writer is bored, imagine the poor reader!

Over the twenty years I've been writing the McCone series, I've made a number of choices and changes, and each of these came from within Sharon's character and her reactions and interactions with others. This involves a firm commitment on my part to remaining flexible, willing to switch directions in midstream. Initially, this was a rather frightening process, but the rewards have proved considerable. If I'm surprised by some event of my own creation, then the reader is sure to be.

For example, Hy Ripinsky, McCone's lover: he initially appeared as a suspect in the twelfth book in the series, *Where Echoes Live* (1991), and was intended to appear in that book only. But Ripinsky has a rather strong personality and wasn't content with his limited role. As I wrote the scenes between him and McCone, I grew aware of a developing sexual tension, and as I allowed that to gain intensity, I also found he was able to connect emotionally with her, drawing out her growing concerns about violent tendencies she felt within herself, as well as her increasing addiction to dangerous situations. I myself had only felt inklings of those concerns in previous books, but Ripinsky, a man who had experienced them personally, was the catalyst for bringing them to the forefront.

Different facets of McCone's character had similarly been revealed to me by her interactions with other characters. A violent confrontation with a man she considered the most evil person she'd ever encountered, and the choice she made in dealing with him, affirmed that she was unable to step over the line into pointless violence. Another confrontation, this time when the lives of people she cared about were at stake, demonstrated that she could take violent action when the circumstances justified it. Her relationship with her employee, Rae Kelleher, has always brought out a softer, mentoring side. She becomes positively maternal with her nephew, Mick Savage, and finds she has difficulty letting go and allowing him to be an adult. And Ripinsky's early inability to open up to her and commit to their relationship caused her to chafe, until she realized that patience and forbearance would serve to draw him closer.

During the past four years, McCone has revealed feelings and attitudes that have dictated radical changes in the overall direction of the series—long before I considered making any. When the All Souls partners threatened to confine her to a desk job (*Wolf in the Shadows,* 1993), I'd originally intended for them to work out some sort of compromise, coupled with expanding the scope of her responsibilities. At the end of the novel, I was still undecided as to the nature of that compromise. But at the beginning of *Till the Butchers Cut Him Down* (1994), while watching for wild mustangs in a high mountain meadow, McCone made the decision for me: she would leave the employ of the co-op and establish her own agency, while retaining offices in the Victorian, thus permitting her to continue associating with individuals for whom she cared.

Only months after her new office furniture was delivered, however, McCone began to doubt the wisdom of her decision. As I was writing a scene in *A Wild and Lonely Place* (1995), I found her saying, "No wonder I avoided having clients come to the office . . . Actually, a lot of things about All Souls were beginning to pale for me." Her doubts mirrored my own, which I'd scarcely confronted until that point. The time had come, she decided for me, to sever connections with All Souls; time, in fact, for All Souls to become defunct. It was an outmoded institution with roots in the 1970s; my attempts to bring it into the 1990s with its virtues intact had failed.

I'd said all I could say about poverty law, and I'd described the big Victorian and San Francisco's Bernal Heights district in every way possible.

But in what direction to go? And where? Certainly not a stereotypical seedy office where McCone would keep a bottle in her desk drawer. (She works at a table, doesn't even *have* a drawer!) And certainly not a suite of offices in a high-rent building in the financial district; she is too frugal for that.

The answer came to me while walking on the Embarcadero, San Francisco's waterfront boulevard, with a friend who was talking about some people she knew who had offices in a renovated pier. We were directly under the span of the approach to the Bay Bridge at the moment; I looked around, spotted the San Francisco Fire Department fireboat station, and noted there was a space between it and Pier 24 that was almost large enough for a fictional Pier $24^{1}/2$. The surrounding area, recently dubbed South Beach, was an exciting one, undergoing a renaissance; artists' lofts, lively clubs, trendy restaurants, and unusual sorts of enterprises abounded. And there was also San Francisco's rich maritime history, which afforded many possibilities. At a time when I feared I might have said all I had left to say about my adopted city, I was presented with a new facet which I could mine for many years to come.

Sharon McCone made the decision to move her offices to Pier $24^{1}/2$ on the spot.

But what of the other long-standing series characters? Would I be forced to abandon Hank Zahn, his wife Anne-Marie Altman, Rae Kelleher, and Ted Smalley (the secretary, who had finally been accorded a last name)? Of course not, I decided. The co-op had paled for Anne-Marie several books before; it would now pale for Hank, and they would decide to form their own law firm, then ask McCone to share a suite of offices with them. As for Rae and Ted, they would need jobs when All Souls went under. Ted would come along as office manager, Rae as the first of what McCone hoped would be many operatives.

Sharon, Hank, and Anne-Marie signed a lease for space at Pier 24$^1/2$ without delay. Rae and Ted began packing.

As may be apparent by now, long and intimate association with well-rounded characters can not only enrich a series, but also an author's life. Over the years, I've found myself moving closer to McCone in spirit. Where she was once the independent, strong, brave half of the partnership, I've now become more independent, strong, and brave myself. (Although I must confess that I'll never quite measure up in the courage department: she walks the mean streets in search of criminals; I research those same streets from inside a locked car. But a few years ago she took up piloting a light plane; I am now learning to pilot a Cessna 150—no mean feat for one who is afraid to go beyond the second step of a ladder!)

It's a strange but gratifying feeling to know that my own creation has empowered me, and I hope she does the same for her readers. For me—for us—that's what the series is all about: to entertain and inspire the reader; perhaps to make someone think more seriously about an issue that's important to McCone and me; and to give escape and pleasure to those who buy our books.

Sarah Dreher

Aiding and Abetting

Decisions about Style

Writing is easy for me. Talking about writing isn't. Talking about writing implies making choices, working from a conscious starting point to make things come out the way you want them to. I could pretend I do that, and perhaps sound very erudite and thoughtful. But I'd only be doing it to impress you.

For me, writing is largely an instinctive, intuitive, and pretty chaotic process. By this I don't mean that I have this "gift" that I simply engage the way you'd put an automobile into Drive and let it take over from there. But I do think we writers are born with something that makes us want to work with words instead of violins or wood, and I was born with an ear for words.

My mother was Welsh. Her parents emigrated from the Rhimny Valley to the U.S. in the late 1800s to work the coal mines. She enjoyed being Welsh and loved the traditional hymns and the sounds of the old language. She'd take me "home" to the coal hills any time she could find an Eisteddfod just to hear Cymraeg spoken once again.

My childhood home was filled with words. Words read and spoken, stroked and savoured. Words explained, defined, refined. Words played with and rearranged until even the slightest event could be described with beauty and humor. We only had radio then, and radio was words. My mother was always talking or reading or listening. She wasn't an educated woman, but she was a teller of stories, a genius at embellishment. She would sit for hours with me on her lap, reading a book or magazine and pointing out the words. At the kitchen table, we would amuse ourselves by picking out words and letters on the ketchup bottles and cereal boxes. She didn't know that, in effect, she was teaching me to read. The day she realized, when I was four, the shock sent her into one of her rare moments of silence.

We had enough books to start our own library. Before television, my mother read voraciously. She was the first person in our small town to read *The Tropic of Cancer* when it was finally available in the United States after being banned for years. She read it all in one sitting, then proclaimed, "Well, I certainly don't know what all the fuss is about." She didn't consider it very *well written.* That was her standard for enjoyment. Was it *well written?* From an early age, my ear was trained to pick up awkwardness, laziness, and incorrectness in the written word.

She also passed down her Welsh sense of humor. And a formidable sense of humor it is. The Welsh detest ego-inflation, and much of their humor revolves around taking the wind out of people who have "gotten above themselves." My mother practised this on a daily basis, especially in church. She would take great delight, when I was a child, in leaning over to me during the most solemn, Lutheran moment of our solemn, Lutheran church services, and whispering rude observations about the service, the minister, or the choir. My father, who had the sense of humor of a badger, would be furious. *His* mother, who made a badger look like something out of Monty Python, would be scandalized.

In my pre-teen years, I wasn't interested in books like *The Tropic of Cancer.* My overwhelming passion was girl sleuth Nancy Drew. Not the current, prettied-up, "Oh, Ned, save me (swoon, swoon)" Nancy Drew. The real, blue-cover 1940s and '50s "Ned, will you *please* get out of the way?" Nancy Drew. She had everything you could ask for: good looks, friends, ingenuity, brains, the respect of her elders, courage, ethics, no mother to get in the way, a father who was usually thinking of something else, impeccable manners, and a convertible.

So when I set out to write a mystery/adventure novel, it was natural for me to think in terms of Nancy Drew for grown-ups. She was, and still is, my role model for the female sleuth, and shaped the way I portrayed my Stoner McTavish. She had to be, above all else, down-to-earth, practical, a doer rather than a dreamer.

A lot of decisions go into writing a novel. First, should the overall style be realistic/naturalistic, surreal, whatever? Being a down-to-earth sort, I think Stoner requires a down-to-earth style. Also, I'm most comfortable with reading and writing in that format. Because, first and foremost, I want my books to tell a good story. I want them to evoke feelings, and for that the reader needs to be able to identify with the protagonist, and that happens most easily when the writing is naturalistic, or realistic. Things can turn screwy later (and usually do), but they have to start out grounded.

What kind of detective would she be? Amateur or pro? Tough or tender? Physical or intellectual? Frankly, the tough or hard-boiled

P.I. leaves me cold. Blood and guts? No, thanks. I get all I need of that in the newspapers. I wanted *my* detective to be a compassionate person, with a wry, Welsh sense of humor. I wanted to provide her with a small, nurturing family of sorts, made up of slightly nutty people—some of whom, I am delighted to say, are based on people from my own life. And I wanted her to not *quite* know what she was doing. That would make her funny, endearing, and easy to identify with.

What kind of story should it be? Highly plotted, with complicated logical twists and turns, a challenge to the reader? Lots of action, with wild chases and breath-taking life-or-death struggles on the edge of a cliff? Whodunit? Whydunit? My personal preference is for the character study, in which the feelings and interactions between the people involved provide the suspense and the emotional ups and downs. There has to be some action, of course, some plot and some suspense, otherwise it's not really a mystery novel. It's a matter of where I want to place my emphasis—after all, I'm a clinical psychologist. My basic nature informs both my career choice and my writing style. It's only natural that this would be where I'd want to cosy down to make up my stories.

The setting I choose for my books also has an impact on my style, often in quite a subtle way. In my first book, the action takes place in a mountain resort. What happens is inside the bounds of "normal" experience, and calls for fairly straightforward, descriptive writing, with a lot of daytime scenes. But my second book is set on the foggy sea coast of Maine, in a run-down town with a haunted house serving as a mental hospital. Here the style is darker, eerier, spooky, and most of the action takes place at night or indoors.

Another important question from the outset when considering style is through whose eyes the story is being told. At first, I wrote entirely from Stoner's point of view. This approach tends to keep things fairly neat and tidy, but it can be limiting. All the other characters have to be seen through her eyes, and though Stoner is pretty accurate in how she sees things (being down-to-earth, of course), sometimes other visions can give us more rounded pictures and allow me as a writer an opportunity to experiment with a variety of styles. And some characters, having become real people to me, insist on being heard. How could I have Marylou Kesselbaum kidnapped at Walt Disney World without knowing what she thinks of it all?

Point of view can be tricky, though. You have to decide whose point of view you want to pursue. In more recent books I've got "into the heads" of one or two other characters as well, and it enhances the amount of information I can give the reader. If I'm in my villain's head, and can show you his or her motives and next moves, it can heighten the suspense. Too many points of view, however, and everyone gets lost in the mob. The reader is overwhelmed and adrift in details. There has to be a balance, and for that I rely mostly on what "feels" right. For the most part, though, I still like to keep Stoner's point of view as the main one.

A couple of minor points, but important ones, I think. I can't write comfortably in the present tense, and don't much like to read it. And I'm most comfortable with the third-person narrative, both in reading and writing. Somehow a book from the "I" perspective all too often begins to sound a little egotistical. In the interest of total honesty, though, whenever I play with the idea of Gwen telling a story about her relationship with Stoner, it fits itself into the first-person format and won't budge.

Finally, I think my style is an expression of who I am. It can't be helped. Back in the dark ages, when it wasn't safe to write openly about lesbians or as a lesbian, I tried to censor that element in my writing. Everything I wrote turned out looking lesbian, anyway. So much so that I lost friends by sharing my work with them. They would read my stories, and say something like, "Well . . . ahem . . . it's well, *intense*." It was a dead giveaway that they were about to become much too busy to socialize with me. And it was stifling, trying to express myself as someone I'm not. So for a long time my writing—

what I could do of it, which wasn't a lot—stayed in the closet and desk drawer. The Women's Movement made it acceptable for lesbians to share their stories with the rest of the world, but it was still a risky business. I wrote my first book not with an eye toward publication, but as a Christmas present for friends, the way others would make pot holders or zucchini bread. I understood the rhetoric of liberation, but that didn't erase a lifetime of fear and watchfulness.

It seems a long time since I wrote the first Stoner novel and created someone I enjoy having for a friend. A lot has changed since then, with practice and as I've lived with these folks. After seven books, the pivotal characters have taken on a life of their own. It's something that happens, I believe, when you've spent so much time in your characters' heads, speaking for them, and feeling the things they feel. They tell me what they want to do. I just write it down and make it real. This sometimes feels very strange, but nearly every time I find myself blocked, it's because I've tried to make someone do what doesn't feel right to her. If we don't agree on what should happen next, my character will close me down. They often make a lot of the stylistic decisions for me now—who wants to share her inner thoughts, who would or wouldn't involve herself in certain actions; sometimes they even dictate where the action will take place (there are certain places that Marylou would certainly *not* be found). In fact, decisions don't seem like decisions at all. Instead of being the Great Creator, overseeing and managing it all, I find I'm simply drifting down a river, going with the current, recording the scenery along the way.

But that's the fun of it.

Chris Niles

Through the Door with a Gun in His Hand

Creating and Maintaining Pace

I wasn't thinking much about pace when I wrote my first novel. I was thinking about jealousy and sex and old-fashioned gumshoes. I was thinking about laconic loners with a love of whisky. I was thinking about spinning a good yarn.

I had what I naively imagined was a plot. Actually, it was less of a plot and more of a final scene. But that final scene was going to be a zinger, oh yes. I was very happy with the place my novel was going to end up. The beginning and middle I was less clear on, so I sensibly decided not to think about those parts too much because I sensed that it was going to involve a great deal of strain.

Instead, I did a sketchy outline that I showed to friends, who kindly kept straight faces when I took them out to lunch and earnestly discussed plot points. The outline was a mess. But that didn't stop me. I was eager to get going. To hell with the details, they would fall into place.

The day I started was like standing at the top of a ski jump. I felt good. There would be an ending to this—it might be a graceful, point-scoring, Olympic medal-winning ending, or it might be a bone-breaking skideroo that endangered the lives of innocent spectators—but it would end.

By that time, I'd even thought of a cracking beginning. My character, Sam Ridley, a radio crime reporter, would use the F-word on air and get demoted to reporting on women's issues. Hey, we were really moving here! I was still hazy about the big bit in between. But I'd made other preparations.

As most writers know, before you sit down at your word processor, you must first do battle with the Inferiority Beast, the crafty creature who knows your weak points and delights in jabbing at them until they are bruised and sore and too ugly to look at and you are a mewing, sniffling creature that lives only in the corners of dimly lit rooms. I'd done battle, and while not exactly victorious, I'd realized it was theoretically possible to shut the Beast up for a couple of hours each day while I got on with other things. That power made me feel silly and light-headed, which is an excellent frame of mind in which to start a half-thought-out novel.

The other factor was that I was working full-time in TV news, which took up a fair chunk of the day. When you subtracted leisure time—watching trashy television, drinking cheap wine, and lying on the sofa thinking of excuses not to write—there wasn't a lot left. So I had to get it done fast. My goal was a thousand words a day.

I started with gusto. I wrote furiously, early in the morning, late at night. On holidays, on weekends, in my lunch hour. I shared a computer with my husband, also a writer, and often had to wait, toe-tapping, while he did his work. But I did those thousand words, even on the frequent days when I sat down feeling sick because I didn't have a clue where my story was going.

There was no discipline in this act—it was desperation. I had to finish before the Beast got the upper hand. Completely focused on getting that draft done, I didn't think anything about technique. It was a bit like my brother's old joke about living like he types—fast, with lots of mistakes.

"Tell me honestly what you think," I said, when I showed it to a writer friend.

"Rough," she said.

I kept going. I rewrote and rewrote, and then rewrote some more. I did so many rewrites that I became embarrassed to tell people when they asked how many. "Two or three," I'd say shiftily, before changing the subject. It was more like six or seven, or could have even been eight or nine. Memory has been kind in that respect.

I smoothed some bits and then others. And then finally, when I was exhausted and sick of it, I stopped, sent it to an agent and took up residence by the phone. He called a day or so later.

"I read it in two hours," he said. Which, along with "Just sold it for five million," is my agent's way of saying he likes something. We were in business.

I should mention at this point that I knew my agent. For several years. I'd been reading unsolicited manuscripts that people like me had been sending him, and writing a short report advising whether or not he should consider them. To get paid for reading and being snippy—well, it was a nit-picking bibliophile's heaven. It was also inestimably useful for learning how to become a novelist, because most inexperienced writers make the same mistakes. And after you've read twenty or thirty manuscripts you can spot them as easily as a herd of stampeding wildebeest. Some manuscript readers joke that they can tell from the covering letter whether the novel is going to be any good or not. Sure, they *say* they're joking, but there's truth in it.

The first and most important thing I knew was that the person who would read my manuscript reads a *lot* of manuscripts, and he or she expected to turn most of them down. So it was important to convince them fast that mine was an exception. I started to think of this reader as someone you would flirt with at a party. I would be light, witty, and interesting. I would be enigmatic, mysterious. Telling jokes, juggling, tap dancing.

All right, not all of those things. But I knew I had to have a punchy start. Good stories start where they have to, not sooner, and I'd read hundreds of manuscripts that fumbled the ball on page one. Even if my protagonist had had a challenging childhood being raised by wolverines in Tasmania, I'd have to put the back story in later.

When I was thinking about how to begin, I studied other crime writers whose story structures I admired. And sometimes I found it useful to watch Hollywood films. The two had a few things in common. One was a catchy opener. An action movie usually starts with a fast sequence, something to grab the audience's attention away from their popcorn and soft drinks and propel them into the story. I'm not saying that books should be written like Hollywood films, but there is merit in studying how they are constructed.

In the first few pages of *Spike It,* I had Sam Ridley get drunk, find a body, and get demoted. It not only established his character and told you what he would have to achieve—getting his job back, finding the killer—it also told you some of what he'd have to fight against—namely his own stupidity and love of the bottle. Like the tape recording at the start of "Mission Impossible," this was where I clearly established what the character had to do.

My editor Beverley, one of those people who reads a lot of mysteries, says she's always intrigued when she begins a story that makes her wonder, "How's she/he going to get out of this one?" An old movie dictum puts it another way— "Stick your hero up a tree and throw stones at him."

The start doesn't have to be an all-action, car-wrecking start. It can be a teaser. Sophocles, while not generally considered to be a mystery writer, did it beautifully in *Oedipus Rex.* The point where Oedipus decides to find out who killed the king is a great hook, and it still feels exciting and fresh even though we've known who done it for nearly two and a half thousand years.

Once I've established a fascinating or action-packed set-up, then I get straight on with the story. This may seem like a rather obvious point, especially for mystery books where there is usually a fairly clear goal to be reached, but it's important. You're still wooing the reader. It's the courtship phase, you don't want them to get bored.

One of the reasons I made my protagonist a radio rather than a television reporter was that, having worked in both media, I knew that radio was faster. Television is a cumbersome thing, and it requires cooperation—a reporter doesn't go anywhere without a camera crew, and all the human and technical complications that involves. There are lights to think about, and batteries, and framing and cutaways and whether the cameraman's sulking because he's shooting a press conference instead of getting that career-making trip to Rwanda. Radio people have only a tape recorder. They work alone. Sam Ridley, I knew, was not the kind of guy who'd be comfortable travelling in a herd and discussing the sound man's personal problems. I wanted him mobile and solitary, and that meant radio.

I believe it can really help with subsequent pacing to have the story start with a bang. That way the protagonist is dropped into the story—he or she has no alternative but to begin the quest. When I started thinking about my second book, *Run Time,* all I knew was that Sam Ridley would wake up next to a dead woman, and that he'd be the number one suspect. I wanted him on the back foot from the word go.

Raymond Chandler used to say that when he felt his story flagging, he'd have a guy come through the door holding a gun, which may be taken literally or figuratively. Literally, it's a cheap trick, so I use it all the time. Figuratively, it's about keeping the story moving, keeping the tension up.

Tension is a slippery thing. You can't have too little of it, and you can't have too much. One of the many ways my editor always improves my manuscripts is by suggesting places where the action can take a breather. She says it's important to stop and recap, so the readers can get a sense of proportion and consolidate the information they've received. If you go too fast, the reader gets confused and probably bored because you're throwing too much at them. From Beverley, I have learned to slow the pace, but not to digress. Sam often pulls into a metaphorical lay-by and has a quick fag, but he doesn't go meandering down a B road because the wildflowers look interesting.

Of course, no matter how many manuscripts you have read, there is no substitute for the lessons you learn when doing it yourself. And one of the big things I learned from *Spike It* was how much time I wasted by not having a proper outline. Pace is about knowing where you are going—if you don't know where you're going, it can make it jolly hard to get there.

I reckon I wrote the equivalent of six or seven books before I ended up with something I was happy with. I was so eager to start writing that I didn't think about how much attention a plot needs. It's a huge task and one that should be approached with respect—something I definitely did not do.

Now that I do prepare properly, I've realized that even with an outline, the story is not set in concrete, you still have options. I usually write three or four entirely different drafts. Remember the brilliant idea for the ending of *Spike It*? It was pronounced boring and predictable by my editor—she was right—so it had to go. I wrote a different ending and a better book.

Run Time went through several incarnations and ended up, as usual, not looking anything like what I'd first imagined. The difference with *Run Time* was that it was easy to make apparently big changes with very little rewriting because the basic story structure was sound. I thought it would be like turning a super-tanker, but in practice all that needed tweaking were a few key details.

Chapters are the frame that holds the story, and the key to making a book a page-turner. When someone is sitting up late, cocoa in hand, thinking, "I'll read to the end of the chapter," you need a few tricks to make them read to the end of the *next* chapter, and the one after that. Chapters are the key to pacing. So naturally, they were the last thing I thought about when working on *Spike It.* I'd write for a bit, then stop, and if I remembered I'd put in a break. This resulted in some chapters being two pages long and others being, say, twenty. I didn't even notice this until my editor politely pointed it out. Obsessed as I was with telling the story, I'd completely neglected the most helpful thing.

The chapter has its own momentum and, used well, it keeps the reader hooked. Each chapter should end, if possible, teetering on the edge of something else—a new direction, a fresh piece of information. This kicks the readers into the next scene. They can't break for tea or feeding the kids or mud-wrestling because they simply must find out what's happenssing next. One writer I know always poses a question at the end of her chapters. I use any ruse, no matter how low-down, to draw the reader on because the point of the exercise is to make them lose sleep. It's a help for the writer, too, because they are obliged to ratchet up the tension. What's next? How can things get harder or more intriguing? If chapters are constructed correctly, then the rocks being hurled at the guy up the tree will get bigger and bigger and it will feel as though he is really going to fall and break something.

Not that every chapter has to be perfect before one can proceed to the next. I'm sure there are gifted people out there who do this, but not in my house. My first drafts are dreck, and wading through it every day is often not a joyous experience. What I've learned is that it's important to keep going. Good ideas often come while I'm knee-deep in dreck, and it's much easier to look at a complete story and see what went wrong. You get an aerial view of which parts of the plot are pulling their weight. The bits that don't, stand out. My rule of thumb is: if it doesn't advance the story or yield a stunning insight into a character, I rip it out and stomp on it until it's dead.

Another important thing to think about when establishing pace and tension, which are two sides of the same blood-splattered dagger, is to make sure the readers care about the characters and what happens to them. You don't want the reader saying "so what" when she hears your heart-rending tale of the guy up the tree having rocks rained on him. I saw this a lot while reading unsolicited manuscripts. The plot may speed along like a stolen car, but if the writer can't make the reader care about the people in it, why they've stolen it and whether or not they're going to get away, then there's no point. Characters have to be identifiable, with lives and ambitions and flaws. They have to be more than the writer's puppets. And they have to speak with real words. Which means good dialogue.

I was terrified of writing dialogue until I started to think of it like television news soundbites. The reporter puts the background in the body of the story and then Mayor X pops up saying something pithy about why his career shouldn't be finished just because some public funds found their way to his Swiss bank account. A soundbite is much shorter than the text around it, but it gives you a flavor of the person. It helps convey a sense of who they are and how they relate to others.

My rule for dialogue is to think of it like packing—I put in as much as I think I need then I take half out. Then I take another half out. Then I prune a little more, because, like cleaning the wardrobe or vacuuming behind the sofa, it makes me feel virtuous. Long, pointless conversations are not conducive to a fast-paced novel.

I also try to keep exposition in dialogue to a minimum. I know that detective novels must have the protagonist interviewing suspects and witnesses, but that's essential to the story. It's the mark of an amateur to have your character say something like: Honey, remember that day we were married—how long ago was it now—ten years? Most people know how long they've been married/in prison/living in Weston-super-Mare. And even if they don't, I never have my characters say it. People might well say those things in real life, but they shouldn't in books. As some clever person once said, novels are life with the dull parts taken out.

If a novel is well paced, then it should hurtle naturally toward a big, strong, logical finish. The climactic scene is the highest emotional point in the plot, where there's no more trouble the protagonist can get into, short of being snatched up to heaven. The tension has built and built and at the eleventh hour and fifty-ninth second she or he can escape—the precise sliver of a second before the balloon goes up.

But I'm still thinking about pace in the scene after that. The one that's less exciting, where I tie up the loose ends. The heroine gets her "reward" for having prevailed—the guy, the money, the ice-cream franchise. Here, we can see her walking into the sunset, gazing lovingly at a pistachio-chocolate double cone. But even though the emotional tenor is less intense than what came before, I try not to let that scene just sit there. I usually put something in which alludes to a future possibility, which is nice in a series—I want my readers to buy my next book—but even if that is not the case, it keeps the momentum. You're saying goodbye, but the characters are going about their business. Life goes on.

I think more about the technicalities of pace now than I used to. But mostly I rely on instinct. If I'm bored when I'm writing, then it's as sure as hell not going to have the reader hanging on by his or her toe nails. I keep asking myself: Where am I going? What is the point?

Does the protagonist need to do this? Would anyone care or miss it if he or she didn't?

I've found that if it feels dull, then it probably is.

Stella Duffy

Writing the Villain in Crime Fiction

If there is no baddie, then Adam and Eve stay happily ever after in the garden and absolutely nothing happens. Which is all very well, but a bit dull and certainly negates the possibility of tarte Tatin. Similarly, without Judas, Jesus simply has a nice dinner with his mates and goes home early to bed. No betrayal, no crucifixion—and no sitting at the right hand of God for ever and ever amen. Jesus doesn't get to prove he's the Son of God if Judas doesn't betray him. Snow White never meets Prince Charming if her stepmother doesn't send her off with the woodcutter in the first place and, without the villain, all the sexy, pacy, spunky, dynamic, determined, witty, and (oh God, when will reviewers stop calling them this?) *feisty* women detectives in the world are out of a job. It's all very well being feisty while running down a dark alleyway or breaking into a triple-locked office—try being feisty sat at home arranging flowers. Without a baddie—be it an individual person, a multinational corporation, an unpleasant attitude, or simply an old, unsolved crime—our heroine doesn't get to show any of her myriad skills or her clever repartee.

In my first book, *Calendar Girl,* I wrote two baddies. I didn't start out to write a crime novel but a book about a relationship. What interested me was the idea of deception in a relationship, in this case between Maggie the stand-up comedian and the un-named "woman with the Kelly McGillis body." But then I invented Saz Martin to investigate the missing un-named woman, and the book accidentally became a crime novel. So, alongside the relationship deceiver I needed a more traditional villain for the crime plot. Enter Simon James. American, good-looking, wealthy, drug smuggling entrepreneur. The bad guy. No reasons, no explanation. Just the baddie. Which, given that the un-named woman was a fully explained miscreant, her "bad" actions analysed and (hopefully) understood, seemed perfectly adequate. One bad girl with reasons, one bad guy with none. Good enough for a first novel anyway.

But not good enough for a second. The notion of someone who is simply bad to make a plot point is tedious enough to me, let alone to the reader, who quite rightly hopes for a real character, not a political cipher. After *Calendar Girl,* I decided that the notion of bloke as baddie simply because he lacks the great blessing of being female, is flimsy at best and dangerously essentialist at worst, suggesting that while men can be bad, it simply isn't in women's nature. This can lead to the awful assumption that when girls are bad, they're really mad. (The world is happy enough to label women as mad instead of bad, so I see no need for other women to jump on the bandwagon, too.) I prefer to believe that we can all be just as awful and nasty and dangerous as each other—boys and girls alike. An equality of evil does also imply an equivalent balance of redemption for both women and men. Casting all antagonists as men is limiting in other ways, too, not least because if all the women are good and all the men are bad, then there's not a lot of room for red herrings and double crosses in your plot. So, having rejected the notion of villain-casting along gender lines (and along class, race, and sexuality lines too—because no one group of people is inherently "good" or "evil," and I want to write believable characters, not stereotypical ciphers), how then do we decide whodunit, whytheydunit, whentheydunit? The contemporary detective or amateur P.I. is more often than not interested as much in what makes people bad as in investigating the actual crime. Certainly the reasons behind the crimes are where my own interests lie.

Having decided it was not good enough to make a character a villain just because he was, my first intention in *Wavewalker* was to use the storyline to investigate why the baddie was a baddie, rather than limiting his or her role merely to a function of the plot. Much as I love my heroine Saz, I know I'm actually much more concerned about the baddies in the books than I am about her. Saz is the constant, she is where I ground the story, but the antagonist provides the reason for the story to exist at all. Hence, Max North in *Wavewalker*—again a wealthy, charismatic American. (It's not that I think all Americans are baddies, but it is easier to cover up a less than savoury past if that past occurs in another country!) But with Max, I wanted to go further than I had in *Calendar Girl*—I wanted to start with someone with clearly good intentions and see how, in time and with the abuse of power, those intentions could be perverted into something quite dangerous.

Bad-guy analysis tends to follow trends in therapy. In the Freudian fifties, it was bad mothering that made a criminal; in the more relaxed sixties we knew enough to blame bad parenting—this time dads got it too. Then there were the dysfunctional families of the seventies. Following political trends, we have also blamed, in their turn, men, straights, and whites in general. The latest flavour of the month—and I think this is a trend taken up more by male writers—is childhood abuse. However, it is a scary theory to link abuse and crime too easily—or to base too many books on this notion. For while many who abuse have been abused themselves, very many more who have survived the experience do not go on to abuse others. The poverty trap is a similarly dangerous concept—while poverty can sometimes breed deprivation, violence, and crime, we ought to be equally aware that a nice middle-class background does not always produce goodness and light. In the end, while I do believe that past events create present characters, I also acknowledge both the power of individual choice and the excitement of completely unforeseen circumstance—the importance of moment. Lady Macbeth could never have done it if Duncan hadn't decided to sleep over that night. Really juicy villains have good reasons, bad reasons, sad reasons—but they also have opportunity. Which is why the bad bitch from hell who might be you or me is such a good villain, such a scary villain. There but for the grace of something . . .

And so to bad girls—a fabulous mine of possibilities. The assumption that all girls are good clearly can't be made by any woman who's had another woman break her heart/lie to her/cheat on her. It could be argued that the lesbian writer is possibly better placed to write women with flaws than the straight writer, having had greater exposure to these flaws (or exposed them herself!) in her personal relationships. And she certainly wouldn't suffer from the straight woman's mistaken belief that relationships with women might somehow be nicer/easier/safer than those with men. Women can be just as lying, cheating, manipulative, and dangerous as the next man—give someone power over your heart, and you'd better hope they use it gently. People in relationships get close, hurt and cheat each other—boy or girl is irrelevant. And no woman—and no man for that matter—can simply be all bad or all good. Gradations of grey are what make people, and volatility, too—good one day, horrid the next: good-looking bad guys and beautiful bitches. The impossibility of pigeon-holing any person is what I want to see in all my characters—including the villains.

In my third Saz novel, *Beneath the Blonde,* not only was the bad guy a bad girl, but the good guys weren't perfect either. And neither was Saz. Of course, these characters are all fictional; of course Saz doesn't exist. (Whenever I am asked if she's like me, I respond that I hope I'm cleverer and a little more circumspect than she is—sadly not as young or thin, though.) What helps to make these characters real is their vulnerability: the heroine who lies to her girlfriend to protect herself; the villain who starts out to save the world and ends up a murderer because people won't let him save it the way he wants to; the woman who lies about her past to protect not only herself, but also her loved ones from the truth. As someone who believes in the redemptive power of absolute truth regardless of the consequences, I don't necessarily agree with characters who lie to cover their mistakes or to protect others—but I do know that it's what people do.

Now that women are writing other women as villains, we are also venturing into the world of the flawed heroine. Val McDermid's Kate Brannigan always makes me think that while I'd be delighted and charmed to be her mate, I'd hate to be her lover, given her treatment of her boyfriend Richard—whatever his faults! While Lauren Henderson's Sam Jones is definitely delicious, I don't know how comfortable I'd feel leaving her alone with my girlfriend—call it my own paranoia but I'm not certain how long anyone could hold out against her evident charms. And as for Kay Scarpetta—suffice it to say that Marino isn't the only person who finds her fastidiousness incredibly infuriating. These character notes make our heroines more endearing not less because allowing the good girls to have a crossover with the bad guys makes them all the more real. And I love that Saz fits this mould—accident-prone, clearly not more clever than anyone else, impetuous, and as likely to put herself in a dangerous position as save anyone else. I don't want to write about someone who knows more than I or others in my life do, I want to write someone as real as possible. I don't always approve of her actions—she doesn't think nearly enough—but that's been very useful for pace and plotting, and immensely helpful in making her engaging. Because I care so much more about character than plot, the excessive and impetuous heroine is a damn sight more attractive to me than Sherlock Holmes' all-knowing arrogance. Or Miss Marple's got-it-in-one smugness for that matter. And the heroine who sleeps with someone she shouldn't, thereby crossing over into the baddies' camp—and then compounds her crime by lying to her girlfriend about it—that's someone I find really interesting. Saz doesn't need my approval any more than the antagonist I may be writing, but she does need to interest me enough to get her on to the next page.

So, if the good girl can become a bad girl overnight, and the heroine and villain may well come from the same place, with the same reasons, what then makes a baddie? I suggest power combined with opportunity. As we've all heard often enough, power corrupts, absolute power corrupts absolutely, and the extent of corruption—or openness to be corrupted—is what makes an ordinary character into a page turner. We live in a society that allows certain people to wield vast amounts of personal power, quite often with few constraints. It makes depressing newspaper reading, but fantastic material for rogues. People need "no-women" more than they need "yes-men," need to be contradicted and challenged. And it's in the challenge that the story is found: the detective who won't let the villain off the hook just because they have a plausible tale; the heroine who sees beneath a veneer of pleasantries to the corruption that lies there—and quite often is only able to see through the mask because she has an understanding of the mask herself. So the protagonist is able to challenge the villain precisely because she understands the less pleasant side of her own character.

Unfortunately, in real life, actual villains (and not only those who are found on the traditional "wrong side of the law") tend not to get challenged, or if they do, they simply remove the challengers. But even then, it can be their very excess of self-belief, that overweening personality power that many villains possess, which makes them interesting—at least from the story-teller's point of view. It's why almost any actor would rather play Goneril than Cordelia in Shakespeare's *King Lear*—so much harder to make the nice girl worth watching. At the most basic level, the crime—the theft, the betrayal, the murder, even—are simply actions. But for me, the story is not about the crime per se, the story is about the why and the what-then of the crime. For my money, the story interest lies in cause rather than effect: who first got the plague and how they passed it on to the next person, rather than how many people died gruesome deaths some weeks later. (Though gruesome deaths do of course have their place—especially in the final chapter!) The account of what happened is reportage, how and more importantly why it happened is what I think makes good crime writing. The fact that the baddie did it is less than half the story.

As we write the villain for the twenty-first century, it's why they do what they do that interests us. Well-written villains are juicy, complex characters—like real people, there can be few of them who are really all bad. Just as the heroine who shags around, makes mistakes, upsets her friends or has a failure of a personal life is more believable because of her imperfections, not in spite of them.

There has been much talk in recent years about the "new wave" of British crime fiction, but this is not quite the homogeneous group the name would suggest. There is, for example, a clear delineation between the male and female writers. In general the boys write extremely graphic violence and while they may allude to sex, they rarely show it (unless it's linked to the violence). The girls, on the other hand, have made huge inroads into the sex lives of their good and bad guys, but show rather a lot less graphic violence. Certainly the newer women writers tend to write more violence than their predecessors, but not, as yet, quite as much as the men. What most of us do have in common, though, is that our baddies matter. They are often as interesting (if not more so) than the hero. We may not even write a hero. And these "new wave" villains regularly get away with it. The cops don't rush in at the end of our books and cart the bad guys off to jail, leaving society the better for their removal. Not only that, but the protagonist the reader is supposed to identify with is often as unpleasant as the obvious bad guy. There is a blurring of the lines between good and bad, between goodie and baddie. Kind of like real life.

And now in the fourth Saz novel, I've written an antagonist who starts out apparently ultra-bad, yet (from exactly the same motives) he ends up benefiting Saz's life immeasurably. And how does the heroine cope when the villain she's decided is an evil bastard turns out also to be her fairy godfather? What makes crime writing fascinating to me is the moral dilemma inherent in acknowledging that in even the nastiest piece of work there must be some good, while every benign character has a skeleton or two in their closet. I love to read other writers for their brilliant plots and intricately worked-out dénouements. To me, that kind of work is both clever and enthralling, but my brain doesn't work that way—I start and end with the character. From the six books and fifteen or so stories I've written so far, it has become clear to me that I only really care to write about truth and lies—which is why my two non-crime novels are also full of the "crimes" of lying and deception. I'm not for a minute suggesting all crimes are forgivable once we understand where they come from, or even that all crimes can be understood—not at all. Rather that for me, the crime is not the reason for the novel, the criminal is. It's the bad guy that gives our good girls a reason to get out of bed in the morning. (And sometimes a reason to get back into it late at night!)

Joan M. Drury

The Wrong Way
My Approach to Plot, Process and Endings

When I was writing my first book, *The Other Side of Silence*, I was convinced I was doing it all wrong. After all, I had been reading mysteries since my girlhood and had spent almost as many years reading articles and books on "writing mysteries," in preparation for the mysteries I knew I would some day write. Everything I'd ever read made it clear to me: in a mystery, plot is the most important element—plot, plot, plot. And here I was, writing my first mystery (or at least the first mystery that was to actually get completed), and I had *no* plot in mind.

What I had, when I began, were three characters: Tyler Jones; her best friend, Mary Sharon Andrews; and a dog named Agatha Christie. And a body in a park. It began with the classic "what-if" exercise. Every morning I walked my own two dogs (neither called Agatha Christie) in a San Francisco park, and I wondered *what if Morgan or Sappho found a body under the bushes?*

I did not know then, when I started *The Other Side of Silence*, how or if this body was connected to my protagonist, let alone who rendered it lifeless, or how it came to rest in a park across the street from her house. I liked the characters as they began to develop in my head. I liked the dog—a real dog who needed attention and had to pee and poop from time to time (ever notice those animals in books who never seem to need walking or feeding or any attention beyond an occasional scratch of the ears?). I thought a dog discovering a body in a familiar place was sufficiently intriguing, and so I just took the risk and started to write.

At the end of the seventh chapter, it was clear that Tyler knew the deceased, but *I* didn't know who he was at that point, only that Tyler knew. I found out, just like the reader would, in the eighth chapter. And so the book progressed pretty much in this manner throughout about half of its length. I fretted constantly—with myself, with friends, with other writers—still convinced that I had to be doing this wrong. But, even so, I just kept writing. And uncovering more and more information as I went along.

It was not unlike *reading* a mystery. I'd write something that appeared to be a "clue," and I'd say to myself, "aha, he did it!" and then develop that idea for a while, until I'd think, "No, no, it couldn't be him. But what about her?" About half way through the book, I figured out "who done it," and I knew, for certain at that point, that this was not just a possibility or a red herring. This was the real thing.

When I tell other writers of this method, many say, "But didn't that involve incredible amounts of rewriting, to get the clues accurate?" The answer is yes and no. Yes, for obvious reasons: I did have to make sure that there was a certain continuity and sensibility aimed toward the ending. No, also for obvious reasons: I had to rewrite anyway. This was, after all, a first draft. Books are never finished on a first draft (unless you're that rare writer—and I've known some—who painstakingly rewrite and rewrite and rewrite each line as it's first written).

That is not how I write. I learned quite early in my writing career, maybe at about twelve or thirteen, that if I attempted to write perfectly the first time, I would give up. It was too tedious, and besides which, I would develop a kind of terror that I couldn't do it well enough, which would, in turn, result in totally blocking my ability even to conceive of what the next sentence should be. So, when I sit down to begin something, I just write it through from beginning to end—be it a poem, an essay, a short story, a novel, because that's the hardest part for me: starting, getting it down on paper, sticking with it to the end, *finishing*. And if I start worrying a lot about how *good* it is, well, what a perfect excuse for just quitting altogether!

So, I get the story, the entire idea down first, even if I don't know what the "entire idea" is when I start—as was the case with that first novel. I just write and trust that the next sentence, the next paragraph, the next chapter will come. Then, I go through the book and rewrite it: distinguish the characters more clearly one from the other; remove a lot of dreck; add some necessary informative and colorful detail; sharpen the dialogue; and direct all the details, including adding clues and red herrings, toward the heretofore unknown ending.

Luckily for me, when I was no more than six or seven chapters into that first book, I attended a panel of nine women mystery writers that was held at a nearby bookstore. All of them talked about their own peculiar methododogy. Although many described creating detailed outlines from which they then wrote their books, two of them admitted they started most of their books with no idea of who did it or why or any other relevant details. I breathed a sigh of relief. And kept writing.

I didn't expect, when I wrote this first mystery, that this was to become my usual style or set a precedent. I did notice that, for me, the writing of the first half of the first draft was a bit more pleasurable than the second half. I realized this had to do with the fact that, when I didn't know the ending, I was more engaged in continuing the writing, the way you would be if you were reading a book and wanted to keep reading to find out what happens next. Once I knew what was going to happen, I was more impatient with the slow process of writing. After all, reading is far quicker than writing. And I assumed, I think correctly, that I brought a certain freshness to the writing because I did *not* know what was going to happen next.

So, when I began the second book of my Tyler Jones series, I did not exactly choose, consciously, to do it in the same way that I'd done the first book. I simply trusted the process at that point and let it happen—got out of the way, you might say. And, again, I did have a body, so I proceeded to build the book around that. And also again, I had no idea who the body was or how he was connected to my protagonist or what all the subtext of the book was going to be. I just started writing and kept writing.

About half way through this second book, *Silent Words*, I thought I knew everything, pretty much as it had happened to me during the writing of the first book. Imagine then, my surprise when I realized, no more than three or four chapters from the end of the book, that I was wrong, that I didn't know everything. The villain was actually someone different from whom I'd thought it was. It was more than surprise, actually; it was shock. And, I have to admit, I resisted it at first. But when I started my rewriting, it was obvious, and I had to get out of the way and let it happen. Again.

I began the third book in this series, *Closed in Silence*, with a completely different attitude and starting point from the other two. I didn't have a body; I had a place. I wanted to write a mystery that was set on an isolated island that would limit the possibilities of suspects. And I had a set of characters, because I knew it was going to be a personal reunion of Tyler Jones and her closest friends from college, twenty years after their graduation.

Starting in this manner made it clear to me that I *had* to do this book differently from how I'd done the last two. I *had* to plan it out, partly because it was such a closed environment, and partly because I wanted to create what I felt was lacking in the first two books—a convoluted, complex plot. This would have to be planned, wouldn't it? So I started the writing, in my by now familiar manner, knowing nothing about the plot but a lot about the characters, setting the stage for this complex plot I was going to create. Right?

After the characters were introduced and the flashbacks were done and the setting and necessary weather conditions were presented, I felt—for the first time in this series—that I could not proceed until I'd actually figured out what was going to happen. A complicated plot doesn't just "happen," I believed. It *had* to be planned.

So I stopped writing at that point, to think it out carefully. I had occasion, because of other obligations, to spend a great deal of time in my car and was ecstatic at the prospect. Much of my problem-solving, for my writing and for other parts of my life, has been accomplished in my car. Somehow, over the years, clearing the deck—meaning removing all other distractions such as the phone, people, plants that needed watering, obscure corners that needed dusting, other work—always resulted in clearing my mind enough to work out knotty problems. Solitary sojourns in my car seem to be almost the only place these conditions exist in my life. So I assumed that I would be able to figure out my labyrinthine plot in all the driving I was being required to do.

It didn't happen. I would try to think about the book, the characters, the conditions I'd created, and my mind, without fail, would skitter off to some other problem in my life that needed attention. I would bring my focus back to my book, and it would then just wander off to some pleasurable dreaming. I would get tough, forcing myself to think about the book, and my mind would also get tough, by clamping down and refusing to consider that matter at hand. No matter how much I tried to concentrate on my book, I kept finding my mind had gone to some other place, time after time after time. I was adamant, though, and refused to write more until I knew where I was going. The result of this was that I didn't do *any* writing for about three or four weeks.

Because I had deadlines to meet, this would not do. So, I finally gave it up and succumbed to my waiting computer with a few introductory chapters on it to see what would happen if I just started writing. And what happened was that, once again, I got another book. The lesson in this, for me, was that this is obviously the method that works best for me. How I write is—I just write, I just do it.

One more thing here: the other element that is constant during my writing is that I try to keep my reader in my mind, *be* my own reader, even. I'm one of those annoying readers who says, "What? Why are you closing that door? You already did that," and then flip back to the previous page to prove my point. Or, "You don't like artichokes!" then paw through pages far earlier in the book until, again, I can prove my point. Mystery readers are careful readers, weighing every statement, every movement as a possible clue, a possible piece of the puzzle. We rarely forget anything. As a writer, I applaud the precision of copy editors, who often catch the inconsistencies that I miss (but my readers will *never* miss), but I'm also aware that I have to do most of this work myself.

Consequently, when I reach the finish of the book, I need to focus on that reader and especially that reader's astounding memory. Many a good plot and fine characterization have been weakened by an inconclusive or vague or too-quick ending. I always strive to end my books with the same weighty respect with which I began them and to remember that my readers want everything credibly explained and neatly tied up.

This is easier said than done. One of the devices I use, although it took until I reached my third book to figure this out, is I keep a "cheat sheet" handy—listing all the details that might be pertinent throughout the book, so that I can refer to this list when deciding how much to write at the end. It's a fine line that mystery writers walk between dragging that ending out and cutting it off too precipitously. I always start with dragging it out too long, because I've discovered that—for me—it's easier to cut back then to add. My background, partially, is in journalism, and so I'm always in fear of writing those crisp, succinct lines that leave out too much of the emotions, the spirit of both the plot and the characters, the background story.

I want to finish with that most important of words, "respect." A writer should treat her characters and their lives with respect throughout the book, and also demonstrate an appreciation of the reader, then merge these two at the end. While it's important to guard against disrespecting readers by overwriting at this point, I find it annoys me much more when I feel the author is just rushing to end the book and, consequently, doesn't seem to give as much care and concern to this final episode. To me, this indicates no respect for either the characters or me, the reader.

With all this in mind, I probably spend more time writing and rewriting my final chapters then I do the entire book—knowing full well that this is the part of the book the reader will carry away, more than almost anything else. I write the ending with love and devotion, tying up all those loose ends but avoiding being pedantic. I also attempt to make sense without insulting the reader's intelligence. And finally, I think about the entire story to this point: the ending should reflect the tone, the quality, the style of the rest of the book. If I do it right, I've discovered, my readers keep coming back.

Abigail Padgett

Midnights Dreary

Creating Atmosphere and Suspense

Morning, a southern Indiana river town shortly after the end of WWII. In a warm kitchen, a couple who married late are trying to persuade a baby girl to eat oatmeal mush. The baby (then and now) detests mushy food and clamps her toothless gums in defiance. But the parents, through God-knows-what sequence of literary trial and error, have discovered the key to unlocking their darling's clenched jaw. The key is Edgar Allen Poe. More specifically, it is the line, "Quoth the raven, 'Nevermore'."

So the parents recite Poe in their kitchen while shovelling spoonfuls of baby food into a mouth that opens like an infant bird's at every incantation of "Nevermore." The baby loves the shivery sounds and cadences of a poem created to evoke abysmal dread, even though her comprehension of the words will not be possible for years. It comes as a surprise to no one when this baby, some half-century later, abandons all other pursuits to become a writer of mysteries.

I "remember" the baby food and the Poe in the way that oft-heard anecdotes are recorded by the brain as actual memory. Especially the Poe. Today as I write, a phantom raven perches atop my computer monitor. His single word battles the fabled California sun outside, the relentless beamishness. A skylight in my office off the garage has a custom shade that admits no light; the sliding glass door has been covered with blue film and is additionally protected by mesh screening guaranteed to "cut sun by eighty percent." Door and window are further hung with blinds through which the fierce light still manages to intrude. Eventually, I will get lined drapes as well.

The raven is fatigued by light, his message dimmed. Away from the foggy autumns and bleak winters of Poe's east coast haunts, I require something like a cave in which to hear again the "Nevermore" which my writing must echo. I am happiest when I write at night.

Five Bo Bradley novels—*Child of Silence, Strawgirl, Turtle Baby, Moonbird Boy,* and *Dollmaker's Daughters,* and two in the new Blue McCarron series—*Blue* and *Blue Plate Special*—have been written from my cave in California, mostly at night. All echo Poe's raven as well as my own personal revolutionary cry to destigmatize psychiatric illnesses, professions, settings, and language through the power of popular fiction.

The storylines in both series must conform to their mystery heritage. They must engender in readers a chill of fear. But the genesis of that fear in my novels may never be found in illness. Rather, it must be found where it really exists—in the inexplicable and sometimes terrifying struggle between good and evil that is our heritage as sentient beings.

Chills of fear, the elements of suspense are, however, not as readily available as one might hope. They tend to be elusive, obscured by the mundane. The washer has overflowed. The insurance agent calls with a reminder that death waits for no woman to get around to buying term-life. The dog has dug under the fence again and can't get back. There's no milk in the fridge, and isn't today the day there's a fine if the car isn't moved away from the curb for the street cleaner? Sometimes, it's just necessary to make up the mysterious scariness, whole-cloth. Often necessary, actually. Maybe always.

So, lacking both real dark and anything remotely spooky, I slosh to my office and its invisible raven through the suds drifting over the garage floor. There I will create, out of nothing but the electrical activity in a brain mercifully kept in perpetual night by its cave-like skull, stories about good and evil, life and death. Stories in which something unknown and deadly lurks perilously close to Bo or Blue, and thus perilously close to the readers who are rooting for them. There is a rustling of spectral feathers, black as the nineteenth-century ink in which they were first penned, from above my computer screen. Time to begin.

And how is this done? Specifically, how is this done with words? Writer and intellectual Brigid Brophy has said that "music has an enviable immediacy of mood—enviable, I mean, to writers . . ." Indeed. Like a half-forgotten scent, a single bar of music can call up a continuum of mood and feeling from anguish to zeal. Metred poetry, too, with its old-brain pulse has the capacity for combining sonorous vowels and rhythm in a sort of music that can override rational immediacy and even capture the attention of pre-verbal babies who hate baby food.

But prose cannot do the same. It is an acquired taste, like Scotch whisky. An appreciation of prose is learned, not instinctive. Prose fiction requires complex agreements between writer and reader about suspension of disbelief, the boundaries of fictional reality (which differ radically from genre to genre—mystery to science fiction, for example), adherence to conventions, and culture-bound taboos which may be anything from political to grammatical. Most, if not all, of this complexity is dealt with subcortically by prose writers who have internalized the terms of agreement by reading other prose writers. Mystery writers understand their particular terms of agreement by reading mysteries in vast quantity long before first setting word to page.

The extent to which I am able to create suspense with words may be traced to a brain genetically predisposed to "spooky" rhythms and sounds, and to a pre-television childhood filled with books. One can only write if one can read. Among many, I have read Dorothy L. Sayers, P.D. James, Carolyn Heilbrun writing as Amanda Cross, and hundreds of other women mystery writers. With the exceptions of Poe, Algernon Blackwood, Carolyn Keene (pseudonym of Edward L. Stratemeyer, creator of the Nancy Drew series), and a few contemporaries such as James Lee Burke, I have not read "boy" mystery writers, finding their twin obsessions with their own genitalia and with violence tedious. So, what I know about writing suspense I have learned from others who write suspense.

From these authors I have learned that suspense hides in everyday situations, and that it may be revealed through the language of mood. Words which establish mood immediately invite readers into a barely seen world beneath the superficial one. A world where the checker at the grocery waits only the imposition of mood, which is a change in perspective, to remember that lone car she saw in the parking lot last night. There was something odd about the trunk, wasn't there? It wasn't quite closed. Something caught in the lid, maybe. Something pale.

In *Moonbird Boy,* I practiced this lesson on page one, introducing a sense of lurking threat by describing a mundane sunny California beach scene. Except the action is offshore, where a great white shark is distracted from her pursuit of a sea otter by the scent of blood in the water. Readers feel the otter's pounding heart and great relief when the safety of a rock is reached, but like the otter they are now forever wary. Something dangerous is nearby!

In *Blue*, my heroine returns to her solitary desert hideaway at night as shadows of wind-tossed plants seem to leap at her on the sandy road. A lone tumbleweed lurches ominously across her headlights, casting stark patterns on the ground. Both Blue and her readers know what these mood-evoking images suggest, and they're not disappointed. Something unforeseen and frightening waits dead ahead. And Blue, her readers right behind her, must confront it. The mystery author's task is to do this, to reveal the suspense hidden in the quotidian and then to diminish it within the boundaries of both the author's and the readers' concepts of right and wrong, tolerable and intolerable. And certain things *are*, to me, intolerable. There are certain things that I don't, and won't, write.

Late morning, and the parents of a blond little boy pace with growing fear in a vinyl-tiled hospital hallway. Over two hours ago their child, drugged and pale, was wheeled on a gurney to surgery. A simple tonsillectomy, the procedure was expected to take no longer than an hour. There has been no word.

Much can go wrong in an operating room. Fatal drug allergies, a miscalculation regarding anesthesia, the sudden hemorrhage that cannot be clamped in time. What in God's name can be taking so long? What has HAPPENED?

Finally the elevator doors open, and a gurney is pushed into the hall. The parents are faint with relief. Their child is on the gurney, stirring slightly as the anesthesia wears off. He's alive! But his skin is even paler now, and a rivulet of dried blood runs from the corner of his mouth to crust on the front of his hospital gown. The gown is the color of washed-out egg yolk with an all-over design of tiny racing cars. The mother will never again see that shade of yellow without feeling a rush of nausea. The yellow has become a shadow cast by the unspeakable.

The surgeon's scrubs are dark at the armpits.

"Tonsils were imbedded," he explains. "They may grow back, but he'll be okay."

The boy's tonsils do not grow back, but the mother, who occasionally publishes poetry and short stories now, knows there is one kind of suspense she will never recreate on paper. The kind that is intolerable, that is too agonizing for words.

One of the conventions generally observed by mystery writers and certainly by me is this: that the gradual accretion of threat which constitutes suspense results in neither the death of a child or a non-predatory animal. Nor the revelation that the cute primary-school tyke or loyal border collie is in fact the very embodiment of evil. Mystery readers are not unaware that some children/border collies can be exquisitely nasty, but as Agatha Christie observed—mysteries are morality plays. The line between good and evil must be drawn with an absence of ambiguity never found in real life. In mysteries, innocence is always avenged, never murdered or defiled.

To that convention I add an additional, personal undertaking. I will not exploit illness, particularly psychiatric illness, for thrills. The mystery genre crawls with "demented killers" and "escaped lunatics" in such numbers that one wonders whatever happened to genuine evil. Schizophrenia, manic depressive illness, and acute depression are treatable medical disorders like diabetes or heart disease, not monstrous tentacles from the heart of darkness. My heroine, Bo, lives with manic depressive illness, usually takes the necessary medications, and manages her life with acerbic wit and not unrealistic competence. She reflects millions of real people living with serious but treatable psychiatric disorders.

I am outraged when mystery writers negatively exploit psychiatric illness (from which I exclude sociopathy) for the suspense-value of its medical terminology and symptoms. The practice contributes mightily to the burden of stigma under which real people with real illnesses must live, and violates the contract between mystery writer and reader, which demands a framework of truth. For the truth is, people with untreated psychiatric illness are most often the victims, not the perpetrators, of crime. To suggest otherwise is to mislead.

Less cruel but as misleading is an excessive use of physical violence in the construction of suspense. I don't believe that readers experience pleasant little shudders of terror when told that "Her right hand had been mangled in excruciating pain when he slammed the car door on it, but with her left she was able to extract the cheap ballpoint pen buried in her neck. She wondered how he'd managed to miss her spinal column, jugular vein, aorta, and trachea with his murderous thrust." I'm sure my readers don't peruse *Gray's Anatomy* for fun on rainy nights and are, moreover, likely to wonder how someone with four broken ribs and a skull fracture could possibly rappel down the side of a mountain twenty minutes after sustaining those injuries. When gratuitous violence isn't repugnant, it's ridiculous, and neither adjective is interchangeable with "scary."

Neither is "sexual." The French definition of orgasm as "a little death" notwithstanding, there is almost no common ground between novels of suspense and novels of sexual passion. Let's face it, a character who is passionately in love will be unlikely even to notice the body hanging in the gazebo, much less to evince any interest in the twenty-odd suspects carefully positioned on the lawn. The character in love is obsessed not with good and evil, but with the beloved. Sexual attraction and the need for love are primal, compelling, and may easily obscure the more intellectual concerns of the suspense novel. The mystery sleuth passionately in love is in the wrong book which is not to say she can't be in love at all. She can.

But her deepest passion must be for the battle against evil. And the spirit beside her in the night must be nothing more than the whisper of a blue-black wing.

Night, a canyon in the Anza-Borrego Desert east of San Diego, California. The author has driven over miles of desolate, rocky road in order to reach a little stream where the last of the bighorn sheep sometimes come to drink. The Kumeyaay Indians once traversed this canyon, as did more ancient people before them, but over thousands of years these left no wound on the desert's face. Now there are tire marks everywhere in senseless patterns that have destroyed plants seventy years in the growing. She sees a beer can in the stream, pulls it out, smashes it with a stone. There are spent shotgun shells and rifle brass on the ground a few yards away beneath a spidery ocotillo, but she doesn't see those. It's just as well.

At dusk, a thousand little birds leave their burrows below ground or deep inside barrel cacti and dart over the stream, swooping and dipping against a mottled pink sky. Motionless among them, she feels their exultation at the dying glare and shares it. But the celebration of small birds at dusk is not why she has come. What she has come for will only happen later, if at all. What she has come for will only happen in the desert dark.

So, the author sets up a camp cot near the stream, unrolls a sleeping bag on it, and slides inside to wait. This land has its stories. She has never seen the ghostly mule train said to cross the desert floor at night, its driver's eyes like burning coals. Neither has she seen a single timber of the Viking ship supposedly lost when this desert was still a shallow sea. The ghost of the young bride who perished of "desert sickness" and was buried in her wedding dress at the last stagecoach stop has never appeared to the author. But she believes in these things, in a way. Because they are the outward manifestation, the word-draped forms of the thing she has come to find. They are mystery.

At some point, she drifts into sleep, and much later, suddenly she wakes. Silence now, broken only by the eerie, tinselly sound made by wind in the resinous leaves of smoke trees. There's something in the clear, dark air. Something inexplicable and therefore terrifying. Not a sound or even a scent, just a feeling impossible to ignore. Here, miles from the nearest artificial light, coffee cup, or human voice, is the revealed heart of darkness. It is her own heart of darkness. The real thing. And it is a paralysis of dread. It slips like an icy film through her hair, over her wide-open eyes, down her arms. It has no name.

But it will.

There are ravens in this desert canyon, distinguishable from crows by the V shape of their shining black tail feathers. In the moment just before dawn, when darkness seems to lose cohesion and merely dissolve, a black form with a V-shaped tail swoops low over the stream and wide-eyed author. In the rustle of its wings she hears a single word, "Nevermore."

Then there is an explosion of barely perceptible grey in the eastern sky, and everything is different. Everything is visible, comprehensible. The author stretches and ventures a foot out of her sleeping bag. Time to go home and wrap words around darkness. Time to pretend again that the thing has a name.

This is how I think the traditional mood and suspense of mysteries are created—by the layering of words over an inchoate and universal dread so unknown it cannot be spoken. The artifacts of this dread drive mysteries, and the artifacts are nothing human. They are a slant of shadow, an inexplicable scent of roses on a snowy wind, the desperate ringing of a phone in a brightly lit but empty room. The artifacts of dread caress the story and move stealthily through it, luring it along, but they are not the story. They are the mystery.

The story itself will be about people. The villain, the embodiment of evil, will turn out to be merely a human being, grossly flawed and probably despicable, but recognizable. Nameable. We readily identify each mystery-villain's motivations because none among us is stranger to greed, envy, lust, betrayal, or any other deplorable inclination. These things have names in every language. We stand smugly in contrast to the villain, believing we have conquered those nameable inclinations in ourselves. But deep inside, we know that the villain, just a mirror of the worst in ourselves, is not in itself enough. The villain will never be enough.

The heinous crime has been solved, and its perpetrator stopped; the sleuth has matched wits with evil and won; the innocent are avenged and safe from harm; and none of this is enough. We must read, or write, another mystery. We must see dread brought to heel by stories again and again.

The origin of the dread which drives mysteries is, I think, irrelevant. Whether an inherited memory of giant lizards stomping beneath our treetop habitat or a more elegant and terrible awareness that the universe is completely oblivious of our existence, dread simply exists. What is relevant is the magnetic attraction its artifacts exert, the endless seduction of its very namelessness. Every good mystery cloaks the unspeakable in a story, pretends that the nameless can be named, and names it. But with each snapped twig, every puzzling message hidden long ago in a crumbling wall, mysteries hint at a core experience only temporarily, if pleasantly, obscured by the intellectual machinations of the story. Mysteries create the illusion of conquered darkness, but remind us through a genre-specific poesy of dread that the conquest is an illusion. Like the blue sheen on a raven's feather, which is only a trick of light. Or the echo of a single word no bird has ever spoken.

Anne Wilson

A Sense of Place

For me, the crime novel doubles as a travel guide. The kind of guide which describes people and places from a knowing, sceptical perspective. Although, as a reader, I look for an intricate plot, likeable characters, sassy dialogue, I will put up with almost anything if a book has a strong sense of place. The place doesn't have to be glamorous, but it does have to be colourful, both in the way it looks and in the people who live there.

I want to be introduced to a local neighbourhood by someone who knows all its secrets. My favourite crime fiction heroines show me around, pointing out the roads and buildings where characters live, or where important action takes place. They introduce me to the people who make up the local community from their own, distinctive perspective. The amateur and professional sleuths of women's crime fiction tend to be women who are "marginal" in some way—they might be from a minority ethnic group or have parents from two different cultures; they might be lesbians or be unconventional in some way. Because of this, they have the ability simultaneously to belong and not belong to the place in which they live. They are in the perfect position to describe and interpret their world to us. They see it with objective eyes, but they are enough of an insider to paint an authentic picture.

As a reader, I want insight rather than straight description. I want the writer to reveal the living, pumping heart of the place—the corner shop, the smaller streets, the ordinary places where people go about their daily business. By the end of the book, I want to feel that I know the place almost as well as the author does. If I ever go there, I shall be able to find my way without needing a map. I shall know, without having to ask, where I can get the best cup of coffee and where to find the friendly bar tender or restaurant owner who dispenses food/whisky/wine and sympathy in equal measure. The fact that my fantasy destination is the backdrop to a murder adds to its spice.

When I first started to write crime fiction, I wanted to create this same neighbourhood intimacy in my books. I decided to stick to the maxim "write about what you know." I think it helps to set a story in a place you know well and about which you have strong feelings. For the novice writer, at least, using somewhere which has personal resonance and memories helps to bring it alive for the reader. But reading the authors I admired and studying how they put across a sense of place, I realized that knowing somewhere in the geographical sense is not enough. The writer is a filter; we choose what to tell the reader about the place and what to withhold. We decide what is important and what is not. The sense of place is an integral part of how we choose to tell the story. It can have a number of functions. For example, we might use the unique features of the setting to feed the plot (a murder inspired by political tensions in City Hall), or to heighten tension (a chase at night over cold, inhospitable terrain). If we write in the first person, a sense of place may be intimately bound up with the character of the narrator—the setting comes alive through her priorities, her observations.

Describing the physical terrain or architecture is something of an effort for me. I am striving constantly to write more visually about places—to paint better images of physical structures, materials, colours, the weather, and the seasons. Depicting the human landscape comes more naturally, since I have always been nosy about other people's lives. I studied sociology for many years, and before I became a crime fiction writer, I wrote a book about identity, which involved interviewing many people from different backgrounds. Like Sara Kingsley, the heroine of my first two books, I am adept at getting people's life stories. Sara, because of her work as a counsellor, has become a little tired of it. But I am a solitary writer, and wherever I go, I am curious about the people who live there.

I chose to set my novels in Acton, a cosmopolitan suburb of West London. It is not, at first glance, the obvious location for a crime story, but has a particular significance for me because I have lived there through many phases of my life. I moved there twenty-five years ago, when I was at university—just weekends at first, to be with my boyfriend, who shared a dirty third-floor flat with three others. In the summer, we would climb the ladder through the skylight onto the flat pitch roof. The view was glorious. Peeping over the side, we could see the ice-cream shop with the factory behind it and the garage where they kept the ice-cream vans. The mechanic had another business fixing gleaming, chromed Cadillacs, left-hand drive and all. On a clear day, we could see right into the West End, to Centre Point and the newly built Post Office Tower. Occasionally, a neighbour emerged from one of the other skylights, and we would smile and wave. On the first floor lived a shrivelled, toothless, old woman, whose rheumy cataracted eyes could barely see, and on the second floor, just below us, was a Chinese family. At night, we were serenaded by the tonal twangs and dips of Cantonese and the sharp click of mah jong; the first dim sum I ever tasted was from a cracked saucer offered at our front door. The savoury fragrance lingers still.

The first flat we owned was in a more suburban part of London, but we missed Acton's diversity and its nearness to the centre. As soon as we could, we went back and bought a house. It was the best, the most perfect house I have ever lived in; I fell in love with it the moment I saw it—a terraced workman's cottage, built in the late nineteenth century, with three bedrooms and a small garden with a lawn bordered by roses. And the street on which the house stood epitomized everything I love about Acton—a rough friendliness, a sense of community, and an extraordinary diversity of culture, class, and lifestyle. There was a tremendous feeling of people looking out for each other. The house used to be ours, but our family grew, and we moved on again; now it belongs to Sara Kingsley. The spirit of this house was happy and benign. Letting Sara live in it is a way of reconnecting with my life at that time and remembering the people and the neighbourhood. When I was looking for a home for her, it seemed ideal—just the right size for a single mother of two small children and plenty of good neighbours on hand to help look after them when Sara is busy with her investigations. And there was the added benefit that I could use memory, rather than invention, for the layout of the rooms.

Of course, the Acton I write about in the Sara Kingsley books is not "real," in the literal sense. I conjure up roads, alleyways, shops, and cafés where there are none. I change geography to suit the plot. If I want a school, a clinic, or a factory, I create one by a process of pick and mix, taking different elements from places I know to create the final amalgam. Sara lives in a place which exists only in my imagination, created from feelings, impressions, and images from the past and the present. The backdrop to any work of fiction is like a stage set which the writer designs to fit the story, and makes with materials drawn from her own experience.

The only problem I have encountered in using Acton as a setting for my books is the reactions of readers who also have local knowledge. A local doctor, for example, sent me a note to say that she had actually checked some of the geography in *Truth or Dare,* and it was *inaccurate*—as if the book set out to be a street map of Acton. Taking liberties with real places to create a backdrop for fiction will always offend some people. Similarly, local readers often claim to "know" my characters, or the person on whom they are based. Yet, with very few exceptions, my characters are rarely drawn from one person. The raw materials for making them are observation and memory; my imagination fashions this into the final form. I have heard many writers talk about the process of creating fictional places and characters and, though each sees it in a slightly different way, most agree that it is difficult to explain to people who have not tried it for themselves.

Like other crime writers, I use elements of the setting to create a certain atmosphere. An industrial landscape of factories and warehouses, for example, can be made to sound quite eerie, especially at night, and so help to build tension and create a sense of menace. In *Governing Body,* Sara makes a nocturnal visit to Park Royal, an industrial estate about a mile north of where she lives:

> Park Royal, at this time of night, was a spooky wasteland. The few street lamps that were actually working cast a limpid yellow glow for a few miserable yards, leaving gaping holes of darkness in between. The area is completely industrial, apart from a cemetery, which sprawls incongruously between two warehouses. The factories crouch side by side in shadows like giants watching over the dead. The industrial estate stretches for about two miles, starting at

> the A40 motorway which runs from the West into Central London. It's mainly light engineering here—nuts, bolts, and grommets—with the odd food or furniture company thrown in. At night, even the main roads are deserted. Once the rumble of the motorway receded, the ragged engine of my Vauxhall Chevette was the only sound, and the rough tarmac, pitted by the wheels of lorries, made every rattle count.

The marks of urban decay—litter, graffiti, broken glass—all add to the grittiness of the book. They remind us, too, that Sara's perceptions of the people and places around her is realistic rather than rose-tinted—she "tells it as it is." She is aware, as I am, that not everyone appreciates Acton's attractions the way she does:

> Saturday afternoon, especially in the summer, is a quiet time in Acton. Most of the male population is either slumped in front of the telly watching the horse-racing or lurching, mildly pissed, out of the betting shop. Just off the High Street, there's a desultory market which fizzles out at about 3 o'clock. The only real sign of life is McDonald's, packed with mums surrounded by kids and bags of shopping, nattering to each other and popping chips in the mouths of toddlers, half toppling out of the high chairs beside them. It's a low-key time, everyone waiting for Saturday night. Some people find the whole place depressing—not me. It's real—not pretty, but alive. *(Truth or Dare)*

I use the multi-racial community in which Sara lives and works in a number of ways. First, it creates a colourful social landscape in which to set the story, and one which reflects my own view of the world. My characters are socially and ethnically diverse because that is the kind of community in which I live, and it also reflects my opinion that Britain is all the richer for its diversity. But I try not make an issue of it. Clancy, for example, one of Sara's co-workers at the clinic, is black and lesbian, but I mention this only in passing since it is not relevant to the action. Some readers may miss it altogether.

Sometimes, however, I deliberately introduce specific social issues into the plot because they interest me, and I think they are important. One has be careful with this, otherwise the story can easily slip into boring rhetoric. In *Governing Body*, I tried to strike a balance between spinning a good story and bringing to the fore some ideas about racism, the police, and black women. In this story, Mona, a black head teacher, is found holding a bloody knife over the dead body of Tony Thornley, the chair of governors, who is a racist bully. In the course of the investigation, certain facts come to light about Mona's sexual past. The fact that Mona is a black, single woman in a job where she is expected to be a role model for the community is highly relevant to the plot. Certain issues have to be addressed if Sara is to solve the mystery—stereotypes of black women's sexuality and Mona's struggle to be respected have to be set against the fact that she had the means, motive, and opportunity to kill Thornley. For the story to be credible, it had to be set in a multiracial community, where having a black head teacher of a large secondary school who finds herself in a situation like this, is, at least, plausible.

In some ways, choosing a location for a crime story—especially for a series character like Sara—is like choosing a place to live. The writer must consider whether the location suits the plot and the characters, and whether the place is sufficiently varied to provide a number of different settings for the action. A good crime story has light and shade, and it may need several changes of pace and mood.

On Sara's first date with John, in *Truth or Dare*, they go out for dinner and then to a famous jazz club in the centre of London. A big city setting means that excitement and glamour is always close at hand.

> We went by taxi, which took the Cromwell Road route into town. It was a treat not to be driving and to watch the city race by, twinkling with the soft edged lights of a summer Saturday night . . . Inside it was just as a jazz club should be—dark, fuggy with small tables crowded together, yellowing lamps illuminating the curling haze. A young black woman, dressed in a skimpy top and silky trousers, was easing her velvet voice round a blues number. I thrilled to the atmosphere and felt naughty and grown up to be there.

In the same book, I use the river to give the story—and Sara—a bit of breathing space. A trip on the Thames gives a sense of freedom and respite—and time to think.

> A fresh breeze off the River Thames whipped back my hair. I breathed deeply, tasting the damp river air, savouring that unique mix of countryside, traffic fumes and the promise of the sea that you get on a boat in the middle of the city. I love the river. I love its sense of history and the way it detaches you from the city's frantic grip. Everything looks different—Battersea Power Station, Big Ben, Tower Bridge . . . the river removes you from the bustle of the streets, shows you a new angle, reminds you that although the city changes constantly, the river Thames is timeless. The bright sun sparkled on the gentle waves, chopping out in the wake of

> the noisy putt-putting engine. I leaned on the railings of the boat, feeling sensuous and romantic in a thin Indian cotton sun dress and reflected lazily that my arms were tanning nicely. On our left, St. Paul's glided past, its glorious onion dome gleaming amongst the shimmering glass of the new City buildings. The sound of bells ringing in perfect rounds drifted faintly across the river.

Many crime writers who have rural or provencial settings for their stories use nature and the changing seasons as texture, or as metaphors for developments of character or plot. Crime writers who choose urban settings may have less opportunity to do this, but it does not mean that we ignore the natural world altogether. Gardens and parks can lend a softer edge to the urban landscape if we want it. Sara even manages to detect a bit of wildlife in her patch of green:

> I opened the back door and leaned against the door frame, savouring each sip of the musky wine. The warm air was heavily scented with night jasmine and honeysuckle which clung tenaciously to the trellis on one side of our tiny garden. On nights like this, David and I used to fetch two chairs from the kitchen, turn off the lights and sit outside, each with a drink in hand, silently listening to the sounds of a summer night. Once a fox came, nosing gently through the hedge, picking a delicate path across our small patch of grass. As a slight breeze shook the trees, he lifted his nose and detected our scent. A flash of eyes, swish of tail and he was off again, stalking his prey in the miniature woodland gardens of Acton. *(Truth or Dare)*

Heat and cold and the changing seasons can still impinge on the lives of city dwellers, and describing them can be an effective way of adding an extra dimension to the story.

I like to think my books tell interesting stories; I hope readers find my heroine, Sara Kingsley, engaging, and I hope they catch some of my enthusiasm for the litter-strewn mean streets of Acton. If my books launch Acton as an ultimate tourist destination for sight-seeing mystery readers, so be it. We can cope. As you will already know if you have read *Truth or Dare*, the Indian grocers stay open until late, and the Horse and Plough pub does a great meat-and-two-veg, with optional stodgy pudding.

Ellen Hart

From Sidekicks to Sword-Swallowers

Unravelling the Mystery of Supporting Characters

It's been said that the three primary elements of mystery fiction are pace, plot, and characterization. While this is certainly a generalization, I think most of us would agree that all of these components are essential. Mystery writers must be good jugglers, keeping each of these balls up in the air at all times, never allowing one to drop. Yet, it's also true that every author has a different take on which is most important, which is most central to her or his own writing.

For me, characterization has always been primary. As a matter of fact, I think the modern emphasis on characterization in mysteries has moved many novels out of the realm of the whodunit into the realm of the whydunit. Modern mystery writers and readers are terribly interested in what motivates human beings to behave the way they do. As a reader I find that, even if a book has the greatest plot and the fastest pace in the world, if the characters are composed of tissue paper, the book falls flat and leaves me feeling curiously empty. I've heard many editors comment that one of the biggest reasons books are rejected for publication is because the characters—including the supporting players—fail to come alive.

What is the distinction, you might ask, between the main character and the supporting cast? For me, the primary sleuth is the central character in any mystery. She is our eye in the book. We experience the story vicariously through her. And while there is an obvious hierarchy of importance in supporting characters—some more central to the plot than others, some continuing from book to book—the main character, for me, will always be the person leading us through the maze of clues to the final solution.

So, put simply, characterization is primary. It's also, without a doubt, the most fun I have when writing any book. Developing my cast takes time and effort, but when all is said and done and I'm finished with my novel, I feel I've spent time in the company of friends. Sure, some of these folks are sleazy, or even downright nasty, but they become real to me as I see them move and speak, as they begin to take on their own life. Make no mistake, your creations do surprise you sometimes.

When I was writing my third book, *Stage Fright*, I recall that I had conceived of a certain supporting character as a rather mousy, middle-aged woman. She was damaged by her past, and in the book I saw her as someone who was not only timid, but also afraid of life. Yet, when I heard her speak for the first time, she wasn't timid at all. She had confidence and a sense of humor, neither of which I'd anticipated. I tried with all my writerly might to get her to behave the way I thought she should, to fit within the constraints I'd envisioned for her, but she simply wouldn't cooperate. In the end, I came to understand that she was a somewhat introverted eccentric, unhappy with the hand life had dealt her, yet able to express an opinion and stand up for herself when she needed to be strong.

Ever since then, the first time a character speaks in one of my books, I feel it is the true moment of creation. Most often, my creatures behave the way I tell them to, but sometimes they just won't stay within my boundaries. And that, to me, is the magic of writing. You have to listen to your characters. Put more simply, you have to love them—not judge them. It's the only way you can get inside a character and truly understand what it is to be that person. It also helps you understand what that person wants out of life. That's a key question. Once you have the answer, you're well on your way. Since I often have less time to develop supporting characters, this information helps me create a dominant personality trait for each of the minor players. Developing supporting characters through the use of a dominant trait thus becomes a kind of literary shorthand, one that works well in the mystery.

I believe firmly that writers have creative access to most human experience. When I begin to examine the person in my book who will commit the crime—the fulcrum on which the plot of the book rests—I have to think long and hard. Unless this individual is a psychopath, someone who doesn't recognize society's rules and standards, someone for whom the term "conscience" has no meaning, there has to be a pretty strong motivation. The idea that one human could take another human's life, end all possibility forever, is an overwhelming thought. Therefore, I have to understand what motivates my character before I can write about him. And to comprehend is to create a certain empathy. A well-known English writer once said that there are no evil people, only people who are pushed to the wall and who see no other way out of their dilemma than to commit a crime. While I don't necessarily agree, I do think that the majority of people who commit crimes, the women and men who populate my books, do so for reasons I *can* understand. Lust. Greed. Jealousy. Fear. Hatred. Even love. Loyalty. The need for justice—motives we might think of as noble. In a sense, we're all working with the same motivations. But each character has a unique set of circumstances, life experiences, and beliefs. As a writer, I don't need to approve of the actions of my villains, or even my heroes, but I do need to understand them.

So, how do I go about creating a supporting character? Some writers create long dossiers on each member of the cast. Much of what they write in these dossiers never actually makes it into the novel, but it's a method by which they get to know this particular individual. I've never used this method, but it's certainly one way to approach the development of character.

In the thirteen books I've written to date, I've created my characters in essentially the same way. Most of the early work I do in my head. I move back and forth between the vital premise of my story—the main idea out of which the plot will develop—and my characters, seeing what's going to happen and what sort of person I need to help me flesh out the action. I suspect many writers spend a great deal of their time on the main protagonist and the main antagonist—the sleuth and the villain—and that's as it should be, and yet a good (read: successful) writer never forgets to develop an emotionally convincing supporting cast. In my case, since I write two mystery series and I'm on a pretty intimate basis with my main characters, I devote most of my time to the villain and the other supporting players.

In a mystery, with the exception of the sleuth and perhaps her or his partner or sidekick, every character you include must have a potential motive for the crime. Put another way, you have to cast your net of suspicion over *everyone*. Some motives will seem stronger than others, but to keep your readers guessing, all the supporting players must be suspects.

The exception to this rule, of course, are the truly minor characters —the woman or man we see only once. These "extras," as I call them, are often used as bridges or transitions, a device to connect one action or episode to another, or they may be used to throw a red herring into the path of the reader. Sometimes, they're needed so that we can hear a story from a different point of view. Or they may simply be used to add a bit of humor to lighten the book briefly. A writer should take care to make the descriptions of these "extras" sufficiently vivid, although the need to understand their internal motivations is generally unimportant.

Once I've placed the supporting characters in the context of the story and have some sense of who they are, the next step is to name them. Names are very important to me because they can reveal much about character. Most often, I go through lots of names before I finally hit on the right one. I may change a name four or five times over the course of writing the first draft. And sometimes, I never do get the name quite right, and I have to go with second best. I love names. I keep a book on my desk and write interesting first and last names in it—ones I find in graveyards, on TV shows, in phone books—anywhere and everywhere. I also have several copies of what-to-name-the-baby books—that sort of volume is absolutely invaluable to me.

Okay, once you've got a good sense of everyone in your supporting cast, the development of your plot line will start to take shape. Whether a character is guilty or innocent, you have to tie the person to the crime. Let's say it's a murder. How did they know the deceased? Were they friends? Enemies? Related? Is there a secret they know that no one else knows? Where were they at the time of the murder? Did they have motive, means, and opportunity to commit the crime? What, if anything, did they stand to gain by the death? You create character the same way you plot: by asking questions.

Once I have a sense of how the person is related to the mystery, I sit down and do a quick physical sketch. It's important to visualize the person before you begin writing about them. Let's call our character Betty. First, what is Betty's body type? Is she short? Tall? Fat? Skinny? Lanky? Athletic? Then, age. Young, middle-aged, elderly? Next comes the face. I try to get as clear a picture as possible at this early stage, but I don't worry if it's not all there.

Next, I take it one level deeper. I begin to get a bit of the history of the person. What's made Betty the kind of woman she is? Where is she from? An only child? One of six children? From a poor family? Middle class? What's her psychological make-up? Is she happy, depressed, cynical, arrogant, distrustful, sly, witty, slow, intellectual, sweet, opinionated, bitter? Remember, what you tell your readers about each character must have relevance to the mystery. A mystery novel is a tight construction in which everything you include about a person's character must relate to the central story, even if it's just a red herring.

At this point, we have a pretty good idea of what Betty looks like, and a little bit about her background. Next comes what I call "original detail." I don't mean a list of character tags, something like: Betty hiccups a lot, always wears something blue, never drinks anything but Coke, and has a pet monkey. That's not a person, it's a laundry list. Instead, think about who Betty is. What kind of music does Betty like to play in the car on the way to work in the morning? What does that say about her? What does she carry in her purse at all times? What does that say about her? Whose picture does she carry in her billfold? Again, you may not use all of this, but it's helpful in visualizing Betty. The better you know her, the more consistently you'll be able to portray her in your writing. And by concentrating your attention on the details—not just a photographic representation—you have a better chance of creating a vivid image, something your readers will remember.

Believe me, by the time you're done with a first draft, you'll know these people inside and out, or at least you should if you're doing your work as a writer. And that's where revision comes in. The second draft of the book is where I square what I know about these characters now with what I knew about them when I first began writing. It's all a process. Nothing is perfect the first time around.

This may seem like a lot of work to do, but trust me, it's important. Again, I believe strongly that a character's identity comes from *your* understanding of how your character views the world. And that takes time to figure out. You will be rewarded by a much deeper and clearer sense of who this person is, and it will also help you to keep their voice and motives consistent, even when on the surface their actions may seem inscrutable. It's all part of the mystery—of your book, and of the human heart.

So, where do we find the raw material to develop our characters? I suppose there are several answers to that. First, some authors have such wonderful, inventive minds that they're able to create stories and the characters to people those stories simply out of their own imaginations, with no ties to the actual or real. Fantasy writers spring immediately to mind. Yet I have a hunch that, to a greater or lesser extent, most writers mine their own lives for material. Sometimes I feel like an actor playing many parts. In a sense, I have to become my characters to write about them, and to become them, I have to find some connection between them and me. I borrow from my life constantly and from the lives of those around me. I study people—their movements, their gestures, their attitudes. I sit in shopping malls and watch people walk by. Sometimes I take notes, sometimes I just let the scene wash over me. It's all grist for the mill. Consequently, while some aspects of my characters are truly fictions, some are also borrowed from the actual. Perhaps it's a bit like Frankenstein's monster—a brain here, a body there. The final result, however, *is* fiction, or it better be unless you want to get sued.

One of my most successful supporting characters, Cordelia Thorn, is a composite of several elements. First, she resembles physically one of my old high school friends. This particular woman is large, attractive, and *very* theatrical. She was a theatre major at the University of Minnesota, and later became the stage manager for a small theatre company in Minneapolis. Cordelia, however, has a humor that is entirely her own. I'd like to say that I'm a lot like Cordelia, but the truth is, I'm not. I understand her, but when I'm writing in her voice, I'm continually surprised by what she says and does.

When I first began the Jane Lawless series, I conceived of Cordelia as the salt in the book—a little would go a long way. Much to my surprise, she's consistently grown in importance, both to me and to my readers. I suppose this is another example of a character taking charge of her own fate. Cordelia simply wouldn't stay put in that theatre I built for her. Somehow, she found herself a way out.

Actually, the chapters that feature Cordelia are always the most fun to write. She provides the humor in the books, and she's a great foil for Jane, a character who, while the main sleuth, is far more cerebral and quiet. That is one of the chief reasons to have strong supporting characters—we get to see Jane *in relation to someone else*, and that facilitates our understanding of who she is. Why? Because we now see a contrast. Jane is more methodical and logical; Cordelia is more intuitive. Jane is conservative; Cordelia is flamboyant. One is yin, and one is yang. Each characterization helps form the other. Indeed, surrounding your main character with flat, cardboard cut-outs is the quickest way to sink the central characterization.

Another supporting character in the Jane Lawless series is Jane's English aunt, Beryl Cornelius. Through Beryl, we catch a first-hand glimpse of Jane's younger life. In the present, we see Jane cared for by an older adult and—perhaps most important—we see Jane's struggle to move away from her more solitary existence and accept another human being into her somewhat lonely life. While Jane has the capacity to be lonely in a crowd of friends, Beryl, like Cordelia, cracks through Jane's formidable defences and helps humanize her.

Now, even though I believe it's important to beware of authors bearing tips, here's one of mine. To be successful, supporting characters must have one important element: they have to be plausible.

The bargain any reader makes with a book is to suspend her or his disbelief long enough to allow the book to unfold—to see where the author is going to take them. Without that voluntary suspension of disbelief no work of fiction would have a chance. Readers would never become involved. If supporting characters behave in an implausible way, it pulls the reader out of the book—"No cop would talk like that," "No private eye would do something that dumb." Consequently, the reader can't escape the fact that she is reading a book. So, a word to the wise. Be careful to make your characters plausible.

A word about caricature. As a writer of mysteries, I don't have any problem with the use of caricature for the "extras." For those briefly seen individuals who are used for a single purpose, caricature can be an appealing option. The art of caricature consists of ignoring the ordinary and exaggerating the remarkable, and while I think that caricature should be avoided with other characterizations because it is an essentially shallow conceptualization, it can be a quick and effective way to draw a bit player.

Now, how does an author reveal character? The most significant way is through action. Characters in conflict are characters that grab our attention—whether they are central or supporting players. Why is action so essential? Fictional characters, like real human beings, often say one thing while they do another. It's only through actions that we see the essential truth of any given person. Again, our murderer, if not a psychopath, is probably someone at the end of her rope—and this makes her a very interesting character indeed. Don't shy away from conflict, from kicking a character when she's down. Giving a character a choice, allowing her to wrestle with a tough decision, is a great way to help the reader see the hidden person. You have the opportunity for action with every cast member—some, of course, more than others. That's why it's important for your writing to be lean and to the point. You don't have a lot of time to develop supporting characters, so when they are on stage, they can't remain static.

Historically, the hard-boiled novel gave us a main character whom we knew very little about. Although it was usually a man, his personal history was almost always ignored. Oh, we knew he liked blondes or brunettes. We knew what sort of whiskey he drank and which drawer he kept his gun in, but in general he was more of a cipher than a fully fleshed out human being. Today, however, we seem to want all our characterizations as fully fleshed out as possible. In short, clever plotting isn't enough—we want some exploration of what it is to be human.

In the famous words of F. Scott Fitzgerald, "Character is plot and plot is character." I think that just about says it all.

Barbara Paul

Putting an End to the Mystery

People who read mysteries hate mysteries. What they like are solutions.

A mystery novel is the only kind of book a reader can pick up knowing that, after some two hundred pages of turmoil, order will be restored at the end. Questions will be answered, problems will be solved, and the disruptive force in the world of the book will be rooted out to allow that world to return to its own norm. Every mystery writer makes her readers a promise: I'll bring you safely home again.

The basic mystery formula never varies: crime → investigation → solution. There can be a great deal of variation *within* that formula (and the more the better, say I), but unless all three of those basic steps are there, you're not reading a mystery. But that, too, is part of returning safely home at the end: the reader knows what to expect. There's a certain comfort in that.

The challenge for the writer, then, becomes one of keeping the novel from becoming predictable, even mechanical. Older mystery novels went in big for surprise endings, putting the burden of counteracting predictability exclusively on the conclusion. Revealing the murderer to be the Least Likely Suspect was a favourite device—a strategem no mystery writer today would dare try for fear of being laughed out of the profession.

But the truth is, a mystery novel succeeds or fails on the strength of its conclusion. Have you ever read a mystery that is absolutely perfect—until the ending? Then something goes wrong: the conclusion is rushed, or the explanations are a little vague, or the "evidence" is unconvincing, or something vital is left out. Quite a few otherwise excellent mysteries have been marred for me when I was left with the impression that the writer was in too big a hurry to wrap things up and meet her deadline.

Every writer has her own way of proceeding, but I never start work on a new mystery novel until I have the conclusion locked down. No, I don't know all the details; I don't outline the ending or anything like that. But I have to know, in general terms at least, what the solution to the mystery is—who committed the murder(s) and why, and that "why" has to be thoroughly thought out. It's a target for me to aim at the whole time I'm writing. That's no guarantee I'll get it right (and if anyone knows of a device that does carry that guarantee, please get in touch with me immediately), but the end must be inherent in the beginning. I'm convinced that's true of all good fiction, genre or not. But it's doubly so in a form of storytelling as plot-driven as the mystery novel. Knowing the dénouement of my story is an absolute must for me before I start writing.

The word "dénouement" properly refers to the part of the plot that follows the climax—the unravelling of the plot, the wrapping up of the details of the solution. But lately the term seems to be used to mean the entire ending of the story: the pay-off, what everything has been leading up to. And that's the way I'm using the term here. A longish sequence following the exposure of the murderer in which the detective explains all those puzzling little details that the reader may be wondering about—that's the old-fashioned way of doing it. It worked very well in the early "puzzle" mysteries of the sort that Agatha Christie did so well, but it's artificial in a modern realistic crime novel.

The reason is distance. Christie kept her readers at a safe remove from the ugliness of murder. Word arrives that the vicar was found stabbed to death in his study last night, and everyone immediately starts talking about where they were at nine o'clock the previous evening. The *horror* of violent death is never allowed to intrude upon the puzzle to be solved.

But that was a different kind of story for a different time. More and more contemporary mystery writers want their readers to feel the sickening fear that murder generates—not just in hard-boiled novels (where it's expected), but also, umm, in medium-boiled novels as well. Puzzle novels are polite; contemporary realistic mystery novels are in-your-face. Any post-climax explanation in a modern mystery is an intrusion; it reads like an afterthought, something the writer forgot to work into her plot earlier.

Only once did I ever write something close to the old-fashioned dénouement, the post-climax explanation kind. It was at the end of *Full Frontal Murder*, and I called it an epilogue. The mystery was solved, the villain apprehended, the details all explained—none of that needed further elaboration. But my two main characters had suffered deeply during the course of the story; and if I left them like that, I knew I'd get letters saying "What happens to Marian and Holland? Are they all right?" The readers would feel unsatisfied, and they would be right to do so; it was a loose end that needed tying up. So I added a scene demonstrating not that Marian and Holland were "all right"—but that they were healing. The scene shows them embarked on a journey of recovery, and that was sufficient; there's no need to spell out every little detail. Order must not only be restored, but restored in a way that doesn't leave the reader feeling short-changed.

Don't take that to mean that all mysteries must have happily-ever-after endings. The mystery novel has often been criticized for tying up the loose ends a little *too* neatly, of resolving conflicts in a way they are seldom resolved in real life. It's a valid criticsm, I think.

One way contemporary writers have dealt with this problem is to leave an issue or two unresolved, deliberately so, to reflect the fact that in real life we frequently have to live with unanswered questions. Not the main thread of the mystery, of course—that conflict must be resolved—but minor threads that were woven into the main plot; sometimes one or two of them can be left dangling. Liza Cody ends *Bad Company* that way, with detective Anna Lee not knowing what's going to happen to two teenage girls she became involved with through her recently concluded case. It's the right ending; that note of uncertainty is the only credible way to conclude a story that devotes much of its attention to the difficulty of reaching an understanding with people who don't want to hear. Leaving a thread or two dangling at the end is also risky for the writer, for you can be sure that some reviewer somewhere will complain about the unanswered questions.

Another way to avoid the unbelievable all-problems-solved ending is to write a resolution that isn't quite as tidy as the characters in the book might like. A good example of that kind of dénouement is P.D. James's *The Skull Beneath the Skin.* Investigator Cordelia Gray learns who the killer is, but she knows she'll never be able to prove it or even persuade the authorities to look into the problem. By the end of the book, the killer is dead, so the murders don't go unpunished; the scales of justice are balanced. But Cordelia is left in a state of utter frustration that she'll never be able to set the record straight. Yet, that feeling of frustration is primarily on the part of the character, not the reader. We sympathize with Cordelia's feelings of disappointment and even defeat, but we ourselves are, on the whole, satisfied. We know whodunit, the disruptive force in the world of the book has been removed, and order has been restored. It's just that it's not restored as prettily as we might wish. A perfect modern dénouement.

The way of avoiding the too-neat ending that I favour is to stress the high price of restoring order. Just solving the puzzle isn't enough; the reader must be kept constantly aware of the sense of loss caused by the crimes that have been committed. And that's not something that can simply be crowded into the ending; there can be no sense of real loss without adequate, book-long preparation. In a sense, I try to start writing my dénouement the minute I type "Chapter I" on a page.

An example? All right—*Kill Fee.* In that book, the villain is a freelance killer-for-hire named Pluto whom I showed to be as tricky as he is callous. His only concern is collecting his fee; he never gives a thought to the pain he leaves in his wake. Pluto is eventually tracked down by two police investigators after a long and disappointment-filled hunt. During a shoot-out on an excursion boat circling Manhattan, Pluto is killed; but he manages to wound one of the investigators in the arm before he dies. The other investigator sees that his friend gets medical attention, drives him home, and unlocks his apartment door for him—unaware that the door is rigged to a booby-trap. Tricky Pluto has the last word.

I stopped the book right there, with the investigator unlocking the door. A scene earlier in the book shows Pluto setting the trap, so the reader knows perfectly well what's going to happen; there's no need for further particulars. In fact, actually showing the bloody consequences of opening that door would only dilute the punch-in-the-gut ending I was aiming for; overdoing it is a cardinal sin in any kind of writing. That ending works as a second climax, one that comes after the reader thinks the story is done and all is well once again.

But this is what crime is—great and unnecessary loss, people getting hurt who don't deserve to be hurt, the blow that you never see coming. I always try to bring my readers safely home again, but I like to show the "home" is now missing a few of its former rooms. Order is restored, but at great price.

Of course, all of this applies only to the modern realistic mystery novel. If we're talking about comic mysteries, all bets are off.

Obviously a mystery written to make people laugh doesn't want to create a great sense of loss, or leave disturbing questions unanswered, or resolve the conflict in a way that's not completely what we might wish. Here we *want* everything tied up neatly. A clever ending is more important than a true-to-life one—so long as it doesn't go over the top. But readers will tolerate a big helping of artifice in a comic novel where they won't in a realistic one.

The reason, once again, is distance. In the realistic mystery, the reader is close to the investigator, perhaps even identifying with her (although I personally think that's a misguided way to read), we're definitely "with" the protagonist every step of the way. In a comic mystery, however, that kind of closeness just gets in the way; it makes it difficult for the reader to laugh at the character. We *like* the characters in a comic mystery, because they keep us amused, but they are something apart from our personal experience, and that distance from them is what lets us laugh.

I can't think of a better example than the characters in Donald D. Westlake's series about Dortmunder, the world's unluckiest criminal. Dortmunder makes beautiful, elaborate plans for illegally enriching himself and his cohorts—and then watches those plans go absurdly, comically wrong. We like Dortmunder and want him to succeed (a little guilty pleasure there), but we never for a moment imagine ouselves doing the things he does.

The Dortmunder books aren't true mysteries; they're "caper" books. Instead of crime → investigation → solution, Westlake follows a scheme of planned crime → attempted execution → comic disaster. This gives his books a whole series of little climaxes as Dortmunder's gang keeps trying to make the plan work, building up to the final comic disaster that ends the story.

I'm using Dortmunder as my example because he's familiar, but I'll wager every avid mystery reader has crossed Dortmunder's path at least once (and if you read one book in the series, you want more). Even though they're caper stories, they offer a clear illustration of the difference in approach between comic and realistic writing.

What Westlake does so well is write dénouements that are logical results of the absurd goings-on that precede them . . . logic within absurdity: quite a trick. Not all writers can do that. I've read quite a few comic mysteries in which the mystery is little more than an excuse for parading a string of eccentric/funny/cute characters across the pages. Some of these books are good fun, but I tend to think of them as near-mysteries. Their dénouements are as perfunctory as the preceding plots are thin. Westlake avoids that problem by keeping whatever sting or burglary or con game Dortmunder is working on always in the foreground, no matter what else is going on—and there's always a lot else going on. As a result, Westlake has built up plenty of momentum by the time he reaches the conclusion of his story, and the reader is more than willing to go along with the final comic disaster, the one that makes further disasters impossible by writing an end to the whole enterprise.

Formulaic? You bet. But Westlake makes it work through sheer inventiveness; readers approach each new book wondering what kind of mess Dortmunder will get himself into this time—and readers in a mood of happy anticipation will tolerate both formula and improbabilities. In fact, we cherish them; it's the absurdity of what happens to the characters that gives the books their special flavor.

I got involved in dealing with the tricky issue of the improbable dénouement myself a few years back. An American publisher started a line of mysteries in which the detective was to be an actual historical personage, and I joined in on the fun. I'd been wanting to write a mystery with an opera background, so I chose the great tenor Caruso as my detective.

Now, if you were to search through the entire history of Western Civilization, you wouldn't find a more unlikely detective than Enrico Caruso. Caruso was a bit of a scaredy-cat, and he was too devoted to high living to take time off to conduct a disciplined investigation of a crime. So, the problem was how to make this lovable, larger-than-life figure into an investigator the readers would accept. The answer was obvious: make it a comic novel.

So, in *A Cadenza for Caruso* the tenor sets out to discover who killed a small-time impresario, because the police suspect his friend Puccini did the dastardly deed; there had to be a personal motive for Caruso to involve himself. He bumbles around, poking his nose into other people's business, asking impertinent questions, making a thorough pest of himself. Without any sort of licensed authority to back him up, his extreme meddling would not be tolerated by the reader unless it was presented in humorous terms. So my task was to make sure that the readers never started looking upon Caruso as the kind of detective they'd like to see in charge of a real homicide investigation.

All of which brings up one major problem. Here we have a detective who has been repeatedly shown as well-meaning and eager but none too able—how does such a detective solve the mystery? How to make such an improbable dénouement acceptable to the readers? There are a number of ways this could have been handled, but I decided to take one of the hoariest clichés of detective fiction and turn it upside down.

Remember all those mysteries that end with the detective gathering the suspects together in one room and then explaining how the murder was done, why the murder was done, and —at last!—

who the murderer is? It was an okay gimmick when Hercule Poirot did it, but it's been imitated to death. And we still haven't completely abandoned it, unfortunately. I think every episode of *Murder, She Wrote* that I watched ended that way.

But that was the ending I wanted to poke fun at. So I had Caruso gather everyone together on the stage of the Metropolitan Opera House for the pay-off scene. There he goes through the rigmarole of relating what he's learned, explaining why the impresario had been murdered, and—at last!—pointing an accusing finger at one of the people on the stage. And gets it wrong. The person he accuses is not the murderer at all.

I'd wanted to write that scene for *years*.

But at the same time I didn't want Caruso to look like a total doofus, simply because he had been so much fun while he was playing detective; I liked this fictional character too much to leave him with egg on his face. Therefore, I had his misinterpretation of the facts prompt a *clarification* of the facts from others on the stage, which in turn leads to the exposure of the real killer. So, while Caruso doesn't come up with the solution to the mystery, he does trigger it. In spite of the mess he makes of his maiden foray into criminal investigation, he comes out of the affair smelling like a rose. Improbable? Yes. Acceptable? Also yes.

My point is that if this were a realistic mystery, I could never have got away with a dénouement like that one. Comic mysteries let writers have more leeway than realistic stories do; what's more, readers expect something a little *outré* to wind up a story filled with high shenanigans. If I'd written a "straight" solution for *A Cadenza for Caruso*, the readers would have been disappointed. And so would I. So that scene was the target I was working my way toward the whole time I was writing. Whether you're writing comic mystery or realistic mystery, knowing the solution before you begin writing is, in my opinion, an absolute must. *You have to be in control of your material.* And you have to know where you're going before you can figure out the best way of getting there.

Contributors' Notes

Jean Bedford was born in England in 1946 and moved to Australia in 1947. She has been a journalist, a publisher's editor, and a teacher of English as a second language and of creative writing. She has published nine works of fiction, including three detective novels featuring private eye Anna Southwood. She lives on the Illawarra coast of New South Wales.

Sarah Dreher was born in a small town in Pennsylvania. She holds a Ph.D. in clinical psychology, is a practising psychotherapist, and began writing novels at the age of 45. In addition to the Stoner McTavish mystery series, she has written a novel and is an award-winning playwright.

Joan M. Drury lives in Minnesota and shares her life with a daughter, two sons, a daughter-by-marriage, and two *perfect* granddaughters as well as dear friends. She is the publisher of Spinsters Ink; director of Norcroft: A Writing Retreat for Women; and author of the Tyler Jones mystery series: *The Other Side of Silence, Silent Words,* and *Closed in Silence*. She writes, she talks, she makes things happen, she dreams, she tries to make a difference in all she does.

Stella Duffy was born in England and grew up in New Zealand. She has written four crime novels, *Calendar Girl, Wavewalker, Beneath the Blonde* and *Fresh Flesh* (Serpent's Tail); and two non-crime novels, *Singling Out the Couples* and *Eating Cake* (Sceptre). She has also written fourteen short stories, two one-woman shows, and *The Hand*, a dance/theatre piece for Gay Sweatshop. She is an actor and writer with comedy company Spontaneous Combustion and teaches improvisation as a creative tool to actors and writers and in the corporate sector. She lives in South London, purely because it irritates North Londoners so much.

Ellen Hart is the author of the Jane Lawless series of mysteries. She has a BA in theology and worked for fifteen years as a professional chef. She lives in Minnesota with her partner of twenty-one years.

Gillian Linscott is the author of fourteen crime novels, eight of them featuring her suffragette detective character, Nell Bray. Before turning to book-writing full time, she worked as a journalist for the *Guardian* and the BBC. She lives in Herefordshire.

Val McDermid grew up in a Scottish mining community and, after university, became a journalist. She worked on national newspapers for fourteen years, spending the last three as Northern Bureau Chief of a national Sunday tabloid. She quit journalism in 1991 and has since been a full-time writer. Spinsters Ink publishes her Lindsay Gordon mysteries: *Report for Murder, Common Murder, Deadline for Murder, Conferences are Murder*, and *Booked for Murder*. She is also the author of the Kate Brannigan series: *Dead Beat, Kick Back, Crack*

Down, Clean Break, Blue Genes, and *Star Struck*, which won the French Grand Prix des Romans d'Aventures. She has written a book of non-fiction, *A Suitable Job for a Woman*, and three thrillers—*The Mermaids Singing*, which won the Crime Writers' Association Gold Dagger Award for the Best Crime Novel of 1995, *The Wire in the Blood*, and *A Place of Execution.*

Marcia Muller created the contemporary hard-boiled woman detective with her first Sharon McCone novel, *Edwin of the Iron Shoes,* and this groundbreaking series is now over two decades old. Much-loved bestsellers, the McCone novels have been translated into eight languages, and there are two million copies in print worldwide. In 1993, Marcia Muller received the Private Eye Writers of America Life Achievement Award. Her novel *Wolf in the Shadows* was nominated for the Edgar Allen Poe Award for Best Crime Novel and the Shamus Award, and won the Anthony Boucher Award. Marcia Muller lives in northern Califonia.

Chris Niles is the author of three novels, *Spike It, Run Time* and *Crossing Live*, all published by Macmillan. She has lived in New Zealand, the UK, Hungary, and Australia, and now works as a freelance journalist in New York City.

Abigail Padgett grew up in Indiana. She has worked in teaching, vocational counseling, child abuse investigation, and mental health advocacy. The last two jobs contributed to Padgett's series sleuth, Bo Bradley, a child abuse investigator who lives with the problems of manic depressive illness, featured in *Child of Silence, Strawgirl, Turtle Baby, The Dollmaker's Daughters,* and *Moonbird Boy.* Padgett's second series features lesbian social psychologist Blue McCarron in *Blue* and *Blue Plate Special.*

Barbara Paul taught drama and literature at the University of Pittsburgh in Pennsylvania until she reached a point where she could not face even one more undergraduate paper and traded in a steady pay check for the exigencies of full-time writing. She has published five science fiction novels and seventeen mystery novels, including a series featuring NYPD detective Marian Larch. A collection of her short stories, *Jack Be Quick and Other Crime Stories*, was published in 1999.

Penny Sumner's first publication was a short story in *Reader, I Murdered Him*. Another story, "Dead-Head," which appeared in *Reader, I Murdered Him, Too* was shortlisted for the Crime Writers' Association Short Story Dagger Award. She has written two crime novels, *The End of April* and *Crosswords*, and is editor of *Brought to Book: Murderous Stories from the Literary World.*

Anne Wilson did a Ph.D. in sociology at the LSE, then became a freelance journalist. She is now a corporate video scriptwriter. She is the author of the Sara Kingsley mysteries *Truth or Dare* and *Governing Body.* She is married with three children and lives in London.

Editor

Helen Windrath has worked in publishing for many years and has edited several anthologies. She lives in London, and has no criminal record!

Praise for Oscar Casares's

AMIGOLAND

"A story rich in humor and sadness and truth and embellishment, full of life's incalculable, unpredictable graces and missteps and inevitabilities. It is the story Oscar Casares was born to tell." — Steve Bennett, *San Francisco Chronicle*

"*Amigoland*'s poignant imagery and wisecracking leads make it hard to put down. Casares is at his best when describing the downfall of the fiercely independent Don Fidencio. . . . Readers will remember this well-drawn crank even after this witty, affecting novel's final page." — Beth Perry, *People*

"Part of the pleasure of the novel: It's different from so much else out there. . . . Casares has crafted characters who are not powerless in the face of infirmity and thus cannot be reduced to caricature. . . . Casares has proven himself to be a writer with a big heart. This debut novel indicates he's also a writer with a big future."

— Edward Nawotka, *Dallas Morning News*

"Passages that shimmer on the page and stick in the reader's mind. . . . Casares makes it look easy."

— Maggie Galehouse, *Houston Chronicle*

"A hysterical and poignant family road trip."

— *The Daily Beast*

"By turns hilarious and heartbreaking, this story of two feisty, aging brothers and their bumpy road trip to the past is a delightful romp. Think *Sunshine Boys* go south of the border, but funnier, much funnier, and infinitely more poignant."

— Cristina García, author of *Dreaming in Cuban* and *A Handbook to Luck*

"Casares's comedy of missed cues and carefully tended rancor makes the revelations at the end of the book . . . testify all the more eloquently to the strange and unpredictable paths that memory can take." — Benjamin Moser, *Harper's*

"Pitch-perfect. . . . Knowing, touching, and true. . . . An exceptional first novel." — *Kirkus Reviews* (starred review)

"Casares lovingly and humorously creates these aging characters, whose humdrum lives and small-scale dramas nonetheless burn bright with a belief in possibilities and a demand for respect." — Kathe Connair, *Minneapolis Star Tribune*

"A pleasant and readable ride. . . . *Amigoland* will not disappoint Casares's many eager fans."

— Roberto Ontiveros, *Austin American-Statesman*

"A winning novel. . . . It's plain to see how love, borders, death — and most of all willful ignorance — are part of everyday reawakenings. With Casares's blessing, you can laugh at them all." — *Publishers Weekly* (starred review)

"Oscar Casares's *Amigoland,* his first novel and a follow-up to his much acclaimed book of short stories, *Brownsville,* is a liberating journey full of warmth and color. . . . The group's impromptu trip to Mexico feels like a refreshing, rejuvenating trip for the reader as well as the characters. And the ending? Bittersweet, unexpected, and undeniably precious. All told, *Amigoland* is full of new friends and makes for perfect summer reading." — Jessica Inman, *BookPage*

"Engaging and humorous. . . . Casares continues to enlighten his readers by showing Mexican-Americans experiencing the usual human conditions." — Teresa Carbajal, examiner.com

Also by Oscar Casares

Brownsville

AMIGOLAND

A Novel

Oscar Casares

BACK BAY BOOKS
Little, Brown and Company
New York Boston London

Back Bay Books / Little, Brown and Company
Hachette Book Group
237 Park Avenue, New York, NY 10017
www.hachettebookgroup.com

Originally published in hardcover by Little, Brown and Company, August 2009
First Back Bay paperback edition, August 2010

Back Bay Books is an imprint of Little, Brown and Company.
The Back Bay Books name and logo are trademarks of
Hachette Book Group, Inc.

The characters and events in this book are fictitious.
Any similarity to real persons, living or dead, is
coincidental and not intended by the author.

"Los Inditos" appears in the book
A Texas-Mexican Cancionero: Folksongs of the Lower Border
by Américo Paredes, University of Texas Press, 1995.

Library of Congress Cataloging-in-Publication Data
Casares, Oscar.
Amigoland : a novel / Oscar Casares. — 1st ed.
p. cm.
ISBN 978-0-316-15969-2 (hc) / 978-0-316-01883-8 (pb)
1. Older men — Fiction. 2. Brothers — Fiction. 3. Mexican Americans — Fiction. 4. Nursing home patients — Fiction. 5. Reminiscing in old age — Fiction. 6. Voyages and travels — Fiction. 7. Brownsville (Tex.) — Fiction. 8. Mexico — Fiction. I. Title.
PS3603.A83A59 2009
813'.6 — dc22 2008045123

10 9 8 7 6 5 4 3 2 1

RRD-IN

Printed in the United States of America

For Becky and Adrian

Ahi vienen los inditos por el carrizal. . . .
¡Ay mamita! ¡Ay papito! me quieren matar. . . .

The little Indians are coming through the canebrake. . . .
Oh mommy! Oh daddy! They want to kill me. . . .

—"Los Inditos"
Mexican folk song, circa 1848

PART I

1

The One With The Flat Face was taking her time coming around with the cart. She had stopped to visit with The Friendly Turtle and the two of them were talking and talking, as if it had been years since they had seen each other, as if it wasn't only a few hours ago that she brought out the cart, as if there weren't other people already hungry and waiting for their dinner.

He sat at the table closest to the side door, which he planned to use as his escape route once he finished his meal. The clock now read 5:05, five minutes past the time they were supposed to bring out the trays. Five minutes normally wouldn't concern him, but he had only picked at his breakfast and then later not felt like eating the turkey casserole they served at lunch, so instead he spent his lunch hour smoking out on the patio, sitting on the padded seat of his walker.

"You're going to get hungry later, Mr. Rosales," The One With The Flat Face had come outside to tell him.

"You think I have never been hungry?" he snapped at her.

"A man your age should not be smoking cigarettes."

"Leave me alone. I smoked my two cigarettes a day for most of my life, long before you or your mother and father were born, maybe even before their mother and father."

"Still, it's not good for you, sir. If you get sick with the flu, your lungs are not going to be strong."

"And what, you afraid I won't make it all the way to ninety-two?"

She finally went back inside and left him in peace. That had been more than four hours ago, though, and since his nap Don Fidencio had kept an eye on the clock. The first thing he did was search through each of his five shoe boxes for any cheese crackers or chocolate candy that he might have forgotten. He found everything but the snacks he was looking for — his five U.S. government–issue pens (two more were missing, most likely stolen by a miserable somebody with nothing better to do than torment an old man); his three Zippo lighters (only one of which still had fluid); his federal employee badge, made of brass and still worth the trouble of polishing; his can of Mace spray (just in case); his extra pair of suspenders (also just in case); his roll of lottery tickets, wound tightly with a pair of rubber bands; his slightly warped cassette of Narciso Martinez music; his baseball that had been signed by a famous pitcher for the Astros but whose autograph was now smudged and impossible to make out; his tiny Aztec calendar on a broken key chain; his spare keys to the car and house, neither of which belonged to him anymore, but just the same, he liked to rattle them inside his pocket; a few random pesos and centavos, along with the silver dollar that he used to carry in his wallet; and his rosary that one of The Jesus Christ Loves Everybody Women had given him when they were going room to room, tracking down innocent souls that had somehow survived this long without their help.

The hunger had hit him more so when he walked into the mess hall. He took out one of his ballpoint pens to jot down the hours that had passed since the last bit of food he ate at breakfast. After listing each hour, he numbered them all the way to eleven. Eleven seemed like a lot, but he was sure he had lasted longer in the past. He thought if he could make himself think of a time when he was hungrier, it might make him feel less hungry now. There must have been plenty of times; the problem was making his old head remember. His best guess was it had to be when he was a boy and they would work along one side of the river one year and along the other side the following year, then back again, so much so that he sometimes forgot they were two separate countries. And then again much later they followed the crops up north. Minnesota, Iowa, Wisconsin, Ohio, Indiana. He could remember picking beets. He could remember the onions. He could remember the cucumbers. He could remember the melons. He must have been hungrier then, he and his younger brothers and sisters crowded into the back of the truck, their mother and the baby in the cab with their father, driving all night so they could make it to the next job. He could see himself crouched in a corner, clinging to the wooden slats, the stars up above him like bits of cotton sprinkled across the dark sky.

He was still thinking about this when The One With The Worried Face rolled up in his wheelchair. The wooden table was tall enough for the armrests to fit underneath and let him scoot forward until his chest touched the edge. After locking the brakes, he placed his elbows on the table, then held on to his weary head as if he were trying to decide the fate of the world. A small monitor with a string attached to it hung from the backrest of his wheelchair and then clipped to his collar, ready to send off a piercing alarm if he were to move too far away and slip out of the chair onto the floor. Though the weather outside was predicted to be in the high nineties for the rest of the week, he kept warm with a green ski cap, a checkered flannel shirt, thick sweatpants, athletic socks, and woolly slippers.

The Gringo With The Ugly Finger was the next one to guide his wheelchair into the dining room, using his heels to spur him along until he reached the table.

"I could eat two horses," he said, which was what he had said at lunch and before that breakfast and before that dinner, and so on and so on. "How 'bout you boys?"

The question got only a half nod from Don Fidencio and even less from The One With The Worried Face, who obviously had too much on his mind to be troubled with something as trivial as feeding himself.

"Say," The Gringo With The Ugly Finger began, "I ever show you boys what happened to me when I worked for Pan Am?"

Only about six hundred times, Don Fidencio wanted to say. But he knew better than to acknowledge the question or to so much as look in the direction of the man's left index finger, which was snipped off at the end like a cigar about to be lit. Don Fidencio pulled his walker a little closer to make sure it wasn't sticking too far out into the aisle. His own hands weren't in such good shape either, with a patchwork of scars and splotches scattered from his knuckles to the crook of his elbow, most of them from bumping into this door or that fence or just about anything else that could tear his papery skin. He tried to remember why he had a bandage covering part of his right hand and when nothing came to him he went back to inspecting the rest of the walker. All four tires, front and back, were made of plastic, but he pressed his thumb into them anyway, same as the men used to do when he drove up to a service station. He rattled the wire basket, where he sometimes carried his #4 shoe box, the one with the chocolates. Then he fiddled with the extensions on the handgrips, first making them longer, then shorter, and finally moving them back to their original position, where they should have stayed all along.

"Now you wouldn't think the tip of a man's index finger would take so damn long to find, but when the rotor on that DC-3 caught me, I was lucky the darn thing didn't end up in Cuba. Wish I could blame it on somebody distracting me, saying, 'Hey, Phillips,' and me turning to look when it happened. But the truth of the matter is that the blame falls squarely on my lap. Just wasn't thinking, had my head somewhere else, in the clouds maybe, when it should have been down on the ground, concentrating on my work. The other mechanics went looking all over the hangar and out on the tarmac, since the doors had been wide open. That's what they told me anyway — I was out cold almost as soon as it happened. Had a chance to see the tip of my finger was gone, and it was lights out. I never was one for the sight of blood, most especially my own. That, I can trace back to my time in the war. Saw things that stayed with me, inside my head, no matter how I tried to get rid of them. Anyhow, I think it was one of the Mexican janitors who finally recovered the tip and wrapped it up in some aluminum foil left over from his lunch."

The finger, the finger, dear God, the bloody finger. Who asked him? Did he think he was the only one who had a story from his work? Don Fidencio had delivered the mail for forty-two years and had a few of his own stories. Lots and lots of stories, about working his whole life, about his eleven brothers and sisters, about growing up on both sides of the river, even about how his grandfather had come to this country with the Indians. Yes, real Indians! Indians on horses! Indians with bows and arrows! And if he could remember any more of it than this, he still wouldn't be sitting around driving people crazy.

A few months earlier he'd had a dream that had stayed with him. He was waiting in a long line at the bridge, driving back from Matamoros to Brownsville, but instead of the bridge being where it always was, they had moved it closer to his old house — either that or they had moved his house closer to the bridge. The point was, he could see his house from the other side of the river, which in real life was no short distance, but in his mind he saw his front yard, the grass nice and trimmed, the large orange tree that shaded most of the backyard and still produced fruit after so many hurricanes. He saw it all so close to him and he couldn't wait to get back. But when he reached down into his pocket for the toll what he found was the bloody tip of The Gringo With The Ugly Finger's finger. And what use did he have for a bloody fingertip when he was already a few pesos short? The tollbooth worker didn't want any part of the bloody coins he was offering him. He didn't care if Don Fidencio had to get home to watch the baseball game. Come back when you have more to offer me than a bloody fingertip, the man told him. Then maybe I let you cross over.

After that night he had gone to bed asking God to please not torment him with these dreams of The Gringo With The Ugly Finger. It was just one more humble request added to the short but growing list of things he prayed for every night: for the staff to stop pilfering his chocolates, particularly the ones with the cherries that he was partial to; for the gout to go away once and for all; for some rest from the aches in his muscles and bones each morning; for some relief from his constant need of having to go make water; for The One With The White Pants to stop finding new pills to give him; and most important of all, for him to find some way to escape from this prison where they kept him against his will; and for his freedom to come soon, even if it should cost him his life, so long as he didn't die here in this bed, surrounded by so many strange and unfamiliar faces.

He had given up trying to remember everyone's name. The night he had passed out in the front yard had left his brains scrambled up so much that it was difficult for him to keep things straight in his head. Instead he had come up with a special name for everyone, usually having to do with some dominant feature, but then kept these names to himself because he still had enough sense left to know that The One With The Flat Face probably wouldn't like being told she had a flat face. Really, it was more her nose that was flat, but once he came up with a name he rarely changed it, so The One With The Flat Face it was. Besides, there was already The One With A Beak For A Nose and he didn't want to get them mixed up. He might have remembered The Gringo With The Ugly Finger's name if he hadn't kept waving his crusty finger at him every chance he had. The One With The Worried Face had a name that reflected his disagreeable nature and yet was different from the strained and troubled face of the old man known as The One Who Always Looks Constipated. During mealtime there was The One Who Likes To Eat Other People's Food, who would scoot up in his wheelchair if Don Fidencio was taking too long to eat his Jell-O or some other tasteless dessert. "So are you going to eat that or not?" he'd ask, then wait around to make sure he did. Some of them Don Fidencio didn't see because they stayed in their rooms, like The One Who Cries Like A Dying Calf, who lived somewhere down the hall, but as loud as he was he might as well have been in the same bed.

The women residents he knew as The Old Turtles. There were so many of them he mainly remembered them collectively, though a few did have special names. The Friendly Turtle sat in her wheelchair near the front door and waved at all the visitors whether she knew them or not, whether it was the first or the fifth time the person had walked in that day. The Friendly Turtle's friend, who also sat by the door but didn't wave, was The Turtle With The Fedora because of the felt hat she wore, even if it made her look less like a Turtle and more like an old man sitting around with nothing better to do. The Turtle Who Never Bends Her Legs leaned back in a larger wheelchair with a cushiony footrest that extended out like a recliner on wheels. The Turtle Who Doesn't Like To Talk sat in her wheelchair next to her husband, The Loyal One, who came by every day to sit with her and massage her right leg and then the stump where the left one used to be. The Turtle With The Orange Gloves said her hands were always cold and took off her coverings only when it was time to eat. The Turtle Who Should Be An Operator sat in her wheelchair next to the nurses' station, yelling "¡Teléfono!" anytime the phone rang.

The Gringo With The Ugly Finger sat up a little straighter when The One With The Flat Face pushed her cart up to the table.

"The doctor plain-out told me, 'Sorry, son, there was no saving the tip of your pointer finger. But there is absolutely no reason in the world that you can't go back to work once you heal up and from then on live a perfectly normal life.'"

Don Fidencio pretended the chatter was no different than the mumbles and gurgles he could hear coming from The Table Of Mutes along the far wall, where no one did more than moan and hum to himself and then every so often shout "Macaroni?" or "Bunco!" He could hear his belly tightening and he was thinking that he might have been hungrier sometime between when the Depression hit and the year he went off to the CCC camps.

The One With The Worried Face finally let go of his cheeks so The One With The Flat Face could strap on the cloth bib that covered the entire front of his shirt. The Gringo With The Ugly Finger puffed out his chest as if she were decorating him with a medal.

Don Fidencio raised his hand when she came around with his bib.

"I already have one." He picked up the end of the paper napkin he had stuffed into his shirt collar when he'd first sat down, ready to eat.

The One With The Flat Face leaned in close to him. "Papi, you know you have to wear one of these."

"For what?" he said, shrugging. "If I have my own."

"That one isn't big enough, papi. Your shirt's going to get dirty."

"I'm not your papi."

"Yes, all right, but you still have to wear the bib."

"No food is going to fall on my shirt."

"How do you know that, Mr. Rosales?"

Don Fidencio looked away and shook his head. "How do *you* know?" he said, and in this instance wished that he could remember her real name — Josie, Rosa, Vicky, Yoli, Alma, Cindy, Lulu, Flor, whatever the hell it was — just to toss it in there for emphasis.

"All I know is you have to wear the bib. That's the rules, Mr. Rosales."

She brought the long white cloth toward him, but he pushed her hands aside.

"Already I told you to take it away!"

The One With The Flat Face stepped back, hands on her plump hips, and glared at the old man.

"I'll be back in a little bit, sir," she said, as if this were supposed to scare him.

When he turned around, the other men at the table were staring at him. The One With The Worried Face shook his head in a disillusioned sort of way; The Gringo With The Ugly Finger looked as dazed as if something had just happened to one of his other fingers.

"What?" Don Fidencio said to both of them. "What are you looking at, eh?"

The One With The Worried Face turned his attention toward the vase of plastic flowers on the table. The Gringo With The Ugly Finger stroked the frayed edge of his bib.

Don Fidencio tugged a couple of times on the paper napkin, making sure it was secure. He knew what he was doing; he didn't need some young girl telling him things. She must have been blind to think he needed one of those towels hanging from his neck. Maybe from now on he would call her The One With The Flat Face Who Is Also Blind.

He sulked back in his chair. His stomach growled as if he hadn't eaten in days. The memory he felt churning inside his belly had taken place in those early days of the Depression. He had found work close to the river, picking tomatoes with some other men, including a couple of hoboes from up north who spent their time complaining that it was too damn hot for a man to be working so hard. They were making so much noise that no one heard when the agents drove up. Before he knew it, they were rounding everyone up but the hoboes, who by then had put down their bushels and were taking a cigarette break. It didn't matter where he lived or for how many years. "Looks Mexican to me," the agent said when he protested. And how was he supposed to explain to the agent that because his parents had crossed over to look for work, he was born in Reynosa, just on the other side of the river, but almost all his life he had spent on this side? Another week and he would have been born in the U.S., same as the rest of his family. Yes, even if he had relatives on both sides, really he was American now and had been for many, many years. Later that same night he was crammed into a boxcar with the others — some Mexican citizens, some just unlucky enough to look it — until the train arrived down in Veracruz. It was his first time so far beyond the other side of the border. He and a few of the men stuck together as they traveled the more than six hundred miles back to Texas. None of them had much money. Over the next two weeks they walked and asked for rides when they could, but mainly walked. And if he could recall any more of this, he would probably say it was the hungriest he had ever been.

The metal doors to the kitchen swung open and two dining room attendants rolled out the food carts, starting at the far end of the room, where most of The Turtles gathered. Of the eighty or so residents eating in the dining room today, only two had guests. One was a tall man with a long stringy ponytail who was sitting with his mother while she chewed her fried fish. The second guest was a woman in her early fifties with slightly tinted hair and a pair of gold-lined teeth. She sat with her much-older husband at almost every meal, sometimes ordering a tray of food for herself.

Alongside the window that looked onto the patio, one of the aides stood in the center of a U-shaped table and uncovered trays for three residents, all of them twitching in their reclining wheelchairs that were more like upright gurneys. She took a spoonful from the first tray and fed a dark-haired woman not more than sixty, and then a second later the aide had to recover the yellowish dollop that had seeped onto the woman's chin.

Don Fidencio tried not to look around the room as much as he had his first two months. For what? He hadn't seen anyone he remembered or who might remember him, which seemed odd given that he had lived and worked in the same town for most of his life. Where the hell is everyone? he kept asking himself. Strangers, all strangers, they had taken everyone he knew and replaced them with strangers. This is where they had sent him to die, with strangers. The gray-haired daughter of one of The Turtles had said she recognized him as the man who used to bring the mail to her mother's house, a white one with light-blue trim that had a large banana tree in the front yard and that stood on the corner near the entrance to the compress. Don Fidencio didn't recall the house, though he remembered a chow biting him near the train tracks, leaving him with a dozen or so stitches on his backside. When the woman said it wasn't their dog, he lost interest in whatever else she had to say.

The other reason he preferred to not look around was that he didn't like thinking about his life, how it used to be, how it was now, and what it would likely become, if God didn't do him the good favor of taking him soon. No matter how much he had lost, or they thought he had lost, he was still alert and understood what was happening to him. How long could it be before they moved him over to the U-shaped table where the aides would be feeding him? When would he not be able to dress himself anymore and have to wear his pajamas all day? One of these nights would there really be a need for them to keep the plastic lining on his mattress?

"Is there a problem, Mr. Rosales?" The One With The Big Ones was standing next to the table. The One With The Flat Face lingered to one side of his wide frame.

"Yes, there is," Don Fidencio said, cocking back his head. "I'm hungry already. Tell them to hurry it up with the trays."

"The food is almost here, sir, but Miss Saldana tells me that today you don't feel you have to wear your bib like everyone else." The One With The Big Ones crossed his arms, which in his yellow polo shirt only formed a deeper cleavage. "This isn't true, is it?"

"For what?" he said, and then lifted his napkin. "Look!"

"That paper napkin is not going to be sufficient, Mr. Rosales."

"How do you mean, not sufficient?"

"We have rules and procedures here, sir. And the rules and procedures state that every resident must wear a bib during mealtime."

"Look what I have here," he said, holding up the napkin again. "Are you blind, like the girl?"

The One With The Big Ones glanced back at The One With The Flat Face, who only raised her eyebrows as she waited to see how he might respond to the comment. The dining room attendant, a younger man with homemade tattoos on his knuckles and forearms, had just rolled the serving cart up to the table. The One With The Big Ones signaled for him to hold off and then turned back to continue his conversation.

"There's no reason to be belligerent, Mr. Rosales."

"Don't you be calling me names."

"Belligerent means to be hostile, to be insulting, like saying someone is blind because they don't agree with you. Miss Saldana is only trying to do her job and follow the rules and procedures. Don't you want to follow the rules and procedures?"

Don Fidencio waited for him to finish. Not only was he forced to argue with the man about his bib but he had to do this in English, which for him meant stopping to think of the right words before he could open his mouth. A building full of old people who spoke mainly Spanish and no longer had any use for English, if they ever had, and this was the one they had sent to run the place.

"I'm just saying the truth. This is a napkin and it works just the same as that horse blanket she wants to put on me. Look at it, and if you don't see it, then maybe you both need to go have your eyes checked. Get in the van and go together if you want. What's so insulting about that?"

The One With The Big Ones squatted by holding on to the edge of the table and the handlebar on the walker.

"Mr. Rosales, the rule is that everyone has to wear a bib." He was now eye-to-eye with the old man. "What you have there is a paper napkin, not a bib."

"And who made the stupid rule?"

"Those are just the rules. It was like this before I started working at Amigoland. I'm just following the rules. Don't you want to follow the rules?" He motioned with his head, stretching his jowls to glance over his shoulder. "Look at how Mr. Phillips and Mr. Gomez are cooperating."

The Gringo With The Ugly Finger sat up when he heard his name. The One With The Worried Face shook his head as if he couldn't believe the misfortune Don Fidencio was tempting.

"Why do you want to cause such problems?" He dropped his forehead into the palms of his hands. He looked up a few seconds later. "Why?"

"I used to pack a lunch pail back when I was with Pan Am."

"Not now, Mr. Phillips," The One With The Big Ones said, keeping his eyes fixed on Don Fidencio. Then he told the attendant to go ahead and serve the two other men at the table.

"And me?"

"I want to give you your food, so does Miss Saldana, but first you need a bib, sir." The One With The Big Ones leaned on the edge of the table in order to stand up again. "I can't serve you until you cooperate."

"I have one."

"Sir, I'm not going to argue with you about your paper napkin. If you want to eat, you have to follow the rules." The One With The Big Ones glanced over at The One With The Flat Face, who nodded back at him.

The attendant was waiting with his last tray of food; after a while he stuck one of his tattooed fingers under the plastic covering and touched the mashed potatoes, just to make sure the food was still warm.

Don Fidencio felt weak; his head was beginning to hurt. They had strayed off the main road and gotten lost in some dense scrubland. By now it had been more than a day or two since their last meal. Close to dusk he spotted something scurrying under a huisache. Before they could surround the shrub, the armadillo bolted out into the clearing and found cover somewhere else. Each time they thought they had it cornered, the animal would rush off past them because nobody had anything to hit it with. They started throwing stones, but most of these missed or ricocheted off the animal's shell. Half an hour went by this way. It was getting dark and they were about to give up on catching it when the armadillo stopped suddenly and dropped dead from exhaustion. One of the men who knew how to cook prepared the meat on a spit over an open fire. Don Fidencio had eaten without thinking of what he was eating or why he was eating it or how gamy it tasted or how tough it was to chew or how the meat was getting stuck between his teeth or if the memory of any of this would stay with him. He just ate.

The One With The Worried Face was working on cutting his corn bread with the edge of his spoon. He scooped up the first piece, but it kept toppling over to one side. After the fourth or fifth time, it was clear to him that he had cut too big a piece. So he worked on it until he had whittled it down to three smaller chunks. In between he stopped to take a sip of his iced tea with the bendable straw. Then he stared at the spoon, as if unsure where it had come from, and a few seconds later switched over to the vanilla pudding.

The Gringo With The Ugly Finger stirred a second packet of Sweet'N Low into his coffee. "Really it wasn't much of a lunchroom, just some metal chairs and an old Coca-Cola-bottle machine, so I usually ate my sandwich out in the hangar somewhere."

"Please, Mr. Phillips, I'm talking to Mr. Rosales right now."

The One With The Big Ones turned back to Don Fidencio. "Well, sir, what's it going to be? Dinner or no dinner?"

"You can't tell me when I can eat," said the old man. "I'm not even supposed to be here. Against my will they brought me to this place."

"You're here for your own good, Mr. Rosales. So we can take care of you."

"This is how you take care of people?"

"Miss Saldana says you skipped your lunch so you could smoke outside. Is that true?"

Don Fidencio shook his head but without looking at the man.

"How can we take care of you, Mr. Rosales, if you won't let us take care of you?"

"I don't need you or anybody taking care of me."

"Your daughter thinks you do."

"And what does she know? If you people let me, I could do everything like I used to. One day you'll see."

"See what?"

"Nothing," he said. "Just give me my food."

The One With The White Pants came around to the table with his own cart. His was bigger than the food cart or The

One With The Flat Face's cart. To begin with, the wheels didn't rattle or get stuck, so it was hard to know when he was getting close to your table. One minute you were eating your carrot cake and the next second there he was, standing next to you, dressed in his white pants and shirt, smiling like he knew you were expecting him and here he was with his tiny paper cup full of goodies.

The One With The Worried Face took the cup and steadily raised it toward his mouth until he was able to tip a purple pill onto his tongue, which was now chalk-colored from the milky supplement he drank with his meal.

"Water?" asked The One With The White Pants.

But The One With The Worried Face already had some and raised his glass as if he were about to toast the beginning of another miserable year. Then he took a swig of the water, cocked back his head, and swallowed. The One With The White Pants gazed up at the ceiling while the old man took eight more pills this way.

"Not yet for Mr. Rosales," The One With The Big Ones said when The One With The White Pants came around the table. "Take care of Mr. Phillips, someone who likes to follow the rules and procedures."

"Now I sure as heck do," The Gringo With The Ugly Finger said and then held it up for everyone to see.

Don Fidencio could feel his stomach grumbling. The One With The Big Ones thought he was making him suffer by not letting him have his paper cup, as if he looked forward to taking so many damn pills. He was doing him a favor. Thank you very much, he wanted to say. A cupful of pills was the last thing he wanted. If he even thought he could find some crackers in one of his shoe boxes, he would have grabbed the walker and headed back to his room. A man who looked like he needed to wear a brassiere shouldn't be talking to him in this way, telling him what to do, when he could and couldn't eat. Only a few years earlier he would have laid him out flat on the floor, made him regret having spoken to him in that way. He didn't know who he was dealing with, what Don Fidencio had lived through in his life.

It was late in the evening when they finally made it back to the river. What little money they had started with was gone now. Don Fidencio and the two other men walked along the dense riverbank, trying to figure out where exactly they could cross. The current seemed strong no matter where they looked. They finally spotted a bend where the river was narrower and it wouldn't take but a minute or so to tread water and reach the other side. Don Fidencio stripped down and rolled his clothes and shoes into a tight ball. But when he looked around, only one of the men had undressed. I never learned to swim, the other one said. He was more boy than man, but he had worked hard to prove himself the last five days. You can hold on to us, Don Fidencio told him. But he refused and said he preferred to remain on this side. He claimed to have family he could stay with. But if he really had family here, then why come all the way to the river with them? They waited to see if he would change his mind and then went ahead and took their first steps into the river, making sure to keep their knotted-up clothes raised above their heads. The water wasn't as high as they had imagined and they were able to stay on their feet most of the way. Don Fidencio wanted to tell the boy he could make it, he would go back for him, but when he turned around he had already lost him.

He closed his eyes and tried to count the extra hours he might have to wait until breakfast. It was past five o'clock, which meant he had less than two hours before they started to turn off the lights. He couldn't remember the last time he slept a whole night, so he would most likely wake up around four in the morning, not including however many times he was sure to wake up to go sit on the toilet. So the five hours since lunch, plus however many hours he said he needed before he fell asleep, was something like nine hours, maybe ten. Then he had to add in the hours since he had last eaten, however many he'd said it had been. If he could just write this down, he could figure it out, not let all these numbers get jumbled up inside his head. He reached for the ballpoint pen in his shirt pocket but then figured The One With The Big Ones would be rushing him as he wrote down the numbers, so instead he kept his eyes shut, left the pen where it was, and pretended to have an itch at his armpit.

No matter how long it was overnight, what he knew was that after he dressed in the morning he would have to wait until they unlocked the patio before he could go outside for a smoke and kill some of his hunger. It was brighter at the front of the building, but he didn't want them coming to take him back inside by the elbow. The sun would hardly be out at that hour. The yardman didn't let himself in through the back gate until later in the morning. If someone were to look outside, all they would see was the burning tip of a cigarette and the shape of an old man attached to the end of it. The package had seemed kind of flat when he was smoking at noon. He maybe had two cigarettes left. Two cigarettes wasn't much after picking at his breakfast and not eating lunch and now dinner. If only his hands were still steady, he could roll his own, but he had given this up years ago when the cigarettes kept coming out looking like broken fingers.

Then after going out to the patio, he would have to wait another hour before they opened the mess hall. That seemed like an extra long time to wait, however many hours that would end up being. He imagined arriving in the mess hall and waiting in one of the chairs closest to the kitchen. Maybe he could find a newspaper or a magazine to distract himself until they brought out the food. Maybe The One With The Net On His Head would do him the favor of serving him a little early. He would be willing to pass the man a small tip on the side, a few extra cigarettes when he had some, just so he wouldn't have to wait any longer than he already had. He couldn't say he even cared for the oatmeal breakfast they served. Every day the same thing, oatmeal and raisins. Monday, oatmeal and raisins. Tuesday, oatmeal and raisins. Wednesday, oatmeal and raisins. On and on that way. He usually spread sugar over the top of the oatmeal and then mixed it in with a little bit of milk until it got creamy, but he could see himself skipping this part of his routine just so he could start eating. The biscuit he would bite into while it was still hot (normally he liked to save it for later, sometimes taking extra care to wrap it up in a napkin, placing it in the center of the paper and folding the napkin end over end until it formed a small brick that he could stuff inside his shirt pocket). No, these people didn't know who they were dealing with. He had been through much worse in his life. The One With The Big Ones actually thought he could keep him here.

Now he was the one smiling. He knew they were all around the table, he could feel their eyes on him — The One With The Flat Face, The One With The Big Ones, The One With The Worried Face, The Gringo With The Ugly Finger, The One With The White Pants, The One With The Net On His Head — staring at him and waiting for his next move. It all seemed possible to him, the waiting, the restless night of sleeping, getting up so many times until he couldn't go back to sleep, waiting for the patio to open up, smoking his one or two cigarettes, and finally making his way into the mess hall when they turned on the lights. Then he realized the first person he'd see would be The One With The Flat Face, coming around with her cart.

2

The urge came with no warning, the third one since waking up. A few years earlier his urologist had said the problem had to do with Don Fidencio's prostate. His urologist was an Indian man, tall and slender, who spoke in a hushed tone as if someone might be listening at the door. He explained that on a normal man the prostate was about the size of a pecan. He drew a pecan on one of his prescription pads. But in the particular case of Don Fidencio, his prostate had grown to what was closer to the size of a small avocado seed. He drew the seed next to the pecan. Clearly there was a problem: a pecan was not an avocado seed. And it was this enlarged prostate pressing against his urethra that was necessitating the frequency of his trips to the lavatory. He drew the urethra on the pad, placing it between the pecan and the avocado seed. The doctor explained that because of the patient's advanced age, surgery was not an option, but there was medication that would help to ease the symptoms. The old man listened attentively, as if he were taking in all this new information, committing it to memory, but in truth he was only amazed how the doctor knew so much from sticking his long, delicate finger in there for what couldn't have been more than two seconds. Not that he wanted it in there any longer than necessary, but still, it wasn't much time to determine that his was the size of an avocado seed. The doctor was good at drawing the nut and the seed and the little tube. Maybe this was what he told all his patients. The old man took the medicine for a few weeks, but he stopped when he didn't notice any real change in how often he had to urinate. He took enough damn medicine as it was. The doctor probably had it wrong. How could he really be sure after only two seconds, maybe less?

Once he undid his pants and suspenders, he held on to the support rail and, with his yellowed and cracked toenails digging into the foam cushions of his orthopedic shoes, eased himself down, down, down, down, until finally touching the pot. Never would he have imagined it would come to this, urinating like a woman. All for falling in the yard and not having the sense to wake up and get himself back inside the house. Earlier that same afternoon he had gone over to watch a Little League game and then stayed in the car where he could drink his beer. Maybe he should've paid more attention to the numbness he felt along his arm, but he blamed it on his medicines, which were liable to cause all kinds of side effects. The blurriness, though, that was something he couldn't ignore so easily and it finally made him give up on watching the game and head home, taking the side streets so he could drive slower than usual. When he got back to the house, he left the two remaining beer cans on the floorboard. He staggered into the front yard, toward the old mesquite, and sat down with his back against the trunk. He planned to rest his eyes for only a few seconds, but the seconds soon turned into minutes as a warm breeze passed over him. From the taller branches of the tree, a group of chicharras serenaded him, starting with a low chirp that grew louder, almost imperceptibly at first, then with time harmonized into a shrill pitch that resounded far beyond the small fenced-in yard, but by which point the old man had already passed out on the grass.

The doctor at the hospital explained to Amalia and The Son Of A Bitch that with some rehab her father could be expected to make an almost full recovery, though he would need extra care from now on. The part about the old man wetting himself, from his crotch to down close to his knees, was probably just an accident, nothing to worry about. Don Fidencio swore no such thing had ever happened to him and never would again, he guaranteed her. She had been trying for years to get him to sell his house and move up to Houston. Okay, so he was finally ready to accept her offer, only right then The Son Of A Bitch stepped in and said he thought her father needed more assistance, in a place where trained people could take care of him, before something else happened.

Don Fidencio could tell his daughter didn't believe that the stroke, however minor, wouldn't happen again and instead believed that if he wet himself once, what was to say he wouldn't wet himself again? And after a while even he started questioning whether it had actually been an accident or if this was simply what he could expect from his worn-out body. Maybe he should be happy that he was only pissing himself and not more. Once or twice he had barely wet the front of his pants, but this he blamed on the slight tremor in his hands. It had happened one morning when he was out having breakfast and went to the restroom to make water. That time he'd marked his pants just below the crotch and had to go hide away in a stall for close to half an hour, until he dried off. Now he sat on the pot to avoid having any other accidents, the way Amalia and The Son Of A Bitch were so convinced he would.

After he adjusted himself on the seat, he grabbed the section of the newspaper he had left down by his pants. He stretched his arms out slightly to get a better look at the photo. The woman seemed too young, only fifty-four years old. In the next column it was easy to see this was an older photo and the man was wearing a navy uniform, probably from World War II. He had to read the paragraph twice before he saw that the man was from 1923, fourteen years after Don Fidencio. Another woman, this one wearing a mantilla, looked younger than the first.

"Mr. Rosales, are you in there?" The One With The Flat Face knocked once, then cracked open the door.

"And somebody tell me why it is a man cannot have some privacy around here?" he said, yanking back on the handle. "Never will I understand why there are no locks on these doors."

"I need to ask if you have Mr. Cavazos's newspaper," she said. "He likes to read it before he goes to his therapy."

"Who?"

"Mr. Cavazos," she said. "You know, your neighbor here in the room?"

"Yes, yes, of course," he responded, though he really knew him only as The One With The Hole In His Back.

"Mr. Cavazos pressed the emergency-call button because he said someone had stolen the front section."

"Do you mean the part with people who have died?"

"If the obituaries are in the front section, yes," she said. "Do you have it, Mr. Rosales?"

"This is the only part I want to read," he answered. "The rest of the news I have read too many times — nothing new happens anymore."

"Yes, but the obituaries is the part that Mr. Cavazos wants to read this morning."

"Does he think his name is in there?"

She didn't respond, but he could hear her saying something to The One With The Hole In His Back, then his roommate shouting something in that booming voice. After a few seconds, she came back to the door.

"Mr. Cavazos said to tell you that your name would come out long before his."

"I checked, but it wasn't there," Don Fidencio said. "Maybe tomorrow."

"Okay, Mr. Rosales, that's enough," she said. "I need to open the door now and get the newspaper."

"Wait."

"Wait for what?"

"So I can be decent."

"Mr. Rosales, I saw you in the shower yesterday morning, remember?"

"The shower is different."

"How can it be different if you don't have any clothes on?"

"For God's sake, I'm sitting down in here."

"You sit down over there, too," she said. "Remember, in the plastic chair, when we wash you?"

"Here I do different things when I sit down."

"Please, Mr. Rosales, I have other work I need to do and Mr. Cavazos won't stop pressing the call button."

"What do you want, for me to walk outside half dressed, like an indio?"

"At least open the door to give me the paper."

"Can you wait long enough for me to be decent?" He pulled himself up so the flush wouldn't splash onto his cheeks. Never would he understand how these women did it every time they had to go.

"Then just slide it under."

"How do you mean, *under?*"

"Down here, Mr. Rosales." And suddenly her fingers appeared from under the door like hungry worms.

The old man held on to the railing as he leaned over, tottering close to the floor. He fed only the edge of the paper into her hand before she snatched the rest of it from him.

When he reached the doorway, he made sure to look both ways before pushing out into the hall. He stayed close to the wooden railing and had no interest in the pastel paintings on the pastel wall. With his eyes focused on the tile floor just ahead of him, he kept shuffling along, one foot in front of the other, one foot in front of the other, the whole time leaning on the walker. He couldn't tell if the specks on the floor were part of the tile or if they just hadn't done a very good job of cleaning that morning. A few more paces, and he spotted a tiny wrapper of some sort that was probably one of his, left behind by these workers who came around only to steal his chocolates. Near the first corner, he veered into the center of the hallway to avoid a linen basket someone had left in his way. A few of The Turtles were parked along the wall outside the showers. The Redheaded Turtle wore a shower cap since she had been to the salon the day before and wanted her coloring to last before it faded back to the shade of her fluttering white eyelashes. She waved at him with her good hand, but he didn't have time to be waving back at Turtles; he was more concerned with keeping the walker's wheels going in one direction.

He was still getting used to pushing it around. They had given it to him at the rehab center, and at the time he figured it would be only for the two weeks that he was scheduled to be there. After that he was sure he would go back to using one of his canes. And maybe this would've been the case had he gone to live with Amalia and The Son Of A Bitch, but here they insisted that he continue using the walker so he wouldn't have an accident. You don't want to have an accident, do you, Mr. Rosales? It seemed these women were just waiting for him to pull one of his canes out of the closet. Then one day the canes disappeared altogether. We put them away for you, Mr. Rosales, in a safe place. You don't want to have an accident, do you? And how was he supposed to answer a stupid question like that? He was lucky to still be walking, period. Why would he want to have an accident and risk ending up like The One With The Hole In His Back? If only they gave him a chance, he would prove to them that he was okay to walk with the cane. He knew what they were doing, trying to make him into a useless old man. They wanted him to become dependent on them for everything, helpless, so that eventually he would forget how to bathe himself or how to take his own medication or how to eat without getting half his food on his shirt. Look, here comes The Useless One.

And *why?* So he wouldn't go anywhere, that's why! They weren't fooling him. If he had to push around this wheelbarrow to get anywhere, then what chance did he ever have of leaving on his own? He had made his first attempt only a couple of weeks after arriving. He'd been smoking his afternoon cigarette under the covered archway where the cars stopped to pick people up. Only two of The Old Turtles had left during the half hour he'd been out there. One Turtle they lifted in the special van used to transport the residents to their doctors' appointments; the other Turtle sat still as her grandson lifted her out of a wheelchair and set her down in the front seat of his pickup like a duffel bag full of used clothes. After that it was quiet for a few minutes until the ambulance came wailing up to the nursing home. Two burly paramedics rushed into the building with a gurney and their bags of equipment, and from there they followed one of the girls down the hall. So much excitement, everyone running around like a bunch of crazies. Don Fidencio stood up like he might follow them and then suddenly turned into the parking lot and kept going, pushing the walker because by then they had already taken away his three canes. This is where his daughter had come to leave him, to die, in a place where they stole your canes when you weren't looking.

Since there was no sidewalk, he was forced to make his way along the shoulder of the road. At least he was walking against the traffic and could still save himself if some drunk were to suddenly swerve in his direction. He would've been more than happy to sacrifice the walker. Ten minutes later he had covered two blocks and was now only one block from the bus stop. All he had to do was climb on board and wait until they reached some part of town he recognized. If he could get across the intersection, he'd be a free man. He pressed the pedestrian button and kept his eye on the signal that would tell him when to walk. After what seemed like five or ten minutes of waiting, the symbol of the little walking man appeared.

Don Fidencio pushed forward, but two or three seconds later the little man turned back into a big red hand telling him to stop. He wasn't even halfway across the first lane before he had to turn around to avoid the oncoming traffic. Twice it happened to him that way, until he finally decided to take his chances. He was only waiting for the little man to come out again when one of the girls took hold of his arm and guided him back to the nursing home. And from then on they had barred him from going out the front door to smoke and later extended this to include the lobby area when one of The Turtles reported that he'd been asking people for rides.

He veered the walker into the center of the hall again, this time to avoid a food cart loaded up with the trays of those residents who couldn't leave their rooms to eat in the mess hall. A little farther up he had to do the same thing for a hamper and a dust mop that one of the cleaning people had left propped up against the wall. When he turned the corner, he found that the therapy room was still locked. He leaned back on the wooden railing and parked the walker to one side. There was no getting away from it. If they hadn't made him so afraid of falling down, he would have left it behind somewhere, gone on without any help.

He held on to the railing with one hand and walked toward the hamper. A few nights ago he'd seen an old black and white about an innocent man who finally escaped prison by hiding inside a pile of dirty laundry that was later loaded into a delivery truck. When no one was looking Don Fidencio peeked inside the large container, then jerked away when he caught a whiff. What a way to die. They needed to drive it out into the country, burn whatever was inside there. He released the foot brake on the hamper and gave it a good shove, sending it rolling toward the end of the long hall. The walker was next, though it traveled only a few feet before it skidded off and collided with the railing along the opposite wall. Before he picked up the dust mop, he thought about sending it off in the same direction. The wooden handle felt as solid as if he were lifting a shovel to dig a deep hole. He set it down, leaning his weight against it.

He meant to push it only a few steps, maybe clear away some of the specks he could still see on the floor, twinkling like little colored stars, but after a while he turned the dust mop toward the nurses' station. He kept his eyes focused on the tile floor ahead of him and changed direction only to negotiate his way around this Turtle or that Turtle who didn't have anywhere better to be than in the way of a man trying to do some work.

"Mr. Rosales, where did you leave your walker?" one of the aides said when he reached the living area. "You need your walker, sir."

"Now we don't want to have an accident, do we?" The One Who Likes To Kiss Your Forehead said as she rushed out from behind the nurses' station. She took him by the arm, and he had to yank himself away from her and her smelly perfume.

"That's okay, Francis." The One With The Big Ones watched from the doorway of his office. "Just let him for now. He seems to be making it okay."

"¡Teléfono!"

A few more aides had gathered by the time the old man circled the nurses' station. "Eloy's going to get mad if you take away his job," one of them said, and they all laughed.

"¡Teléfono!"

He was about to complete the wide circle and head down the long hall to the right. Just then The Turtle With The Fedora inched forward in her chair, causing him to jig to one side. "This one thinks that somebody's going to pay him so he can buy more of his dirty cigarettes."

"¡Teléfono!"

"You're doing an excellent job there, Mr. Rosales," The One With The Big Ones called out. "Keep up the good work."

Don Fidencio focused on the space ahead of him and pretended he hadn't heard any of their comments. They thought it was all so curious and funny, an old man cleaning the floors. Never mind that he was doing them a service, something they should be doing themselves. Instead it looked like they had cleaned the floors with their feet. What kind of place were they running here anyway? So much for their rules and regulations. He pushed the dust mop out in front of him. There were three more halls, just as long, and after that the mess hall and recreation room. Wait until they saw the work he had done, then we'd see who was laughing.

3

The old man opened the #3 shoe box for his cigarettes and lighter and stuffed these into his pocket. Then he pulled out the pack so he could count how many were left. The over-bed lamp reflected off the darkened blinds and onto the ruffled sheets across the mattress. He staggered back to the closet, leaning against the edge of the bed for support, and retrieved the #1 box and placed it on the overbed table with the other box. He did the same with the #2, #4, and #5 boxes. It was part of his morning routine now to do an inventory count at the start of every day. How else was he going to know when these people were dipping into his shoe boxes for another piece of chocolate or to take one of his pens or simply to move things around in an effort to make him think he couldn't keep track of his things? The One Who's Losing His Mind.

He suspected they were helping themselves whenever he was on the pot or out of the room for longer stretches of time and there was little chance of catching them in the act. Just the other day he had remembered to get up in the middle of his meal and head back to the room, but they must have known or been watching him because the room was empty except for The One With The Hole In His Back, who had fallen asleep eating his meal. Worse still was that by the time he pushed the walker back into the mess hall the attendants had already picked up his tray.

The thieves must have been busy with the other residents last night because all the boxes seemed to be in order. He clicked his government-issue pen so he could record today's inventory in one of his old pocket-size address books, the leather exterior as worn and cracked as the hands that were holding it. There were only a few blank pages left in this particular book and soon he would need to find more space for his notations. He thumbed through the rest of the pages, but they all seemed to be taken up with one name or another that he couldn't place. It wasn't until he turned the R–S tab and saw his own family name that the entries began to correspond some with his faded memory. Vicente had died from a bad heart, still in his fifties. Baltazar they shot in Reynosa, something having to do with a woman he was seeing after somebody else had seen her first. He couldn't remember how Enrique had died anymore, only that it was sad. Luisa was from the cancer, but what kind he couldn't say. When he turned to the next page he saw Celestino's name. Of eight brothers and four sisters, only the two of them were left. At least he thought it was still the two of them. The youngest and the oldest, almost twenty years separating them. That the youngest was alive would make sense, he supposed, but what good reason could there be for the oldest to be alive and for the rest of his brothers and sisters to be gone? What sense did it make for him to be still walking around? For what? For him to be stuck here, waiting to die? At least if Celestino was alive he was probably out there living his life like a free man. *If* . . . They hadn't actually spoken in years. Why, though?

He sat down to wait for the hour that they would let him go outside for his first smoke. After that it would be only a few minutes until they served him breakfast. He opened the address book again. If he wasn't mistaken, Celestino was the one who used to cut hair. Either he or Martín, but he thought it was more likely Celestino. And whatever it was, why they hadn't talked in so many years, had something to do with cutting hair. He raised his cap and smoothed down his hair. Of all the things in this world to have an argument about. *You call this a haircut? I told you not to touch the sideburns!* It seemed ridiculous to him now, whatever started it. For only the two of them to be still alive and not talking.

He had to dial twice, since the first time he misread the number and had to listen to a recording of some woman telling him he didn't know what he was doing and that he needed to hang up and try his call again. The second time, he concentrated, keeping his thumb under each number next to his brother's name and then using his other index finger to stab at the tiny digits on his phone.

It rang. He was happy to not hear the woman's voice. It rang again. She acted like he was the first man on earth to call the wrong phone number. Just wait till she turns ninety-one and see if she doesn't dial a number wrong now and then. It was a common enough mistake. Nothing to criticize. Nothing to scold him about. They didn't even have phones down here when he was born, that's how old he was. No phones! None! Not even one! At least, not his people. Who knows what they had on the other side of town? But where he was, if you wanted to talk to so-and-so, you had to walk to wherever so-and-so was and do your talking. Not like now. The other day some young man, all dressed up in a suit with a tie, came to visit his grandmother, one of The Turtles, but he spent most of his time pacing up and down the hall talking to himself, like maybe he should be living in the part of the building where they locked up The Ones Who Like To Wander Off. Then Don Fidencio noticed the young man had an earpiece with a long white cord that connected to a tiny phone attached to his belt. Who would have imagined such things? A man talking to another man somewhere else and neither one of the two actually holding a phone in his hand. Not like he was doing now with the receiver pressed up to his ear. Only God knew how many times it had rung when he heard something click and a woman's voice come on the line. She was different from the first, but still. It wasn't seven a.m. and already he was about to get scolded, yelled at for the second time that morning. No sir, not Fidencio Rosales. He refused to listen to whatever she had to say and hung up. Yell at the next guy who marks the wrong number. He didn't know why he'd picked up the phone in the first place, what was so damn important. Then he looked back at his thumb stuck inside the little address book.

4

Don Celestino heard the phone ringing in the living room and wondered who would be calling him in the middle of the night. When he glanced at the digital clock on the nightstand, the numbers looked as blurry as if he were underwater. He groped around trying to find his eyeglasses and finally had to get his face up close to the clock to see it was already 6:45 in the morning, much later than he normally woke up. Especially when he went to bed so early, as he had the night before. The phone was still ringing. He looked at the clock again. And here he had thought that by going to bed a little early he'd have that much more time in the morning. Now he had less than half an hour before he needed to be there. The bridge wasn't so far away, but he would hardly have time to shower and shave or even take care of his hair.

He sat on the edge of the bed and used the bedpost to pull himself up. The ceiling fan was on, but he was sweating all the same. Maybe all he needed was a little orange juice in his system and he would be fine. He headed toward the kitchen, staggering a bit, until he had to lean up against the wall before he could go on. He could feel his heart beating as fully as if he were still out working in the yard. It made no sense, not after a full night of sleep. It occurred to him he should sit down, but he worried that he might not be able to stand up later. And besides, the phone was still ringing. He was almost sure it wasn't Socorro calling him. Whoever it was would probably wait while he drank his orange juice. It wasn't more than a few sips that he needed anyway. Two or three more rings at the most. Don Celestino had barely opened the refrigerator door when it occurred to him that she could be calling to tell him she was delayed or that something had happened to her mother, that she wouldn't be able to come today, or that, yes, she was coming, everything was fine, she would be there at the bridge like she had every other Thursday morning, only that this time she had shown up a little early and was waiting for him, and to please come for her now, or something else, something important, something that he would only ever know if he picked up the phone before it stopped ringing.

He could hear the ringing in his head now. His chest seemed to tighten a little more with each ring. He was only two or three paces from his recliner, where he could sit to take the call. Whoever it was would wait that long. He'd never felt this way in the morning and he thought it might have to do with not eating enough the night before. It had only been a few months. How could they expect him to remember everything he was supposed to do along with checking his sugar level? The orange juice would help. Maybe he should have served himself the glass first. But right then the answering machine clicked on and the prerecorded voice announced that he wasn't available at the moment and to please leave a message and he would be sure to call back. He was waiting for the caller to say something, waiting to see if it was her voice, when suddenly the line cut out.

PART II

5

Near the far end of downtown, a street cleaner lumbered alongside the curb, whirling up a torment of dust and trash. The few drivers out at this early hour avoided the machine and the billowing cloud left in its wake. Most of the dollar stores and fabric shops would not open for at least another hour. By now the shopkeepers on the other side of the river were tossing buckets of soapy water onto the sidewalks in front of their businesses, sweeping away the dust that had gathered overnight.

Socorro glanced at her watch and then down the boulevard that led to the bridge. A flock of wild parrots squawked as they formed a green tapestry against the grayish sky. The group maintained its pattern, flying in the familiar direction of his house, then dipped beyond her line of vision. Socorro tugged on her skirt and looked down the street. She had woken up early to give her mother the medicine and then make breakfast and still have time to get ready. It took her several minutes to find a nice skirt and blouse that she could work in, and afterward pinned up her hair instead of simply keeping it in a braid. She debated before the mirror whether she should just wear her usual blue jeans. She had taken the black skirt off twice when she noticed the time and had to rush to catch her bus.

Now Socorro wondered why she had rushed. All that worrying for nothing, as if she were some young girl. Behind her, the bridge was backed up with drivers crossing over to work or shop or bring their children to school on the U.S. side. Across the street, a few taxi drivers leaned up against their cars and vans, waiting for the next fare. Beyond them stood the hall where she had seen couples walking together to the dances on the weekends. She was still looking around for his car when a silver truck pulled alongside her and the driver waved, trying to get her to smile back. "Let me take you to breakfast," the man said. She turned away, as if she hadn't heard him. Just beyond the side mirror, black cursive letters informed everyone of the vehicle's proper owner, but she saw this only as she searched for somewhere else to focus her attention. A figurine of a saloon girl on a tiny swing was dangling from the rearview mirror. He tapped the figurine with his finger, watching it sway to and fro. "Why work today?

We have all our lives to work. Take the day off and come with me." His thick mustache and long, dark sideburns looked as if they had been drawn with a piece of coal. She held on to the strap of her purse and turned her attention to traffic along the boulevard. Any second now her ride would be pulling up. Already it was past the time that he usually came for her. "A woman as pretty as you should not have to work so hard for her money." The saloon girl rocked back and forth, her tiny red heels tapping against the smudged windshield. He liked what she was wearing. "The way it fits you," he explained. "I don't like my women too small, without enough to hold on to." She dropped her left hand, tugged gently at her skirt. She heard a distant fluttering, and then another flock of parrots glided across the muted sky. "Why don't you come over here, sit here next to me? You look about the right size." He could tell she wanted to. "Only to spend a little time getting to know you, mamacita," he said. "Look at all the room I have here for you." He patted the vinyl seat. "Why do you want to be this way? There's no reason to be afraid." She felt flushed in that way she hated. Tiny beads of sweat were gathering along her neck and down between her breasts. She pulled at the collar of her blouse, hoping for any little breeze. She glanced behind her as if someone had just called her name. The sunlight shimmered off the razor wire above the back gates of the immigration offices. The serrated blades seemed newer and less rusted than the ones that lined the bridge. "Look, they just paid me last night. Come closer. Look, mamacita." Some of the taxi drivers were staring now and one of them was saying something that they all found especially funny.

"Mamacita, I want to talk to you. Why do you treat me this way, what are the people going to say?" He reached out for her and she pulled away, walked a few steps toward the end of the block. He followed her, stopped each time she stopped, inched forward with each step she took, then backward when she reversed her direction. "And why not, mamacita?" He reached for her again, then a third and a fourth time. Socorro knew that if he touched her, she was going to do or say something that she would regret, maybe even before she managed to get it all out. Just one more time, she kept thinking. Just one more time. It was only when she crossed the street that he finally left her, but not before he called her a puta and then other ugly words that she herself might have said if he hadn't driven away so fast.

She exited the bus, rubbing the key between her thumb and forefinger. Don Celestino had given it to her several months earlier when he dropped her off at the house one morning and then hurried off to make it in time for a doctor's appointment. Maybe that was it — that he'd had an early appointment with the doctor. There could be so many reasons he had not come for her. Socorro knew it was a bad habit of hers to always imagine the worst. She walked a little faster and tried to put these thoughts out of her mind.

Along the boulevard, the 18-wheelers surged to and from the bridge. She thought she could hear what sounded like a siren in the distance but couldn't tell if it was getting closer or farther away. From the bus she had to walk only two blocks past the school before she was on his street. She also cleaned the house of one of his neighbors, which was how she had come to clean his. La señora Muñoz lived midway down the block in a small clapboard house surrounded by all shapes and sizes of plants, as well as the two papaya trees, a small palm, and a large ebony that dropped its pods and tiny leaflets near the street. Socorro could see a little boy crouched along the curb in front of la señora's house. He had stopped to cram as many of the pods as he could into his backpack. The elementary school was several blocks away and he seemed too young to be walking alone. Socorro wondered where his mother could be. He was lost in his little world as he worked to stuff the pods into his backpack. She was about to ask if he needed help when the little boy finally stood up, but it was only so he could look past her at the ambulance that was headed this way.

6

Close to noon, after doing the cleaning and washing, Socorro packed his shaving kit and some clean clothes into a paper bag, then walked down the street to ask for a ride.

"The thing is that he should not be living by himself," la señora Muñoz said as she drove. She had come out in her housecoat and open-toed slippers.

"Some people like to be alone." Socorro looked out the window at the palm trees along the median. They were traveling up one of the main streets in Brownsville, the same one he'd taken to show her the barbershop where he had worked so many years.

"But he shouldn't be one of those people, not at his age. His wife would not have wanted him to be alone — that I do know. Don Celestino has been lucky until now."

"And his family?" she asked, hoping it didn't sound like the cleaning woman was asking more than she should.

"One of his daughters tried to get him to go live with her in San Antonio, but he wanted to stay here, in his own house." La señora slowed down for the speed bumps leading up to the hospital. "No matter how nice a man he might be, you have to remember he is still a man and very thickheaded."

She stood outside the entrance, watching her reflection disappear and then reappear in the sliding glass doors. Before driving off, la señora had scribbled the hospital-room number on the back of an old receipt. Now Socorro held on to the receipt and the paper bag filled with his clean clothes. Just beyond the sliding glass doors, a thick-necked security guard sat behind a large desk, eating the last bit of an empanada. His dark uniform reminded her of the men and women who every morning asked her to state her purpose for wanting to enter the country. To clean your house, she felt like saying. Why else would she be there practically every day of the week? She waited next to the sliding doors, allowing others to walk by her. This wasn't like the clinics on the other side of the river, where they had taken her mother when she started complaining about the terrible headaches and about her hands, which she could hardly open anymore. Or later after her first attack, when they had to rush her to the hospital. At least then Socorro knew she could open her mouth, defend herself if necessary. Not that she'd ever had any real problems coming across; she knew this, yet she hesitated as if someone would suddenly run her off, tell her she had no business here. Even dressed nicely, she was still a cleaning woman from the other side. She could see this every time the sliding glass doors came back together. And as if it were not already obvious, the hem of her skirt was smudged with some dust that she had tried to wipe away. She thought about leaving and simply walking back to the house or the bridge, but then the guard's phone rang, and as he was cradling the receiver on his shoulder, searching through some paperwork, she had just enough time to scuttle past the desk.

Once she arrived at the elevator, a maintenance worker explained to her how to find the room. Socorro stayed close to the plastic railing, making herself small as she walked by the nurses' station. When she was almost at the room, she stopped altogether. She asked herself why she was doing this and if she shouldn't have stayed at his house and finished the washing and cleaning, what he paid her to do. The rest of it, what had occurred those Thursday afternoons, was between them. And all of this was agreed to without either one of them having to say a word, as if they both understood that they had crossed some clear and definitive line. Only it had continued to happen. And so the line between being his cleaning lady and his lover had blurred before she realized it, and yet because no one else knew about them, the line had become more entrenched, like a moat intended to keep them apart.

Earlier that morning on the bus, she had sat next to Tere,

a girl who lived around the corner from the apartment, and she thought about telling her everything, the meals and talks they would have at his house, the way she started finding more work for herself so their afternoons wouldn't end so quickly, the first time she thought he might be interested, the first time they kissed, the first time they were really together, but mainly about all the things that worried her now. After the bus dropped them off, she had another chance to tell her during the walk to the bridge and even during the walk to the other side, and then again when they were both waiting for their rides on the street. She didn't tell her for two reasons: the first was that Tere was just a girl who lived around the corner from the apartment. They had spoken a handful of times when they happened to be on the same schedule or they ran into each other at the little store down the street, each buying something for her mother, but this was the extent of their friendship. Maybe she would've had someone to tell if she hadn't spent all her time either working or at home. Which was the second reason she had stopped herself from saying anything to Tere: she didn't want it getting back to her mother and aunt. Already she could hear them accusing her of offering herself to him. Explaining it wasn't like that and that things had started innocently between them would do little to help her mother understand what had happened.

She'd learned her lesson with Rogelio. The first years were difficult because of his temper, which seemed to be set off with the slightest disagreement. Her mother had told her to be more forgiving, that he would change once they had a family. It would be natural for him to want to be patient with their children. And perhaps this was true, but after four years she still wasn't pregnant. He didn't want to hear about her body. He didn't want to know about her cycle or anything else that did not directly concern him. That was for her to talk about with other women. He was not a woman — he was her husband. And no, there was no money to go see a special doctor. If they were ever going to have a child, it would be the same way every other man and woman did it, not with the help of some doctor. And so she prayed for God to bring them the child they had been waiting for. The miracle happened shortly after their sixth wedding anniversary, only not for her. Rather than stay with him at his family's house, she moved home. Her mother tried to convince her to go back, speaking of him as though nothing had changed and he was the same polite boy whose older brother and father had walked over to ask for her hand. The truth was she couldn't stop blaming herself for his wandering and finding someone else who could give him what he wanted. With a baby on the way, he started crossing the river again to look for work. She never liked the idea of him swimming to the other side, but it had never been in his nature to agree with her, so as usual he continued doing whatever occurred to him. As time passed she came to accept that this baby and its mother were not going to change things: Rogelio was still her husband; she was still his wife. After a couple of weeks away, she decided she was ready to move back. She was waiting to tell him this when his naked body turned up, floating in the steady current beneath the bridge.

Just thinking of that time made her want to leave the hospital. She stalled by looking inside the bag, pretending to search for some item she might have forgotten. After all this effort she knew she couldn't leave now, not when it had taken her most of the morning to work up the courage to ask for a ride. Perhaps she'd imagined it, but it seemed as if la señora had hesitated, as if she might not have heard correctly — *The cleaning woman wants a ride to the hospital so she can visit the man she works for?* Socorro wrestled with the feeling that she might be stepping beyond what was considered acceptable or proper, and in this way revealing what he had wanted to keep private. She asked herself how it would look if she went to the hospital for any of the other people whose houses she cleaned, some for much longer periods of time, but then decided it was better to not wait around for the answer.

She stood at the door, not wanting to interrupt what the doctor might be saying or wake the patient if he happened to be resting. Maybe she would just leave his clothes at the nurses' station. When she did look around the corner, it was a nurse who was standing next to the bed and writing some notes on a metal clipboard. Don Celestino was lying back in the bed against a couple of pillows. His disheveled white hair from earlier that morning was now combed back in the way he normally wore it, and it looked as though he had shaved, maybe even trimmed the edges of his mustache.

"Is that you, Socorro?" he asked, squinting through his tinted glasses. "You came all this way to visit me in the hospital?" He used both hands to adjust himself and sit up straight in the bed. "Look at how they attached all these wires to me. All I needed was to eat a good breakfast so my sugar would be back to normal again. Now they want to run some tests, just to be sure about my heart. Please, Socorro, tell this young man here that I have many more years left in me. Tell him Celestino Rosales is not going anywhere." He held his hands out for her to come closer.

She walked to the bed and kissed him on the cheek. It was a common enough gesture, one she had repeated countless times throughout her life, though never with anyone whose house she cleaned. And as his white whiskers brushed against her cheek, she wanted more than anything to believe that the differences in their ages and positions were gently being swept aside.

7

Salinas was coughing on the other side of the curtain. The greenish glow of the monitors added the only bit of light to the dark room. Don Celestino had briefly introduced himself when they'd brought the man in that afternoon. He might have spoken more to him then, but the man's wife stayed around until late in the evening, leaning back in a recliner and watching novelas and talk shows. She wore at least one ring on almost every finger and a gold fifty-peso medallion that rested on her broad chest like the hood ornament on an expensive car. Occasionally she talked back to the philandering men or the scantily dressed women on the screen, but otherwise hardly any sound came from the other side of the retractable curtain. The few times he had caught a glimpse of Salinas, the man had looked back in a tortured sort of way.

Sometime after midnight Don Celestino stepped off the bed to go relieve himself. He waved as he passed his neighbor's bed, but the man was turned away as if trying to fall asleep.

On his way back, he noticed him staring at the ceiling. "Trouble sleeping?"

"Already for a long time," Salinas said. "Maybe when that old woman of mine comes in the morning."

Don Celestino only nodded as he pulled along his IV unit and climbed into bed.

"And you," Salinas asked, "are you married?"

"My wife died last year," Don Celestino replied. "I'm alone now."

After a moment Salinas cleared his throat. "Forgive me."

Don Celestino fell in and out of sleep, for a time gazing out the window and later just lying there with his eyes shut. It struck him that if he were to pass during the night, his family wouldn't be there to even notice he was gone. This was the same hospital where they had come when Dora had been feeling sick, and her doctor, after so many other tests, couldn't figure out why she had become so bloated. It had taken opening her up to find that the cancer had by then spread throughout most of her stomach. One day he had been married more than half his life, and a few weeks later he was alone. And alone he had stayed for the first couple of months, rarely leaving the house and refusing to go see his children when they pleaded with him to at least come visit. A man who had never lived by himself and suddenly he was doing his own cooking and cleaning. It was his own illness that finally drew him out some. His doctor urged him to attend the diabetes classes and take control of the disease. For a few days he questioned if it might not be better to stay at home and ignore the new diet. With no one there to watch after him, it wouldn't take long before his health declined. Which might have happened had the doctor not arranged for a nurse to come help him for the first couple of weeks, until he was comfortable with checking his sugar level and taking the insulin. Then his neighbor recommended a young woman who could come clean the house for him.

Until their first afternoon together, he'd been afraid Socorro might see him only as the man who paid her $35 every week but beyond this had little interest in him. It had started this way, as a curiosity more than anything. Was she, could she ever be, interested in a man more than thirty years her senior? Not that he necessarily showed signs of his age (other than this unfortunate visit to the hospital). The fact that his hair had turned completely white on him when he was still in his fifties did little to change his overall appearance. The front still rose into what once might have been called a pompadour, though on a mature man he believed it presented more of a distinguished look. Whether it had been because of his appearance or his manner around her or his interest in her life outside of work, it had been enough to draw her closer to him. Since then, though, he hadn't been sure what he was supposed to do next. He was, after all, supposed to be mourning the loss of his wife, who at the time had been gone only a few months.

Close to an hour had passed when he heard a slight cough from the other side of the curtain. "Still awake?"

"I thought this medicine was supposed to make you sleep," Salinas answered. "You never know with these doctors."

"When I was a young man, we had different ways of curing a person."

"You see me here in this bed only because of my wife. She's the one who has people on this side. I come from Saltillo."

"Close to Monterrey."

"You have come to visit the city?"

"No," Don Celestino said, "but my family came from Nuevo León, close to the town of Linares."

"For many years I had business in Linares." Salinas used the control pad to adjust the bed into a reclining position. "Maybe I met some of your family."

"My grandfather came here sometime around eighteen fifty."

"Only yesterday, eh?" The man laughed to himself.

"He used to tell us a funny story about how he was kidnapped by the Indians and brought here, over to this side."

"One of my uncles used to tell stories like that," his neighbor said. "But you know how people like to talk, share stories about their families. One never knows whether to believe them, if they're not just stories made up to pass the time."

"It always seemed made up to me, but my grandfather liked to say it was true about the Indians."

"And now all your family is from over here?"

"From here, only that my daughters and my son moved away a long time ago."

"But you must have some other people that live close by?"

For a second he considered mentioning his one remaining brother, but they hadn't spoken in years. "I used to," he said finally. "One of my daughters lives in Chicago and I have two more in San Antonio, and my son is close to Dallas, all with their own families."

"And they came to visit you here?"

"I didn't want to bother them — the doctor said he would let me go home soon, maybe tomorrow."

Salinas cleared his throat as if he were looking for something to say or maybe just the best way to say it.

"When they were bringing me in this afternoon, I saw a young lady leaving the room."

"That was a friend of mine," Don Celestino responded, hoping he wouldn't have to say much more.

"My wife would never let me have a friend like that," he said, and shook his head.

"For now that's all she is."

"And someday," Salinas said, "you think she might be more than your friend?"

"There are some people who would think she was too young for a man like me."

"She looks young, but not too young. The better question is not whether she's too young, but more whether you are too old."

Don Celestino gazed at the silhouette across the partitioning curtain. "That sounds like the same problem."

"Not really. If she's too young, it means she is not mature enough and ready to give herself to you. But if you're too old, it means you have nothing left to give her in return."

"And if we're not living together, how am I supposed to know if I still have enough to give her?"

His neighbor sat up a little more, tucking the pillow behind him. "Are you asking me how you find out if it will last, but without taking any risk?"

"Something like that."

Salinas laughed to himself again. "Then what you really want to know is how to fry an egg when it is still inside the shell."

When Don Celestino didn't answer, the man continued.

"There's nothing strange about wanting to avoid the risk," Salinas said. "It only means you are human."

They quieted when a young nurse walked into the room. She smiled at Salinas and then pressed a series of buttons on his monitor; afterward she walked over and did the same to the machine near Don Celestino's bed. He lay silently as the woman did her work. On the other side of the curtain, Salinas readjusted his bed to the horizontal position and a short while later fell asleep.

Don Celestino stared out his window for some time after the nurse had left. He wondered if he shouldn't have told the man more about his time with Socorro. Why should he be afraid to tell people? At least here he had a person who was willing to listen to him. Maybe Salinas would understand. Don Celestino had his children to consider, not that they were going to tell him how to live his life, but still he wanted their feelings for him not to be strained because he had found another woman, and a much younger one at that. And this wasn't taking into account how soon it had all happened. Their mother in the ground only a few months and here he was with another woman in their same bed. And yet this other woman was the one who had come to visit him and the only one who would have known if anything more serious had happened to him. He wondered if he shouldn't have let someone else know about his condition. It reminded him again of his brother, not that he and Fidencio had ever been so close, especially with how disagreeable the old man could be. A few months ago he'd heard that he was living in a nursing home. It had been more than ten years since they had talked, though, and as things turned out, this was probably for the best.

The traffic lights flashed red against the condensation that had gathered on the windowpane. No one else knew about him, that was the point, no one except someone who he probably shouldn't be thinking about so much. Maybe there was a reason that he had gotten sick, to remind him that he was old and she was not. He could have gotten sick any other day of the week, but it had happened the morning she would be at his house to witness them taking him away in the ambulance — half dressed and with his hair a mess — to see with her own eyes that he was old and she was not. To prove to her, and to him, that they had no business together, a young one with such an old one.

He had lived a complete life, and somehow that life and the world he had lived in seemed so distant. There was a time when the boulevard just outside his window used to be a dirt road. People rode into Brownsville, some still in their wagons, and shopped at the Jimmy Pace Store. And even later there was Don José, who sold fresh bread from the back of his horse and buggy. This is the world he had come from. Now the four-lane thoroughfare was lined with businesses he had never stepped into: large grocery stores, gas stations, nightclubs, car lots, motels, restaurants, drive-through hamburger places, video stores, immigration offices. What not so long ago had been a gentleman's club now announced on its marquee that Saturday was APOLLO MALE DANCER NIGHT. Never did he imagine seeing so many changes in his little town. His grandfather coming from a ranchito in Mexico couldn't have experienced such a difference in his lifetime. What could there have been before a dirt road and one or two stores? How different could it really have been for him? He probably never so much as entered a hospital. Don Celestino could remember being five or six years old and the family gathering the evening when he passed away at the house. There must have been some connection, however tenuous, between the world he had arrived in and the one he saw before finally passing away. Lying there in the hospital bed, Don Celestino found it hard not to feel as if he were cut off from all that had come before him and, in some ways, all that still remained of his life.

8

Socorro stopped just as she reached the halfway mark on the bridge. After rifling through her purse, she uncovered the tollbooth receipt and read the day to make sure it said jueves, her usual day to clean his house. She was putting away the slip of paper when she noticed something move out from under the opposite side of the bridge. A Border Patrol agent in a green-and-white jeep cruised along the bank of the river and stopped alongside another agent in a jeep headed in the opposite direction. The two men rolled down their windows and talked in their idling vehicles. After a while one of them handed the other a cigarette, then a lighter. Farther down the levee an old negro, wearing camouflage fatigues but no shirt, pushed a loaded shopping cart. The basket leaned to the right with all the crushed aluminum cans and piled blankets and pillows and empty milk jugs that dangled from that side. The negro used a crutch to help him with his bad leg, but the cart's wheels kept getting stuck in the soft dirt and he had to jiggle the entire frame back and forth, side to side, until he freed it.

She stayed gazing down at the water through the chain-link fence. The current eddied in a couple of places, then continued forward, indifferent to people on the bank or the bridge that stood in its way. The sun reflected off the river in a way that made the water appear to be not quite as green and putrid as she remembered it.

A gust of cold air washed over her as soon as she opened the glass door. A dozen or more men and women waited in the two lines. An older female officer stood behind a computer station, scanning each card. She had dark pockmarked skin and grayish hair cropped as short as the male officers'. The men and women in line looked forward, some with their heads bent and their eyes cast at the floor, as if awaiting Communion. The first woman in line wore a pink blouse, a gray cardigan frayed along the bottom, a plain black skirt, and black cushioned shoes. She carried a plastic woven bag that held her purse and her work apron, which was tucked away to one side. How long do you plan to stay? the female officer asked. Just for the day, to shop, she answered. The officer waved her on and motioned for the next person, a young woman holding an infant with tiny studded earrings, to step forward. The officer asked if the child was hers. The woman said yes, that she didn't have anywhere to leave her while she did her shopping. But the baby was born on this side, the mother assured her. From her purse she pulled out a plastic sandwich bag that held the folded birth certificate. The officer looked at the document, then at the mother, then over at the baby, as if the child might be able to corroborate the story. The officer halfway smiled and gestured for the mother and child to continue on. By the time Socorro reached the station, a new group of women had lined up behind her. The male officer only glanced at her card before motioning for her to continue on her way, even adding, "Tenga buen día."

She felt a stitch of worry when she walked outside and didn't see his car. They had kept Don Celestino in the hospital a few extra days to run their tests, and this would be her first time to see him since then. She calmed herself a few minutes later when he pulled up, then rushed around the car to open the door for her. For a second there on the curb she had thought he might kiss her on the cheek, as she had done in front of the nurse, but it was something that would maybe happen only once.

"But you feel all right?" she asked when they were back on the main boulevard.

"Yes, yes, one of my girls called as I was leaving the house. I shouldn't have answered it, that was the problem. She likes to talk. This was the youngest one, Sonia."

"She must be worried about you."

"Even when I told her all the results came out fine," Don Celestino said, craning his neck to get a better look at the exchange rate outside one of the casas de cambio. "You see why I didn't want to tell them? And now she wants to check on me every morning. Finally I told her that I had to go, that someone was waiting for me."

"Someone."

"Eh?" An 18-wheeler had pulled alongside them.

"Someone?" she repeated a little louder.

"She knows that you come do the cleaning on Thursdays."

"Then you told her my name?"

"Maybe when you first started. I can't remember now, after all this time, five or six months. But they know you used to clean the house for my neighbor and that was how you came to clean here at my house."

"Seven," she clarified, after they had passed the 18-wheeler.

"Okay then, seven months, so you can see it has been a long time."

"But already more than two months since the time we got together."

He neither acknowledged nor denied her last statement and instead let it linger along with the gas fumes that had seeped in through the crack in the window.

They had been sitting in the car at least five minutes, maybe ten. He wanted to glance over at the console, but she might ask if he was in a hurry. Fiberglass siding covered the walls on either side of the carport, starting about waist high and leaving some space for a man to walk under, if he wanted to get out that way. Parked inside the carport, he could easily make out the ceiling through the exposed rafters. The carpenters had used longer nails on the roof than necessary, and now hundreds of rusty tips pricked through the ceiling and formed what looked like a bed of nails.

"I told my mother," she said finally.

"All of it?"

"Enough, what she needed to know — how we met and how long ago, about your business, how you are, the things you say. She was only going to protest if I told her more."

"Then you can imagine how it would be with these girls."

"Girls."

"To me they will always be my girls, no matter the age."

"I even told my brother Marcos when he called," Socorro said. "And now he wants to meet you when he can come to visit."

"If we still talked, I could go tell my brother."

He glanced at the side mirror and spotted his neighbor Mrs. Harwell across the street behind her locked gate. The old lady held up the hem of her dress as if she were wading through a flood, then looked up to see how much farther she had to go.

"You never told me you had a brother."

"You never asked."

"Because you made it like you were the only one left, that the rest had already died. Why would I ask if I thought you had no brothers?"

She could feel the feverish sweat forming on her neck and

chest again, and she tried to find some relief by pulling away from the seat back. If she didn't know better, she would have thought he had turned off the air conditioner.

"With this one, it's almost like that. He doesn't call me and I don't call him, that's how it is. How could I go tell him about us if me and him haven't talked in years?" He glanced into the mirror, and the old lady was now staring this way as if she had witnessed a crime and was trying to commit his license plate to memory.

"Even if you didn't tell him, you could have told me you had a brother. What would it hurt to tell me that one little thing? Why keep it from me?"

"You say it like I did it to deceive you. But there was nothing to tell you. What could I say? *I have a brother, but it's like I don't have a brother. I have a brother, but he is like a stranger to me? I have a brother, but he would never care to know about my life or who I spend my time with?*"

She could hardly listen to him anymore. What she wanted was for him to turn up the air conditioner, but at the same time she didn't want anything from him. It was just a little misunderstanding between them. Later, things would be fine again, like always. She knew this, and yet right then all she wanted was to get far, far away from him. She moved her face up closer to the air vent and left it at that.

"I never said anything about telling him."

"Then?"

"Just why you kept it from me, Celestino, like it was a part of your life that didn't concern me."

He tried to brush a strand of hair from her face, but she leaned away from him. Even upset, she looked more attractive than he had imagined her this morning when he was hurrying to get to the bridge.

"Why would you care about some old man you have never seen?"

"Your brother."

"Yes, all right, my brother, so now you know."

"Yes, now I know," she said, but somehow he had the feeling they weren't talking about the same thing.

9

La señora Muñoz was sitting back in the recliner, watching the novela she had recorded yesterday. Socorro took another shirt from the laundry basket and spread it across the ironing board. If she timed it right, she would finish with the clothes about the time it took them to watch this episode of *Mi destino perdido.* La señora liked to say the tragedies weren't any less sad the second time she saw them. In today's episode, for instance, poor Gabriela lies still in the hospital, thick gauze pads covering each of her eyes. What this beautiful young music teacher doesn't realize is that the doctor who saved her life and with whom she now finds herself falling in love, desperately so, is also the man who caused the accident that robbed her of her sight. Gabriela caught only a glimpse of Dr. Hernan Lozano Ramos as he sped up to pass her and then inadvertently cut her off and sent her car swerving toward a ravine. She is lucky to be alive. The doctor reminds her of this as he stands along one side of the bed and caresses her hand. He says it as a way of pacifying her, as well as discouraging her from trying so hard to identify the person responsible for her condition. A young police detective, much closer in age to Gabriela than the doctor, stands on the other side of the bed. He has come around again to help her recall some detail of the driver who didn't have the decency to render aid after causing this terrible accident. Eduardo, as the detective insists she call him, also has feelings for the victim. The fact that Detective Eduardo, as Gabriela prefers to address him, has been less than friendly and courteous toward the doctor has not set well with her. The doctor has stated, in no uncertain terms, that his patient should not in any way be upset. She is lucky to be alive. Of course, there is little for him to worry about as long as she cannot identify the other driver. And so the respected surgeon remains the only person who knows he was speeding with his unconscious wife in the passenger seat, sedated from the cocktail he prescribed to help relieve her latest case of nerves. Gabriela blames herself for the accident. Distraught from having just discovered her fiancé in bed with her half sister, she had been driving home in a confused and erratic manner that caused her to overreact when the other driver pulled out in front of her. She is lucky to be alive.

Socorro held up the dress shirt and sprayed starch on the

back. She was about to start on the sleeves when she turned to glance out the window.

"Are you waiting for someone?" la señora asked.

"No," she said, pulling away. "Why do you ask?"

She sprayed more starch on the shirt.

"Because already that's the third time you look outside."

Socorro could feel herself getting red and hoped this was from her ironing. "I just wanted to see who was driving by."

"If you're so curious, you should go over there."

"Over where?"

"To check on my neighbor," la señora said. "What else would interest you so much on this street?"

"We changed days, and tomorrow I need to clean the house for him."

"You miss him?"

Socorro turned down the temperature on the iron until it reached the permanent-press setting, then a moment later turned it off completely but continued with her work all the same.

"Tell me," la señora insisted, a little louder now. "You miss him?"

"I work for him."

"And because of that, you can't miss him?"

"Ay, señora, how can you say that?" She tried her best to laugh at the question.

"You think you would be the first woman to feel something for the man she worked for?"

"But he's much older."

"Men forget how to count when they see a young woman — look at the doctor with Gabriela," she said, pointing the remote back at the television.

"Yes, but he would never be interested in me."

"You want me to believe an older man like Celestino Rosales wouldn't be interested in a young, attractive woman?"

"Maybe, but not me." She pretended she was having problems with the pleat on the back of the shirt, so she pulled it off the board to flap it open a couple of times, enough to produce a tiny breeze.

"I saw that you came over two times last week."

"Only because I didn't finish all my work and then one of his daughters was coming to visit him. He wanted everything ready for her."

"I want you to know you could tell me if he was," la señora said, "or even if you were."

Socorro chose to keep her eyes focused on her work and turned the temperature back up on the iron. "Thank you, but there's nothing to tell."

"And nothing has happened?"

"Like what?"

"You know, what happens between a man and woman when they are alone all day in a house."

"Ay, señora."

"You could tell me."

"There's nothing to tell."

"Are you sure?"

"Yes, of course."

"*Sure* sure, or just a little bit sure?"

"*Sure* sure."

La señora didn't seem convinced, but she went back to watching the rest of her novela anyway. Socorro hoped that she wasn't too obvious about her feelings. She could imagine the old lady spreading the news across the neighborhood. And then there were his children that he was always worried about. He said the youngest one talked about her mother as if she were still in the hospital and would be coming home soon. How would they feel if they learned their father had found someone else, and so soon? Her own mother had remained alone after her father died, which was part of what had made it difficult for Socorro to tell her what had really occurred between her and the man whose house she cleaned every week. How could she begin to explain this to a woman who had been without a man for more than twenty years?

Before her first afternoon with Don Celestino, she had never imagined doing such a thing: she used to look down on those women who cleaned houses only because they wanted to find a widower with money. Some of these women married and stayed with their husbands for a few years, until the old man died or grew so ill that his children took him to a hospital, where finally he died. It must have seemed a small price to pay in order to arrange their papers and from then on have a comfortable life. With a little luck the old man might leave them with some money, maybe a house or a car, depending on whether he had arranged this beforehand and his children didn't claim it all. Other women remained unmarried but the old men paid them generously, as if spreading their legs was simply another chore they were doing, like mending a shirt button or replacing a spent lightbulb.

At least she knew that her interest in him had nothing to do with what he could give her. She wanted only what they could share as a couple, if he would let this happen. Since they had become intimate, her life had turned into two lives. One that she lived on the other side of the river with her mother and aunt, still cooking and cleaning and shopping and going to the pharmacy for these pills or that salve that her mother might need. And her other life, on this side of the river, where she rushed about her day trying to finish early so she could spend some time with him in the late afternoon, before she had to walk back across the bridge. Times like this, she tried to remember what she had imagined her life would be like if they ever got together, because surely this hadn't been it. To live her life in secret? As if she were playing the role of the mistress, only the role of the married man was being played by a widowed man? Not that she didn't enjoy her time with him, because she did, but it also seemed like some fantasy that lasted only as long as they were together and then ceased to exist when she wasn't in his car or house or bed.

But after waiting for so long to find someone, she asked herself if she should be making demands of him or if she shouldn't just be happy they were together and not care if these moments were fleeting at best. All these years of waiting, the men she knew had fallen into one of two categories: those who disappeared from one day to the next, and those who stuck around, but only because they were biding their time until something more promising came along, after which they disappeared from one day to the next. Maybe she was meant to be alone? It had crossed her mind again recently. Why else would God have sent her a husband who just wandered off like a mule without a rope? And then sent her an older man who wanted her but wouldn't tell another soul about them, not even his own family? Was their friendship so shameful that he couldn't at least tell his brother, the only one he had left? Neither one of them probably remembered what they had fought over. How much effort would it take him to at least do this for her?

"Ay, he wants to fool you!" la señora called out at one of the women on television.

Socorro hurried to finish the rest of the ironing so she could get paid and leave for the day. It was bad enough la señora was comparing her to these poor women in the novelas. She wasn't mixed up with a man who was trying to deceive her or hurt her in some way. She wasn't married to a man who got so tired of waiting for her to get pregnant that he found himself another woman. And she wasn't involved with a man who wanted to run off on her. She didn't have to figure out who was telling her the truth anymore. She knew the truth; she just couldn't tell anyone.

10

He had never been one to walk around in short pants, showing off his legs to the world. So while the others wore shorts or exercise pants, Don Celestino preferred his blue jeans and an old short-sleeve work shirt. His black cushioned shoes were easier on his feet and still looked like proper shoes. The girl at the store had tried to sell him a pair that fastened with Velcro straps, but he chose the laces because he didn't want to get in the habit of doing things the easy way.

Cooder, on the treadmill to his right, wore running shoes, athletic socks that reached just below his knees, long pleated shorts, and a sagging muscle shirt that allowed tufts of his white chest hair to billow over the top. His black fanny pack hung loose on his hips like a loaded holster. "Ready to be young again, Rosales?" he asked.

Don Celestino was turning side to side as if loosening his back before a long run. "What do you mean, *again?*"

Cooder patted him on the shoulder. "Good answer."

Then each one hit the start button on his treadmill.

Cooder jogged at a slow enough pace that it might have been confused with a fast walk. As he trotted along, he leaned forward as if he were carrying a sixty-pound car battery and desperately looking for a safe place to set it down. He chose the machine on the right because it was closer to the mounted television and the game show he liked to watch, though he generally jogged with his head down, his eyes focused on the black conveyor belt whisking beneath him.

Don Celestino kept his finger on the speed button until it reached 2.0, the setting for the comfortable pace he preferred to walk. He reread the inspirational poster on the wall in front of him: STAYING HEALTHY, MAKING THE MOST OF LIFE! In the poster a gray-haired couple strolled in a wooded park and laughed about something only they knew about. He could look around if he wanted to, but he chose to concentrate on what he was doing and instead stare straight ahead at the gray-haired man and woman. Once or twice he had lost his balance and then caught hold of the railings in time to correct himself. Later he blamed the machine for somehow speeding up when he wasn't expecting it. Anyone would have been caught off balance. He hadn't reported the malfunctioning equipment only because he didn't want to get anyone in trouble.

"Who is Zachary Taylor?" the old man shouted. "Who's General Zachary Taylor?!"

Don Celestino focused on moving his legs at the pace of the machine; by now he was used to Cooder yelling while he watched television. He had more trouble with just the idea of being here with these old men and women. He knew he wasn't old like some of them. Other than his plume of white hair, there really wasn't anything that showed his age.

"Who is Pershing?! Black Jack Pershing!"

And it wasn't just his appearance and physical strength, because he knew his mind was sharper than those of much younger men. You wouldn't find him repeating the same story over and over. He could still describe how the dagger-shaped icicles hung off the truck's bumper that night in 1949 when he had to go for the doctor and how Dora was already holding the baby in her arms by the time they arrived back at the house. And before that, he could remember attending barber school for almost three years because he kept having to leave with his brothers to follow the crops up north to Ohio, to Minnesota, to Iowa, to Michigan, and then by the time he did get his license, the army was ready for him. The foggy morning of June 24, 1945, he and eighty-seven other young men headed to Fort Benning, Georgia, for basic training. He remembered sitting directly behind the bus driver, and when the sun was barely rising over the King Ranch, he pulled out a small notebook and began writing what he imagined might be his last letter to Dora. And when the war ended before he had actually made it overseas, the army shipped him back home, and in Houston he boarded a commercial bus that eventually stopped at a roadside diner near Corpus, and while the rest of the passengers were free to enter the restaurant, because of the times he was forced to sit on the back steps of the kitchen and eat a cheeseburger so greasy it stained his uniform. All these stories and more still came to mind as though he had experienced them only yesterday, no different than they would for a much younger man.

"Who's Johnson?! Who's . . ."

Cooder's fanny pack had slid around to the front and he had to step off the machine to adjust it. Inside the pouch he kept several ballpoint pens and a tiny spiral notepad, where he recorded the distance and time of his walk. He'd shown it once to Don Celestino and later turned to the section where he logged the miles he and his wife traveled in their motor home between here and Belton, Missouri, where they lived during the summer months. Cooder claimed he didn't mind the cold, but his wife's arthritis did better when they traveled south for the winter. They were about to celebrate fifty-six years of marriage, only two years more than Don Celestino had been married to Dora. He had thought they would still be together. He felt so alone in those days after she left him behind. It seemed like he would stay this way, but his life took an unexpected turn and suddenly he went from being married to the same woman for more than fifty years to being with a young woman who herself was still a long way from fifty. It troubled him that Socorro didn't seem to appreciate what this meant for him and instead pretended they were like any other couple that had fallen in love. Their situation was more complicated than that, at least for him it was. And now this business with his brother. If she only knew what she was asking of him.

According to the control panel on the treadmill, he had walked only a little more than a mile, though it felt as if he had already reached his goal of two miles. At this pace he would be here all day. It was Wednesday, his day to wash the car, and if he didn't hurry it was going to get dark on him. He needed to spend some time vacuuming the inside, especially the space between the driver and passenger sides. He increased the speed to 3.0 and began taking longer, more purposeful strides.

Before he retired and learned his diabetes had grown worse, he figured he was getting enough exercise just being on his feet at the barbershop. That was where he had spent most of his days and where he had last spoken to his brother. If it hadn't been for the barbershop, he might not have seen him at all. He referred to him as his brother, but because of the years that stood between them, he had thought of him as an uncle or cousin who came around to the house more often. Don Fidencio was in his early eighties and by this point living alone. Even after retiring from the post office, he had continued to show up early in the morning on the first Saturday of the month.

The last time Don Fidencio had come by, Don Celestino had pulled up to the barbershop at twenty minutes after eight, which was unusual for him since he was in the habit of turning on the lights and the pole a few minutes before the hour. Don Fidencio was waiting inside his car, staring straight ahead as if he were stuck in a long line of traffic.

"I didn't know if you were still in business," he said, then glanced at his watch as he got out of the car.

"We went for coffee," his brother said.

Don Fidencio looked surprised when another man parked his car behind his brother's car and walked up to where they were standing. The man was short and he squinted through one eye as though he couldn't see so well.

"This is my neighbor. Sometimes we go for coffee." Don Celestino turned back toward the man. "This is my older brother."

"Your brother?" He squinted a little more. "Bill Harwell. Good to meet you."

Don Fidencio looked at him a second before finally switching his cane to the other side and putting out his own hand. The two men stood at the entrance of the barbershop, neither one speaking as they waited for Don Celestino to unlock the door. When they were inside, he flicked on the pole and then the lights in the room.

"Did the Astros play yesterday?" he asked, thinking baseball was something the two men might have in common.

"Going to, but they got rained out," Harwell said.

Don Fidencio only nodded.

"They said it was going to rain here today," Don Celestino said, pulling up the blinds. "But I don't see any sign of it."

"I went ahead and cut the grass yesterday," Harwell said, "just to be on the safe side."

"If it's not too much trouble, you think I can get my trim now?" Don Fidencio asked in Spanish.

His brother turned around to find him sitting in the barber's chair, the wooden cane hanging off the armrest.

"I already told this man I would take care of him first."

"And me?"

"It won't take long, then you can go next."

"I was the one who showed up first, not him."

"Yeah, but he called me last night." He tugged on his brother's arm, hoping to nudge him out of the chair, but the old man pulled his arm back and stayed where he was.

"Now you take appointments, like a beauty parlor?"

"That's fine, if you want to start with him." Harwell had sat down in one of the chairs against the wall.

"You see?" Don Fidencio said. "The gavacho agrees with me, even if he doesn't know Spanish. He knows I was here first."

Don Celestino looked at his neighbor, realizing the man had lived here long enough to know when he was being talked about.

"I can come back a while later," Harwell offered, then actually stood up.

"So, how is it going to be?" Don Fidencio said. "For him to go before me, like you don't have a family?"

"Just let me take care of the man."

"You forget, that's the problem."

"Don't start."

"You act like one of them. And to hell with your brother, he doesn't matter. 'Just let me take care of the man,'" he mocked. "'I have to take care of the poor man.' Because how can you think to make him wait a few minutes, like I waited half the morning out there in the car, like some dummy? But how?"

"Ya, Fidencio."

"I got here before him, that's all I know," his brother said, placing his hands on his knees and standing up on the footrest. "It should count for something, being the first one here."

"I promised him."

Don Fidencio glanced over at the other man and then back at his brother just before he grabbed his cane.

"Then both of you go to hell," he said, this time in English.

He must have found somewhere else to cut his hair because he stopped coming around. Then several years later Don Celestino read in the paper that Don Fidencio's wife had died. Though she had moved out years earlier, she had never actually divorced his brother. Don Celestino debated whether to go to the services; Dora argued with him that they should at least attend the Rosary. Wouldn't he want his family to show up if something happened to his wife? And then a year later something did happen. By that time he figured his brother would have let go whatever bad feelings there were between them. But when he failed to show up for Dora's services, this slight, from his one remaining brother, only stirred his sorrow. He knew it was the old man paying him back for his own lapse. But he reasoned that Don Fidencio hadn't been living with his woman when she died. She had left him years ago, wouldn't even talk to him, practically divorced him. How could that be the same as a husband and wife — under the same roof, in the same bed — for more than fifty years? It didn't compare back then, and it didn't compare now.

Don Celestino glanced back down at the control panel and saw he had half a mile to go on the treadmill. If he trusted the machine a little more, he might have raised his arm to see what time it was on his wristwatch. He pressed the speed button until it reached 3.5. Thinking about some old man wasn't helping him any. He still had lots of work to do at home before tomorrow came around.

11

She curled over onto her side, toward the wall, tossing the covers away from her. Just beyond the bedroom door, she heard him flush the toilet. The curtains were drawn and, except for a bit of light slipping in beneath the sheet of aluminum foil that covered the windowpane, the bedroom seemed dark enough for it to be the middle of the night and not the middle of the afternoon.

Socorro used to think his queen-size mattress was so big. Growing up, she had spent years sleeping on the sofa so her four brothers could have the bedroom. Her first real bed had been the one she shared with Rogelio. But this was only a full-size mattress and it was impossible to move without entangling herself with his body, which on most nights she wanted to avoid, especially after she suspected he was lying down in another bed. When she started cleaning houses and saw her first king-size mattress, she assumed it was two beds pushed together. She couldn't imagine why a husband and wife would need such an enormous bed. It seemed a couple could lie there and never touch each other the whole night, as if they had been arguing about something just before falling asleep and had each grabbed his own blanket and rolled over on his side with his back to the other. And if that was the case, then what was the point of sleeping in the same bed with your husband?

Though she had been married before, she felt as if she knew very little about how to be with a man. A few years earlier, while cleaning a lawyer's house, she found a stack of magazines with men and women together in bed and other places where she'd never imagined people would want to be together in that way. She didn't want to look at first, but she couldn't help herself, no more than she could turn away when she saw a newspaper photo of a dead person found somewhere in Matamoros. She would close the magazine, feel some shame for what she had just done, swear she wouldn't open it again, but then open the one right beneath it. Almost all the men in these photos were americanos, but the women were all different, some americanas, some negras, others chinas, and others mexicanas. They had them on the carpet, in the shower, on the kitchen table, on the hood of a car, in the swimming pool, in a stable. She finally forced herself to put the magazines away, but now she knew people had other ways of being together. The few years she'd been married to Rogelio, she had done what he told her to do, and that was to lie down with him in a normal bed, where married people lie down. But even this way she could remember only one time when she had ever actually enjoyed being with him.

They had gone to church at noon — something he rarely did, but he had agreed to this one day to make her happy — and later spent the afternoon in the plaza. It was a beautiful day, with all the families sitting on the benches and children chasing one another around the bandstand. A group of musicians, older men with brass instruments and a woman singer, were getting ready to perform. She and Rogelio sat on one of the benches under the trees and shared a fruit cup. After they sat there a few minutes, a pretty little girl came up to Rogelio and handed him a white balloon. She couldn't have been more than two, and she was playing with him in the way little girls do when they want attention from little boys. He accepted the balloon and then offered it back to her. She accepted it, then a few seconds later offered it back to him. Rogelio asked her who'd given her such a big balloon. But when she opened her mouth, they couldn't understand her garbled words. After a while Rogelio said the little girl looked like her. Socorro couldn't see how, but he insisted that she must have looked like her when she was that age. Maybe so, she said. No maybe, he said. He became very serious and said this was how their baby would look. Socorro smiled. The little girl was pretty. And then he said he wanted to go back to the house and make a little baby, a beautiful one just like her. He threw away the rest of the fruit cup and they left for the house.

But it was as if she couldn't walk fast enough. Everything had to be right away with him. Already more than a year had gone by and still there was no sign of a baby. She'd heard his mother asking him why it was taking so long. They were lucky that when they got to the house his family was still away, buying groceries. He had his pants down below his knees before she could pull the green shower curtain that covered the entrance to his bedroom. But after this he slowed down, slower than she could remember him ever going. She started feeling something funny that she hadn't experienced before. At first she wasn't sure if she was supposed to feel this way and she wanted him to stop, but the more she let him, the more she didn't want him to stop. She imagined they were creating their baby, their little girl, and she was being made from their love. It was as if they were swimming just above the bed, the baby floating between them and the whole time she and Rogelio feeling the same exact thing. They breathed together, they moved together, they made the same sounds. But somehow through all this she heard the front door. She whispered to him that his family was home, in the next room. This had been a problem, living in the same small house, but usually they waited until late at night or early in the morning, before anyone else woke up. She could hear their voices, their shoes on the floor. Stop, she told him. She wanted to get up, except he was holding her down. He was her man and she wanted to be with him, but not this way, with his family right there. She couldn't stop breathing so rapidly, but now she felt nothing. She just wanted to stop what they were doing. They could stay lying there, as long as he stopped making his sounds and pushing the bed against the back wall. Por favor, Socorro begged him. Por favor, Rogelio. But he put his hand over her mouth. She felt as if she were suffocating. She was trying to get up, but he pushed harder. Out of the corner of her eye she thought she saw something move, and later when she looked again one side of the curtain was pulled open and his father was watching them. He smiled back at her because he knew there wasn't anything she could do. Rogelio kept pushing.

Sometimes she wondered if not always enjoying her time with him had made her a bad wife or made it so that they never had a baby, but she also knew that, aside from that one time, she had never told him no whenever he'd wanted to be together — as she did now with Don Celestino. At least she could say he made her feel something again and that she simply wanted to be closer to him, though now after almost three months she wanted to know if he felt anything similar or if she was still only the girl who cleaned his house and then stayed around after her work was done. Somehow she had imagined a man his age would be proud, maybe a little boastful, to have a young woman and to want to present her to his family and friends. Wasn't this part of what all men were looking for?

She could hear him brushing his teeth now. At first she found it difficult to stay interested when they were only starting and Don Celestino would suddenly stop and say he needed to go to the bathroom. A couple of times she had fallen asleep waiting. Then one morning she was cleaning around the medicine chest when she found some pills inside a plastic sandwich bag tucked behind a bottle of talcum powder. It seemed strange to her because he kept his medicines in a daily dispenser that stayed on the kitchen table next to the salt- and pepper shakers. When she asked him about them, he told her that they were vitamins, if she had to know, but that he wasn't asking her about everything she carried in her purse. Socorro apologized and said she was just curious. Another week went by and she found the same plastic bag in the bathroom cabinet, this time wedged behind the hot-water bottle. He must have thought he had hidden it well enough, but he forgot that she'd been cleaning houses long before they had become intimate and there were few places a cleaning woman didn't look. All this time she had assumed his trips to the bathroom had to do with a sudden urge to relieve himself, as a man his age might need to do. But now she noticed how he came back more eager than before he left and somehow he seemed to have as much or more energy than a man half his age. And then she remembered the little blue pills — his vitamins.

Socorro was facing the wall when he opened the bedroom door.

"Still awake?"

She stayed in the same position and adjusted the pillow. While she was still wearing her skirt and blouse, he'd come back from the bathroom in only his briefs.

"Sometimes it can be hard to fall asleep alone," he said.

She mumbled something back.

"What was that, mi amor?"

"Nothing."

"Tell me."

"Nothing, just talking to myself."

"Saying what? Tell me."

She inched away when she felt his bare chest against her back.

"I said, 'You act like you know what it is to be alone.'"

"I was alone for almost half a year before I found you," Don Celestino said. "That wasn't long enough?" He kissed her along the shoulders, as he had been doing before he excused himself.

"I thought it was."

"Then?"

"Maybe other people would think it was."

"What people?" He nuzzled up and set her hair to one side so his lips could reach her neck.

"Your brother, maybe he would think it was a long time."

"He's been alone already for years."

"So then he knows what it's like."

"Only because she left him." He moved his hand across her hip and then down toward the little rolls of skin near her belly, but she moved her arm in a way that blocked the rest of his path.

"Then his alone is different from your alone?"

"They were separated, she didn't want to see him."

Socorro turned to face him. "And you think you know everything that happens between a man and his woman?"

"No, I just know they were not together and for years not even in the same town. Why do I need to know the reasons?"

"He was still married to her, Celestino. He was still her husband."

He liked how she said his name more intimately now, without the "Don" attached to it, and sometimes it was difficult to remember when it had been any other way between them. He was savoring the moment when he realized she was still looking at him, waiting for a response.

"Why do you want to talk about other people right now?"

"Your brother."

"Yes, I know who he is."

"Then maybe you can tell him that we're friends . . . more than friends."

"Please, Socorro." He reached for her as she pulled away.

"What would it hurt to at least call him?"

"Please, no more," he whispered to her. "Can we just stop talking?"

She thought about this for a moment, then twisted back around, leaving a space between their bodies.

"Is that what you really want, for me to be quiet?"

"Yes, please, no more." He kissed her on the shoulders as he had earlier. He tried to inch over and get past the pillow she was holding.

"Then maybe we should just take a nap," she said.

"How do you mean?"

"You know, a nap, when you close your eyes and sleep and then wake up later feeling rested. That's one of the other things people do in bed." She turned over with the pillow now between her legs.

Don Celestino looked at her back and wondered what it would take for her to turn around. A couple of minutes later, he rolled over and gazed at the ceiling-fan blades, which continued to whirl about with no regard as to what was occurring a few feet below them on the bed.

Socorro could hear him sighing behind her as if he might be exhaling his final breath and only she could save him. She had no intention of turning around, though. He could stay awake the rest of the afternoon, and with that rolling pin between his legs to keep him company. He was lucky she didn't go flush the rest of his vitamins down the toilet.

12

This time it happens early in the morning. Don Fidencio sees himself pushing the walker down a long street. And here he thought he would never get away from that place where they kept him locked up. Only now he wonders where he might be headed. He has on only the bottom half of his old work uniform with his red suspenders holding up his pants. No shirt, no undershirt. What has his life come to for him to be walking around in public without a shirt? Was this the only way to escape without anyone noticing? I might as well be a homeless one, un trampa. Later his mailbag falls some-

where along the way but when he looks over his shoulder and then back he is pushing a wheelbarrow and not the walker. He arrives at the first house and knocks. A beautiful dark-haired woman opens the door wearing only a towel. Have you seen my mailbag? The woman says she has something for him. He thinks it might be the mailbag and if not the mailbag then maybe something having to do with her towel, but then she shows him a large manila envelope. He tells her she needs the correct postage before he can take that from her. But instead of taking it back she rips open the end of the envelope and pours some dirt into his wheelbarrow. Then she closes the door. The same thing with the next house, only this time the man is wearing overalls, the same kind that old man Lucas used to wear on the farm so many years ago. No one has any idea where his mailbag could be, no one has the correct postage. Dirt is all they have for him. House after house. Most times they hand him a manila envelope. But some people also have the standard-size envelopes or airmail envelopes. One has a postcard with a little mound of dirt balanced on it. He can never guess what kind of letter the next house will have or what the dirt will look like. It goes from black dirt to reddish dirt to yellowish dirt and once even comes out as mud but all of it turns into plain brown dirt once it gets mixed in with the rest of the pile. When he asks the people what the dirt is for they tell him to keep walking. But where to? How far? By now the pile of dirt is several feet high and so tall that he has to look to one side just to see where he is going. At the end of the long block he turns to the left and now he pushes the wheelbarrow through an open field. At one point he reaches up to wipe his brow and realizes the wheelbarrow is moving without his actually pushing it. He holds on to the handles only to keep from losing his balance on the uneven ground. When he reaches the shade of a large mesquite the wheelbarrow stops altogether. Next to the tree is a deep hole, long enough and wide enough for a man to lie down in, but inside it he sees his canes. Tangled roots bulge from the sides like varicose veins. All that time searching in closets and under beds and behind furniture, and this is where they came to hide them. There's the aluminum one with the four prongs at the base. He used to take it with him when he walked in his neighborhood just in case he needed to defend himself against one of the stray dogs. The wooden one with the knots along the shaft is lying on its side and he can see where he had his initials burned onto the pommel. The black aluminum cane with the foam-cushioned handle is in there but he can barely see it because it is leaning against one corner of the hole. He holds on to the tree and guides himself down onto one knee. Then he lies on his stomach to see if he can stretch his arm down into the hole. He is less than an inch from touching the handle of the black cane when the wheelbarrow tips forward and the dirt pours out.

13

The morning light shined brightest in the far corner of the therapy room. One of the girls had stopped to buy pan dulce, and the white bag lay torn open on the kitchen table. The pink cake had been the first to go; someone was still picking at the chocolate mollete and had left most of the sugary crumbs on a paper napkin. The boom box atop the refrigerator was tuned to a Tejano station, which was loud enough to be heard at the other end of the room.

Don Fidencio sat next in line to The One With The Hole In His Back. Earlier he had been first in line, but The One With The Puffy Cheeks came up and said that The One With

The Hole In His Back had to go first because he wasn't supposed to be in his wheelchair too long on account of his wound. Don Fidencio had to do as the man said and move over. Never mind that he had made special efforts to be there early, wolfing down his tasteless oatmeal, limiting his time on the pot, pushing his walker there ahead of time. And for what? So The One With The Hole In His Back could cut in front? It wasn't fair, but he had come to understand that very little was fair if a man happened to live in a prison. He ate only when the aides told him to eat; he watched his baseball games at the volume he wanted only until one of them came around and told him his neighbors were trying to sleep, no matter if it was extra innings or not; he bathed only when it was time again for them to wash his parts, and never as good as he would have done it himself; and he was allowed out of the main building by himself only to sit on the back patio for a smoke, and only during certain hours of the day.

Of the eight people waiting in line, he was the one person sitting in a regular chair and dressed in clothes decent enough to be worn out in public: black orthopedic shoes, khakis, checkered flannel shirt, red suspenders, red-and-black Astros cap. The One With The Hole In His Back wore his usual maroon pajamas and tan moccasin slippers, but now also with his beige cowboy hat that normally hung off the headboard.

He motioned for his roommate to come closer.

"WHAT DAY IS IT TODAY?"

Don Fidencio pulled away when he remembered the volume of his roommate's voice. "Tuesday."

"EH?"

"Tuesday. Today is Tuesday," he said a little louder.

"TUESDAY?"

"Yes," he answered, and nodded at the same time. "Today is Tuesday."

"ARE YOU SURE TODAY IS TUESDAY?"

Don Fidencio stared at his watch, focusing on the enlarged numbers and the date. "Yes," he said more confidently. "Tuesday, the first of February."

"THEY BROUGHT ME IN ON A TUESDAY."

"Pues, that must have been another Tuesday."

The One With The Hole In His Back raised his cowboy hat and scratched his head, pushing the wisps of white hair to one side.

"LAST TIME I ASKED THE NURSE WHAT DAY IT WAS, SHE SAID TUESDAY. EVERY TIME I ASK, THEY TELL ME THE SAME THING: 'TUESDAY. TODAY IS TUESDAY.' YOU TELL ME, HOW MANY TUESDAYS CAN THERE BE? ARE THERE NO MORE DAYS OF THE WEEK? DID THEY CHANGE THE CALENDAR SINCE THEY PUT ME IN HERE? HOW CAN IT ALWAYS BE THE SAME? TUESDAY, TUESDAY, 'TODAY IS TUESDAY,' THAT'S ALL THEY EVER TELL ME."

Don Fidencio looked blankly at him.

"Ask tomorrow and I bet you get a different answer."

The One With The Hole In His Back flicked his wrist as he turned away.

This was the only time of day Don Fidencio saw his neighbor outside of their room. They served him his meals in bed and he didn't spend any time in the recreation room or out on the patio. While in the hospital healing from his hip surgery, he had developed a bedsore on his backside. By the time he arrived at Amigoland, the bedsore had worsened enough that his body now needed to be rotated from one side to the other in order to relieve any pressure on the wound. Every two hours an aide came to turn him partially onto his side and then slip a couple of thick pillows under him so he would stay propped up in that position. The One Who Likes To Kiss Your Forehead stopped by once a day to change the dressing. A few weeks earlier, she'd come around, given The One With The Hole In His Back his usual kiss on the forehead, and forgotten to shut the retractable curtain all the way. Don Fidencio barely had to lean back to see the bedsore was located near the tailbone and appeared to be about the size of a fist, with the exposed meat infected around the edges, as if a small animal with very sharp teeth had spent the night gnawing out a hole. He winced as he pulled away from the curtain, cursing himself for not minding his own damn business.

"Okay, Mr. Cavazos, it's your turn now." The One With The Puffy Cheeks crouched down and pulled the old man's wheelchair closer.

"LEAVE ME ALONE."

"Come on, Mr. Cavazos, this is going to be fun," The One With The Puffy Cheeks said, stretching his big face into a smile. "Don't you want to have fun?"

"THIS IS FUN FOR YOU, TO TORTURE AN OLD MAN?"

"We just want to make you feel better, sir."

"THEN YOU SHOULD LEAVE ME ALONE."

It took both therapists to lift him from his wheelchair up to the specialized walker. They helped him place his forearms on the padded armrests and wrap his hands around the two foam-covered handles. Once he was positioned, he gazed down at his fluffy moccasins.

"You have to look up, Mr. Cavazos. Up at me," The One With The Puffy Cheeks said, facing him, ready to walk backward. The second therapist was standing behind the walker, holding on tightly to the cinch they had strapped around the old man's chest. "With your head up, Mr. Cavazos, like you and me are dancing a polka."

"YOU THINK THIS IS EASY?"

"Nothing comes easy, Mr. Cavazos. We all have to work hard to see results."

The old man sighed and took a couple more tentative steps.

"Spread your legs out a little, sir, and stand up more straight. You're leaning too much on the walker."

"DON'T BE TELLING ME WHAT TO DO." He took another two paces, stepping pigeon-toed, and barely moved beyond where they had started. He was leaning most of his weight on the armrests and his back end was hanging low, as if he were carrying an anvil inside his diaper.

Don Fidencio stood up to leave. If he was going to waste his morning sitting around, he preferred to do it in his own room. He had already grabbed hold of the walker when The

Filipina Who Looks Like A Boy came up to him and stood a couple of inches from his face.

"And good morning to you, Mr. Rosales. How are you feeling today, sir?"

"Good morning," he said as he strained to read the name stitched on her baggy scrubs. He had never met a person named Mandy, but he guessed it must be a woman's name. She was small, like a woman or a frail boy. The scrubs were too big on her and he couldn't tell if she had a pair of chiches in there somewhere.

The Filipina Who Looks Like A Boy helped him sit back down, then gave him a long rubber cord with handles on both ends. He held one of the handles in his right hand as she hooked the other handle around his right shoe.

"You remember how we do these, Mr. Rosales? These are the ones for your arms." She demonstrated by standing in front of him and curling her skinny little arm toward her chest. "It's easy, right? Can you do ten like that for me, sir?"

He nodded, not really sure what the girl had just asked him, but he agreed so she would stop with all her questions.

"One . . . two . . . three . . . very good, Mr. Rosales, very good . . . four . . . five . . ."

He continued on when she turned to help one of the other therapists with a resident. He wasn't quite sure how pulling a rubber cord up and down was going to help one bit; the problem was with the strength in his legs, not his arms. But this was about the only thing there was to do at this hour, unless he wanted to go back to the recreation room to watch the talk shows with their guests that didn't interest him, or take part in some silly group activity like playing volleyball with a balloon, or singing and clapping with The Jesus Christ Loves Everybody Women who came around every morning, tempting people with their free doughnuts. At least here he thought he could show the therapists how much he had improved, and then, God willing, they might tell the other ones to give him back his canes. And if he got his canes back, he was that much closer to leaving this place.

"So good, Mr. Rosales. Very strong," The Filipina Who Looks Like A Boy said, leaning in close to his face. "Can you do ten more for me now, the same way?"

If she wanted him to do twenty, he didn't know why she didn't say this from the beginning. She needed to make up her mind, instead of expecting him to follow her commands like some trained animal.

"Eight, nine, and . . . ten! Very good, sir!"

Next she wanted him to keep his arm curled and extend his leg, stretching the rubber cord in the other direction. This didn't feel any more strenuous than the first exercise.

"Three . . . four . . . way to go, Mr. Rosales . . . five . . . six . . ." She patted him on the arm. "You're doing very good, sir."

After a while he lost himself in the singsong way she counted off the repetitions, and then counted them off again when he did the extra ten she asked for. He could have been up to fifteen repetitions or he could have been up to seventy-eight, he knew to stop only because she told him to and took away the cord and replaced it with something else, like the big yellow ball that he was supposed to hold between his legs and squeeze, over and over, as if he were a chicken laying an enormous yellow egg. None of it made any sense to him, the squeezing, the curling, the extending. All he knew was there was a time when his arms and legs were so strong that he could walk the whole day, sunup to sundown, even if he'd had to deliver the mail while carrying this skinny filipina on his back. And now here he was, doing these exercises so he could hold on to what little of him was left and maybe someday take this with him when he got out of here.

"Last exercise, Mr. Rosales," she said suddenly. "Over here, sir, on the table."

Her voice had startled him. He looked up when she took away the big yellow ball and gently grabbed hold of his hands to help him stand.

"Don't forget your walker, Mr. Rosales. Remember, no walking without the walker."

He shuffled across the room toward the matted table. He parked the walker to one side and sat on the edge of the exercise station, waiting for the girl to help him lift his feet so he could lie flat.

"I'm going to take your baseball cap and put it right over here so you don't forget it, Mr. Rosales."

He lay still as she hung the cap on one of the handles of the walker. The mat felt just as firm as his mattress back in the room.

"Almost done, sir," she said a little louder. "Don't fall asleep on me, okay?"

She lifted his left leg off the mat, then gently bent the leg in the direction of his chest, stopping when he moaned, then extended it a ways and lifted it up a few inches.

"Can you move your leg down, sir? Pushing against my hand?"

He tried to nod but found it difficult with his head on the mat. After struggling for a moment, he managed to push his leg down an inch or two. He could feel the tendons stretching and coming to life with every little bit that she moved his leg back up.

With all the bending and extending, his khakis had risen and The Filipina Who Looks Like A Boy was now touching his bare skin. Her little hands felt soft from the lotion she must have rubbed on them that morning. He tried to remember the last time a woman had touched him. The showers and sponge baths didn't count as touching since the aides were wearing gloves and working so routinely that at times it felt as though he were going through a car wash with a half dozen other old men waiting in their wheelchairs behind him.

"Very good, Mr. Rosales. Getting stronger every day."

The Filipina Who Looks Like A Boy moved his bent leg slowly backward, stopping when she saw him straining, then extended it a ways and bent it forward only slightly. He liked the way she smelled, the scent of her hair, even if it was cut so short like a boy's. After a while he relaxed a little more and allowed her to move his body through the exercises.

It wasn't Petra who had touched him last, that he knew. She barely got next to him and didn't so much as sleep in the same bed those last few years she was in the house. He couldn't say exactly when this had started, though he had an idea it had something to do with one woman or other he'd been seeing so long ago that it shouldn't have mattered anymore. She never actually caught him, only suspected or heard talk of him here or there. He wanted to remember being with a woman who lived near the highway, on the 78520 side. Earlier he'd had her up on the kitchen counter, until this wasn't working for him, and he had carried her that way, his work pants still caught between his ankles, so they could get down to the carpet on the living room floor, where after a few minutes he finished with a furious thrust that made her scream out and then laugh loud enough to be heard in the next trailer.

"And that?" Petra asked later that night.

"I fell walking up some steps." He had just taken off his pants and tossed them on the chair.

"Did you get hurt?" She came to take a closer look, but he turned as if he needed some privacy to pull up his pajamas. Even after washing himself off again in the restroom at the post office, he knew he couldn't be too careful around her.

"It was nothing, just a little scrape." He yanked back the covers and climbed into bed.

"To both knees, and it was nothing?"

"Leave it already."

"Why won't you show me?"

"I need to go to sleep."

"You're acting like you do when you want to hide something." She was still standing at the foot of the bed.

"Yes, Petra, I am always hiding something from you. That's why I get up at six o'clock every morning, to hide things from you."

"Then tell me how you could fall and not get hurt."

"Turn the light off and come on to bed."

"And not just one knee."

"You try walking around all day carrying the bag, see if you don't fall down sometimes. I wish you could, just so you would know. Maybe one of these days I'll pull you away from the sofa so you can come see what I do all day, what I like to hide from you."

"You never fell before."

"And how do you know?"

"You never said anything."

"Y qué, I have to report this to you? 'Petra, today I fell because a big dog was chasing me and I couldn't run with the bag.' 'Petra, today I fell because they sent out the Sears catalogs.' Like that, is that what you want?" He shook his head at her ideas.

She turned off the light and climbed into bed. He rolled onto his side, away from where she was fluffing up her pillow. Finally some peace, he thought. He reached down under the covers and felt where he had scraped the skin off his knees. Tomorrow morning, while she was still asleep, he would rub some ointment on the burns and in a few days they would heal up like new. By then she would let it go. He rolled back over, squinting, when the light came on again. Petra was standing next to the chair, holding up his uniform as if presenting a piece of evidence to the jury.

"He falls, scrapes both knees, but somehow he doesn't tear his pants," she said, and turned off the light.

Never mind that he had walked mile after mile, year after year, and always come home with his paycheck, for her, nobody else. And after paying the bills, she could spend it however she wanted. With nobody looking over her shoulder, asking so many questions, as she did to him. She chose to forget that part when she finally went to live with their daughter. Afterward he wondered if she had ever been happy, maybe at least for the first few years. He would have asked her, but he was afraid of what she might say, and then the next time he saw her was years later at her funeral.

"Eh?"

"I said, 'This far is very good for a man your age, Mr. Rosales.'" The girl was moving his leg up and down, up and down, like she was changing a flat with a tire jack. "These exercises are going to help with your flexibility."

Maybe it was one of the young waitresses at the cafés he used to go to after he retired. They were tricky, that he remembered. It wasn't so easy knowing which of them might be interested and which were talking to him, patting him on the shoulder, letting their hands linger a bit, only so they might get a more generous tip. He wanted to recall being parked to one side of a café, around from the grease disposal, and she still being in her uniform and scooting over next to him. He'd gone to the flea market to buy a gold-plated bracelet and have her name engraved on it, as a way of getting her to come outside during her break. What her name was, what she looked like, what she smelled like, what her mouth tasted like, how she kissed him or undid his pants or what might have happened after that, or if anything did, was lost to him now. He must have been still in his sixties, before women started treating him as if he were a harmless old creature and what he had once carried between his legs had now shriveled up and fallen off, which was only slightly better than those who avoided him altogether, as if his advanced age were contagious.

Don Fidencio closed his eyes and tried to think of what he could do to fill the rest of the day. It was still another two hours until lunch, which was long enough that he could easily fall asleep for a nap. He didn't like wasting his day in bed, though. Maybe he could go sit on one of the sofas near the nurses' station. If he dozed off there, at least he wasn't in bed. There were some days that the mail came in before 10:30, the time when everyone started moving toward the mess hall for lunch. He was waiting for the day when they would switch mail carriers and get one with a more pleasant nature who wasn't always rushing off and didn't mind sitting for a while to talk.

"How does that feel, Mr. Rosales?"

He opened his eyes, and the girl was gently lowering his leg, cradling his calf in her little hand.

"Good, it feels good," the old man said, straining to make out the name on her scrubs.

PART III

14

He had been reading the morning paper in his chair when he dozed off and before long his head slumped over onto his chest. It wasn't his favorite way to take a nap, but it happened often enough that he was used to it by now. It was hardly worth all the sacrifice it took for him to change into his pajamas and crawl into bed, and then call so one of the girls could come raise the bed railing. These naps never lasted long anyway. Whether it was on the hard bed or in the stiff chair, he usually woke up feeling just as weary and like he needed another nap. Only this time when he opened his eyes,

The Stranger With The White Hair was standing at the closet door and opening his #3 shoe box.

So now it had come to this. He couldn't rest his eyes for a few minutes while he sat in his chair, not five feet away from where he kept the last of his belongings in this world, because somebody was liable to sneak in and try to rob him. Never would he have imagined this would happen with him in the room, that they'd be so brazen as to do this under his nose, as if he were already stiff in the chair and only waiting for them to roll him out the back door.

Except that The Stranger With The White Hair was wearing a maroon guayabera, short-sleeved, with tan slacks, pleated and cuffed, and not the loose-fitting scrubs that would have given him away as one of the nurses or aides he had been waiting to catch in the act. So maybe he was a guest of one of the other residents, not that many of them had guests, except on Mother's or Father's Day, which they were aware of only because someone had finally shown up. Or maybe he belonged to The One With The Hole In His Back and had wandered over to see what he could make off with. At least if Don Fidencio had one of his canes, he would have a way to stop him, defend himself if it came to this.

"And who the hell are you?"

"I thought you were asleep," The Stranger With The White Hair said, turning around. "You didn't answer me when I called your name."

"That gives you the right?" The old man began to stand up, until he realized how much effort this might take and finally sat back. Then he shifted in the chair, but only so he could adjust his pants.

"I didn't want to wake you."

"I prefer to be woken up than have my things stolen." He used his shirt cuff to wipe a trace of spittle from one of the crevices where his face drooped the most.

"Do you recognize me, Fidencio?"

The old man blinked a couple of times. He hadn't heard his own first name in months, however long it had been now since he'd arrived in this place. With the helpers it was "Mr. Rosales" and "sir"; with the other ones it was whatever they could remember, Filemón, Fernando, Fausto, Fulano, as if he cared; with Amalia it was Daddy or My Daddy; and with The Son Of A Bitch it was nothing because he never came around except to say, "Your father needs more assistance." But here The Stranger With The White Hair had said his name as if they knew each other or they had worked together, which seemed unlikely given his look. Then again maybe so, if he had worked only at the station, sorting the letters and whatever else they did back there all day, because this man wasn't out delivering, that Don Fidencio could guarantee. Even if the man had somehow avoided wearing the hat, which would have been hell during the summer months, he never would have been able to get his hair to stay in place the way it was doing now. It seemed to rise up like a frothy white wave and then eventually ebb toward the back of his head. There was only one other time he could remember seeing hair like that.

"You look like a brother I used to have," the old man said. "The younger one, Celestino."

"You remembered my name."

"I'm old, not stupid," he said.

They looked at each other for a moment, both unsure what to do next. Don Celestino noticed that the man on the other side of the retractable curtain was in bed asleep, but his head kept twitching as if he were dreaming.

"I thought you might still be mad," he said, "because of our disagreement."

As if he hadn't heard him, his brother gazed at the ceiling for a moment, then leaned back. "And what disagreement was that?"

Don Celestino only looked at him, wondering if he should remind the old man of what had happened in the barbershop and, if he did, what good it would do. "It doesn't matter anymore," he said finally, then took a seat at the edge of the bed. "I can hardly remember myself, already after so many years."

"Sometimes it takes me a long time to remember what I used to know."

"You look strong, the same as always."

"And getting stronger each day," Don Fidencio replied, tapping his palms on the armrests of the chair. He tried to calculate exactly how long he had been here. The calendar on the wall said it was December, though he was pretty sure Christmas had come and gone.

"You used to be a barber, didn't you?"

"For many years I had my own business."

Don Fidencio stared at him now, as if he might have mistaken him for someone else. "And where was that exactly, this barbershop of yours?"

"Close to the stadium." He pointed out the window, in the general direction of the shop, as if this might jar his memory.

"Where your boy used to play football?"

"Yes, not far from there." He motioned again with his hand. "You used to come on Saturday mornings for your haircuts, before work."

"Forty-two years I delivered the mail."

"People knew you all over Brownsville."

Don Fidencio adjusted himself in the chair and looked out the window. An attendant paused in the doorway and then continued pushing a laundry hamper down the hall.

"They come clean your room every day?" Don Celestino asked.

"Only because of The Son Of A Bitch." The old man slammed his palm on the armrest. "The one my daughter lies down in bed with every night!"

"¿QUE FUE?" The One With The Hole In His Back stirred out of his sleep. "WHO THE HELL IS OUT THERE? COME OUT LIKE MEN, SHOW ME YOUR FACES!"

"Maybe we should talk outside the room," Don Celestino suggested.

"Ignore him." Don Fidencio flicked his hand in the direction of the retractable curtain. "He wakes up and then thinks his dreams are real."

"YOU THINK I CARE WHO SENT YOU? COME OUT HERE LIKE REAL MEN! TRY AND SEE IF YOU CAN HANG ANOTHER INNOCENT ONE." The One With The Hole In His Back banged his bedpan on the bed railing. "LET ME SEE HOW MANY OF YOU COWARDS THEY SENT IN THE MIDDLE OF THE NIGHT TO KILL ME!"

"See what I told you?" He twirled his index finger near the side of his head. "Ignore him, he's just another prisoner."

"That part of you hasn't changed."

"And can you tell me where you live?"

"In the same house as always."

"Alone?"

"Yes, alone," he answered. He wasn't exactly sure how he was supposed to mention Socorro.

The old man turned toward the window.

"Sometimes I think God forgot about me."

"God doesn't forget people."

"I'm not talking about other people. I said that He forgot about *me,* Fidencio Rosales, the one in this room, that He left me here with all these strangers. That wherever it is that He writes down all the names, my name has been forgotten or erased, something. That by now he should have taken me."

"So now you want to complain because you haven't died?"

"How do you explain that I am here, almost ninety-two, and still giving people trouble, so much trouble that nobody wants me in their house? My time should have come years ago. This morning they had eight dead ones listed in the newspaper. Guess how many were as old as me?"

Don Celestino kept looking at his brother.

"Don't break your head trying to guess." He held up his hand and slowly bent one arthritic finger after another until he managed to curl his thumb and forefinger into a zero. "You remember Dr. Hernandez?"

"I heard that he had been sick."

"He was thirty years younger than the old man you see here. He came to the hospital the last time I was so sick. He talked to Amalia, and I heard them just outside the room. They thought I was asleep, but even with my eyes shut I could hear them. And he told her, 'At his age, your father is like a candle, his life is only flickering to stay alive.' He said it, I heard him. And now look where he is and look where I am and tell me, tell me that God hasn't forgotten me."

"Still, that you are alive doesn't mean God has forgotten about you, Fidencio."

"You can say that because you don't live here, because you have your own house, because you think you know how it is to live here, where you cannot walk two paces beyond the door without somebody coming to take you back inside by the arm. They tell you everything: how to walk, when to eat, when to watch television, what time to go to sleep, the days to take a shower, when to make cacas."

"There must be some who like it here."

"I DON'T CARE WHO SENT YOU DOWN HERE—YOU HEAR ME? THIS LAND HAS ALWAYS BELONGED TO MY PEOPLE!"

"Yes, like this one!" He motioned toward the other bed. "You should take me to live with you. Take your brother from this prison. If you have space for another person, why not?"

"And how do you think I would take care of you?"

"I don't need nobody taking care of me. I can take care of myself, same way I used to. I still could, if they would let me. Take me, and I will prove it to you."

"And if something happens? You think I'm so young that I would be able to help you?"

"But that's what I am trying to tell you, that if something was going to happen, it would have happened already. But here you see me, no different from the first night they came to leave me in that bed right there. All they want is to keep me alive for another fifty years. Tell me, tell me why it is nobody wants me, but nobody wants me to die either. Answer me that one."

"They must have had a reason," Don Celestino said. "So these people could take care of you and nothing happens."

"Yes, exactly! That is exactly what is happening to me — -nothing! Every day a little more of nothing is happening to me! Tell me how much longer I have to go on this way. Even something bad would be better than more of nothing!"

"Mr. Rosales?" The One With The Flat Face was standing at the door.

"These other ones, they don't know what happened to them! But I know, I know where I am, where they left me!"

"BRING THEM TO ME! WATCH HOW THEY RUN AFTER I SHOOT THE FIRST ONE!"

"Mr. Rosales, you need to be quiet," The One With The Flat Face said. "You woke up Mr. Cavazos, and we can hear both of you all the way to the nurses' station."

"See, what did I tell you?" He cocked back his head. "They send this girl to tell me when I can talk."

"You can talk as much as you like, Mr. Rosales, just in a quiet voice, for inside." She raised her finger to her lips. "Shh . . ."

"Now you tell me, when was the last time they sent a young girl to your house to tell you, 'Shh'?" He wiped the corner of his mouth with his cuff, then turned away and looked out the window.

Don Celestino stood up from the edge of the bed and patted his brother on the shoulder. "We can talk more later, whenever I come back for another visit."

"Mr. Rosales, next time you can get together outside on the patio, where you can talk as loud as you like."

The old man wished they would just leave him already. He ignored them both and continued to stare out the window. The One Who Likes To Kiss Your Forehead was helping one of The Turtles stand up from her wheelchair and get into the front seat of a waiting car. He stayed watching until after The Turtle was buckled and the car had pulled away and another arrived in its place.

15

The next time Don Celestino stopped by, he brought his green-and-beige tackle box and set it on the overbed table. The extending tray held four shears, a pair of combs, and his straight razor. Down below, in the main section of the box, he kept his two clippers: one with a narrow blade for trimming sideburns and around the ears; the other with a wider blade for trimming hair in the back, either squared off or rounded, or even tapered, depending on the man's preference. Each machine came with an attachable cord for when the batteries were running low. He kept a bottle of hair tonic sealed tight inside a plastic bag to prevent any leaking onto the shears or the black cape that was folded into a square shape at the bottom of the box.

"Why do you want to cut an old man's hair?" Don Fidencio asked. "You cut it this morning and I could be dead later this afternoon — all that work for nothing."

"You're not going to die."

"And if I do?"

"Then you still need a haircut," Don Celestino said. "You want me to do it or somebody at the funeral home?"

The old man sat back and looked at his brother in the mirror.

"If you really wanted to help me, you would get me out before I die here with all these strangers."

"So I can be struggling with you at the house? We would have to hire somebody to come help you, and then if you got sick on me in the middle of the night? No, you're better off staying here."

"It sounds like the one who would be better off is you."

"You know what I mean."

"It would be good for you to have company, someone to talk to."

"I already have someone to talk to."

"Who?" Don Fidencio asked.

"A friend."

"Who?"

"Just a friend."

"A woman friend?"

"I don't know," Don Celestino said, "maybe it is a woman."

"You haven't checked?"

"This isn't so you can go telling everybody."

"Yes, like I have so many people I could tell your news to."

"Still."

Don Fidencio rubbed the bill of his cap, then shook his head.

"You didn't waste no time, eh?"

"It just happened, without us planning it."

"Does she have a name, or is this a secret, too?"

"Socorro," he answered. "Now are you going to let me cut your hair or not?"

Don Fidencio removed his baseball cap and waited for his brother to snap open the black cape.

"We need to find another chair," Don Celestino said. "The back is too high on this one for me to reach your neck." He turned to the resident in the next bed. "Excuse me, but can we borrow your chair?"

"TAKE IT, TAKE IT," the old man said, flinging his hand in the air. He had a couple of pillows tucked beneath him and was tilted toward the opposite wall. "IF I NEED TO GO SOMEPLACE, I CAN TELL THEM TO BRING ONE OF MY HORSES."

But when Don Celestino pushed the wheelchair to the other side of the room, he found his brother motioning back and forth with his index finger like a tiny windshield wiper on its lowest setting.

"No, what?"

"No to that chair."

"Just for me to cut your hair, Fidencio."

"For nothing. Not for a haircut, not so you can clean the wax out of my ears," he said calmly enough and put his cap back on. "For nothing."

"You see what I mean about struggling with you?"

"Because I refuse to sit in a wheelchair, for that reason you want to leave me here?"

"What is it going to hurt you to sit for a few minutes?"

"They already took my canes from me."

When it was clear his brother wasn't moving, Don Celestino walked to the nurses' station and a couple of minutes later returned with a chair with a lower backrest. Once they had switched chairs, he removed his brother's cap for the second time, draped the cape around him, and rolled the new chair closer to the mirror hanging from the back of the closet door.

The old man looked at his brother in the mirror. "So this woman, Socorro, she's why you don't take me to live there at your house?"

"She has her own house, Fidencio."

"But she passes the time there with you, no?"

"She comes to clean the house."

"A cleaning woman? You want to leave your only brother locked up in this place so you can be alone with the cleaning woman? She must have told you not to bring me around."

"It would be the same if she wasn't around," Don Celestino said. "And anyway it was her idea that I go see you."

"Only her idea?"

"I was already thinking about it," Don Celestino said, combing back his brother's hair. "Now tell me how you want it."

"The usual way."

"Ten years later, and you want me to know what the usual way is?"

Don Fidencio stared into the mirror. Tufts of wispy gray-and-white hair were bunched up around his ears, joining up with his broad and unruly sideburns. Though his hair was thin, the strands reached from the top of his forehead to beyond his crown. In the back, his hair had curled into ringlets that fell to just above his shirt collar. He wondered how he had let himself get to this point. Maybe this was why his brother didn't want him inside his house. He should have done a better job of taking care of himself. A barber came once a week and set up in the room where The Turtles got their hair done; Don Fidencio had stopped by once or twice when he saw the other old men parked along the wall in their wheelchairs. After a while he looked up again and found his brother standing behind him in the mirror.

"Just make it look good again."

Don Celestino started by combing the sides, just to have some idea of how much he needed to cut. The top was long, but he planned to trim just an inch so the hair maintained some of its weight. The sideburns looked worse than they really were; the trimmer would take care of them in no time. The back seemed to be the area that needed the most work. The curls reminded him of how wavy his brother's hair had been when he was a young man.

He was surprised at how nimble his fingers were after not cutting hair for a couple of years. When he sold the barbershop, he figured he would never cut hair again. He had brought his barber tools home in the tackle box and stored them in the hall closet next to his shoe-shine kit. Every time he polished his shoes, he thought about bringing out some of his tools, but he knew this would only make him miss what he had left behind. Eventually he pushed the box to the back of the closet, where it wasn't always in the way when he was looking for something else.

Yesterday, when Socorro was over at the house, he had opened the box on the dresser so she could see his barber tools. Other than his driving her past the shop, she'd never really seen this part of his life. He pulled out the first pair of shears from its velvet sheath and let her hold it for a second. Then he took back the shears and, after placing her hand over his, showed her just how rapidly he was still able to move his fingers, all while his little finger remained delicately unfurled as if he were sipping tea in the middle of the afternoon. Later he told her a story about when he was in barber school and how one night four pachucos cornered him, wanting to rob him or worse. This happened in an alley downtown, near the cathedral, where he had to either fight or try to outrun them in the opposite direction. Instead he took off his jacket, wrapped it tightly around his forearm to protect himself, and flipped open the straight razor he had started carrying in the front pocket of his shirt. He stood up from the bed to show her exactly how he had held the straight razor above his head, in plain sight for all of them to see. "So who's going to be my first customer?" he had called out. It took only a few convincing slashes for the pachucos to move aside and for him to continue on his way home.

"And you weren't afraid?" Socorro asked.

"What was there to be afraid of, if none of them were barbers?" he said.

She seemed impressed with his daringness, and he took the opportunity to recount some of his other adventures as a young man, hoping she would trust that he still possessed the same courage today. If for no other reason than to share this part of his life with her, he was thankful there had been an excuse to bring out his barbering equipment. When they finally went to bed, he felt more confident than he could remember being since they had started spending afternoons at the house.

Now he wanted to tell his brother the story about his fight with the pachucos, but the old man had fallen asleep with his head tilted forward. Don Celestino turned off the clippers and tapped him on the shoulder.

"I finished with the back part. You need to keep your head up now."

Don Fidencio glanced down at the clumps of silver-and-white hair on the floor. "Are you sure you're not cutting it too short?"

"Since when did you get so particular about your hair?"

"My ears already stick out too much."

"Stop worrying," he said. "You act like this is your first time ever getting a haircut."

Don Fidencio stayed quiet for some time, looking into the mirror and watching his brother work, though later he seemed to be gazing at something more distant. Then his brother came around to the front so he could check how far some of the longer hairs reached onto his forehead. When Don Celestino moved again, the old man was still staring into the mirror.

"I can remember some of it."

"Some of what?" Don Celestino asked, brushing the hair off his brother's shoulder.

"My first haircut."

"You barely remember that I called you on the phone last night."

"It was a tiny barbershop in Reynosa, only one chair in the whole place. This barber's chair was made of wood and the arms were carved with different figures — with horses and bulls, and on the other one, a rooster. The footrest I remember had the name of the barbershop carved on it — Primos. But there was only one other place to sit if you were waiting to get a haircut, and that was on a wooden crate. Papá Grande told the barber exactly how he wanted his hair, and later he did the same when it was my turn."

"You were maybe only four or five years old, Fidencio."

"Did he take you for your first haircut?"

"He could barely walk by the time I was old enough to go."

"Then you see why — you weren't born yet," Don Fidencio said. "I was there. I was the one named after him, I was the one he would take everywhere with him, I was the one who was there with him when he died. Me, not you." He kept staring at his brother until the other finally turned away.

"This first time he took me was when we lived on the ranchito up the river, close to Hidalgo. We went in the wagon and I sat next to him all the way there, just me and him. The only time we got off was when we reached the ferryboat so we could cross to the other side. One of the boys pulling the ropes was too young to be working, maybe only twelve years old, and I remember Papá Grande got behind him and helped him pull."

"Are you sure that wasn't our father?" Don Celestino asked. "I remember we used to cross that way sometimes."

"You think I would confuse him with my grandfather?"

"Just because they named you after him doesn't make him only *your* grandfather."

"I know what we used to do together, what me and him talked about."

"I was just saying, if he was really helping to pull."

"Already I told you it was Papá Grande," he said, and brought his hand out from under the gown and made a tight fist. "He was still strong in those days."

Don Celestino held his brother's thin hair and trimmed the very tips, then whisked away the remains with his comb. There was no point in arguing with him. He came around the chair to get a better look from the front. The left sideburn needed a little more adjusting. He cupped his brother's chin and turned his head a few degrees to the left, then back toward the center, and then ever so slightly to the right. The only thing left to do was snip some of the hairs along the rims of his ears and growing out from his nostrils. After he finished he reached into the bottom of his tackle box for a small oval mirror. Then he swiveled the chair around so the old man would have his back to the larger mirror hanging from the closet door.

"Tell me if the back looks good, the way you like it." He handed him the oval mirror but ended up holding it himself when his brother had trouble keeping his hand steady enough.

Don Fidencio peered into the small mirror, trying to make his eyes focus on the reflection of his image. He felt confident that his brother had done a good job with the back, the same as he had with the front and sides, but he wanted to see this for himself. He stared into the mirror and turned his head this way and that way, as if he were really examining the finer details of his brother's work and not the cloudy image of what appeared to be the back of a man's head, though not necessarily his own.

"So, what do you think?" Don Celestino turned the chair back to its original position. "Is it good that way or you want me to cut a little more?"

"IF IT WAS ME, I WOULDN'T LET HIM TOUCH ANOTHER HAIR."

They turned around to find The One With The Hole In His Back sitting up in bed. The Gringo With The Ugly Finger and two nurse's aides were also watching from the doorway.

"¡Qué guapo!" The One With The Flat Face said. "Mr. Phillips, don't you think he looks handsome with his new haircut?"

"It might surprise you ladies to know, but I had a very similar haircut when I was working for Pan Am," The Gringo With The Ugly Finger answered. "Back then, I was what they used to call 'a looker.' "

Don Fidencio turned toward the larger mirror again and kept gazing into it until he could see the faint traces of a face he had almost forgotten.

16

There was an old lady she knew by the name of la señora Jenny. Her daughter would drive by the bridge on Saturday mornings. One Saturday Socorro would clean the large house where the old lady lived alone; the next Saturday she cleaned the daughter's house, where she lived with her husband. Then one Saturday they drove to la señora Jenny's house, only she wasn't there. Before the daughter left for the day, she explained to Socorro that her mother had had an accident getting out of the bathtub. She made a sign to indicate the old lady had broken her hip and then she winced as if it were happening to her there in the kitchen. Socorro kept coming every other Saturday to clean la señora Jenny's house, though obviously there wasn't much cleaning to do, considering no one had been in the house for the last two weeks. Still, she washed the unused sheets, swept the spotless kitchen, vacuumed the untouched carpet, scrubbed the clean toilets, and dusted off what little dust there was on the furniture, as if the old lady might show up at any moment. Eventually the daughter sold the house and told Socorro that her mother had found a new home, where there were people who could take care of her. Up until now this had been Socorro's only experience with a nursing home.

Don Celestino found a space at the far end of the parking lot, near a narrow road used for deliveries. The one-story building was made of tan-colored stucco that formed a long Spanish facade stretching out in either direction before its corners turned sharply toward the back. They entered through the arched driveway and from there continued through a passageway surrounded by wilting brown grass and thick palms. As they were approaching the lobby door, she noticed someone waving at them. The old lady sat hunched in the wheelchair, wearing a Philadelphia Eagles sweatshirt that hung off her like a green-and-silver gown. Once they were inside the lobby, she seemed not to recognize them and adjusted her thick glasses as if she'd spotted someone else at the far end of the passageway.

Don Celestino had to slow down when Socorro stopped to say hello to the old lady. Through the windowpane that separated the lobby from the living area, he could see an old man in a wheelchair pumping his right leg up and down so he could pull off his pajamas. The old woman next to him seemed oblivious to it all and was more concerned with licking the outside of a Kleenex box. Don Celestino waited for an aide to dress the old man, then he tugged on Socorro's hand.

"I have to go now," she told the old lady.

"Yes, of course, go enjoy your visit. I have to wait here for my son."

Around the corner from the lobby, they stepped aside for a one-armed man wearing a World War II cap who inched his wheelchair down the middle of the hall. The closer they moved to the room, the harder it became to navigate around the old women parked in their wheelchairs near the nurses' station. Don Celestino tried to explain to her that they all liked to wave, but she wasn't listening. It continued this way until they arrived at the room and he knocked on the doorframe.

"Come in," Don Fidencio called out. Though it took some effort, he insisted on standing to greet his two guests.

"Fidencio," his brother said, "I would like to introduce you to Socorro."

She leaned in to take his hand in both of hers and right away the old man noticed how nice she smelled, as though she'd taken a shower just before they came to visit. And she was young! Much younger than he had imagined when he thought about his brother spending time with the cleaning woman. A girl really, at least compared to the two of them, but given the chance to be out of here with someone on his arm, he would take her at whatever age she came to him.

His brother walked to the other side of the room and brought her a chair.

"Please, sit," Don Fidencio said. "I wish I had more to offer you."

A faded newspaper photo of men playing baseball hung on the wall behind him. A white telephone sat at the edge of an overbed table; two phone numbers were taped to the back of the receiver. The line was tangled around the bed railing and the cord used to alert the staff at the nurses' station. Socorro sat back but then leaned forward so it wouldn't look like she was too relaxed or uninterested. Here she had been asking to come visit his brother and now she didn't know what to say to him or how to sit properly. She was still trying to get her mind off the unpleasant smell coming from the other bed.

"For weeks I have been telling Celestino that I wanted to come visit," she finally thought to say.

"Sometimes my little brother likes to pretend he's going deaf, but I can imagine he would have to listen to such a pretty girl."

Don Celestino shook his head as he sat on the edge of the bed.

"Do you like the way your brother cut your hair?" she asked.

"He did a good job," Don Fidencio replied, running his fingers along the hairline in the back. "The women who work here, the helpers, they were still talking about it this morning when they gave me my shower."

Socorro smiled. The old man sat up a little in the chair and tugged on his shirt collar. "I could bathe myself — better than they can wash me — but here they won't let me do it alone — nothing, not take a shower, not serve my own food, not walk unless I push this thing around." He kicked the walker aside.

"How nice that you are still healthy and strong at your age."

"That's what I have been trying to tell my brother, that I'm strong enough to be living somewhere else besides here in this prison. Only because I got sick one time, for that they left me here. But this was in the past and not anything so serious, just what happens when you get old."

"If you get sick, this is a better place for you to be, where they can help you," Don Celestino said.

"Yes, help me, even if I don't want the help anymore. And what if nothing happens to me and I just continue this way forever?" the old man said, and then turned to the girl. "Tell me the truth: do I look sick to you?"

She hesitated, first looking up at Don Celestino and then back at the old man.

"To me, you look fine," Socorro said. "But my mother also has days when she feels good and later she gets sick on us."

"But at home?"

She nodded.

"You see?" Don Fidencio said. "That's what I mean, that I'm well enough to be living at home. And then if I get sick, he can bring me back. He can leave me there at the curb if he wants, not even get out of the car."

"Ya," his brother said. "She didn't come to hear your complaints."

Don Celestino was afraid this might happen and had called earlier that morning to tell him that they would be stopping by to visit but that he didn't want to hear him begging to come to live with him. He explained all the reasons why, again, including that he himself wasn't in the best of health. The old man seemed to accept this, though at the time Don Celestino understood that his brother would pick and choose what he wanted to remember.

"I was only talking about my health," Don Fidencio said. "A man should be able to talk about his health if he wants to."

"You look good to me." Socorro noticed he had shaved that morning but had missed a spot just below his chin.

"And really the one thing I have trouble with is my memory, but the other day some things came back to me."

"About your life?"

"He thinks he can remember his first haircut," Don Celestino said.

"This one doesn't believe me, but it happened that way. And then more came to me last night."

"I remember a lot from when I was a little girl."

"Wait until you get to his age."

"Only because he was not there," the old man snapped. "Because he didn't spend time with our grandfather like I did. That's why he refuses to believe what I say. He thinks he has to be there for the world to continue. But I know what I am saying. I was with Papá Grande and I remember everything he told me." He used his index finger to tap on the side of his head. "For weeks he had been promising that he was going to take me for my first real haircut — no more putting a bowl on my head and cutting around it, the way my mother liked to do." He pretended he had a pair of scissors in his hand and was cutting his bangs. "'Ya, you are getting to be a man,' he would say, even if I was only four years old. But he said if he was going to take me, I had to promise not to cry the way he had seen other little boys do. If I was going to cry, then it was better to wait until later. 'Real haircuts are for men, not for little boys.' I said I wouldn't cry, but what did I know if I had never had a real haircut in a barbershop? When it was my turn, the barber put a board across the chair and I climbed on."

"The other day you told me there were animals carved into the arms of the chair," Don Celestino said. "How would you know that if there was a board across the top?"

The old man stopped to look at his brother and then over at the girl. He felt disoriented as he glanced about the room, as if he had been roused earlier than usual from his afternoon nap. His brother was always doing this to him, making him question what he knew to be true, what he had lived. Last night in bed, he had gone over and over what he would tell them this morning when they came to visit, how he would say it to them to make it all sound more believable, so his brother wouldn't always be doubting him and would finally take him at his word.

"I know because I saw it before he put the board down," he responded. "And because that wasn't the only time I went to that barbershop. Later he took me again and I sat in the chair without the board."

Don Celestino seemed less than convinced, but he let him continue.

"At first I was all right and not nervous, but it was when they put the sheet over me that I started getting scared, like I didn't know what the barber was going to do with those sharp scissors. My mother had put a sheet over me, but this barber wasn't my mother. Papá Grande was standing by the chair and he kept talking so he could distract me."

"Saying what to you?" Socorro asked.

"Nothing to me, really. He liked to talk to the barber and the rest of them who were waiting for their haircuts." The old man glanced around the room again and this time closed his eyes and lolled his head.

Socorro sat back in her chair. Now she wished she hadn't asked the question and instead just let him keep talking. "The important thing is that you can remember how he took you," she said. "Most people would never be able to, already so many years ago."

Don Fidencio blinked a few times before fully opening his eyes. "And later when the barber had finished with my hair, he asked him if he had cut enough. Papá Grande told him to cut just a little more in the front, but 'not too much,' he said, 'because one time I saw an Indian scalp a man.'"

Don Celestino shook his head at this.

"No, what?" his brother asked.

"No, not those made-up stories."

"So now an old man is not allowed to talk about one of the few things that has stayed with him."

"The only ones who believed the story were little children," Don Celestino said, then turned toward Socorro. "Our grandfather used to tell us that when he was a little boy growing up in Mexico, some Indians attacked the ranchito where he lived with his family. The Indians killed most of the adults and took off with some of the children, kidnapped them and rode off to the north. And he used to claim that that was how he got over to this side of the river."

"It sounds like something from a book or movie," Socorro said. "Even a novela."

"This was one of those kinds of stories."

"If he said that the Indians took him, then the Indians took him," Don Fidencio said. "He saw them kill his mother and father. What more proof do you want? Tell me why would he make up something like that, about riding all night with the Indians and the Mexican army chasing them." The old man stopped to wipe the spittle from the corner of his mouth. "Not only that, but you forgot to tell her that the man they scalped was still alive." He used the edge of his hand as if he were slicing back his own scalp, the same as his grandfather would do when recounting the story.

She made a face as she pulled away in the chair.

"Our grandfather was a little old man who liked to talk." Don Celestino sat back near the corner of the bed. "He thought that because the stories happened so long ago and over there, on the other side, that people would believe whatever he said.

Everything was more dangerous back then, everything was more exciting back then. The men were different, the women were different. Always, always with the way things were."

"You say that only because you were born over here. How would you know how things were back then, if you hardly spent any time with Papá Grande? I was the one who would go spend days with him. It was the last story he ever told me. By then he had told it to me hundreds of times, but I let him tell it one last time. He told me like he had only just arrived here. It mattered to him that other people remembered the story, even those who would never believe it. He told me that if he had one regret in his life, it was that he never went back, at least to see if anyone had survived or what was left of the ranchito. Then he said to me, 'Tocayo,' because we were both Fidencio, but he hardly ever called me by my name. 'Tocayo, someday when you are older you should go back and see how things are now, what there is of my ranchito. Tell them I always wanted to go back.'"

"At least he had you there with him," Socorro said.

"He died that night in his bed. Later I thought about going back like he said, but I was always working or busy with something else, and by the time I could go, I had forgotten what he said, until last night when it came back to me."

"And now you want to go back," Don Celestino said, crossing his arms. "And you want me to take you."

"What's so wrong with that, if you have the time?"

"That I'm not here to do your errands," his brother said. "I wasn't the one he told to go looking for the ranchito."

"And why not," Don Fidencio asked, "if this is our grandfather?"

"Why do I need to go searching through Mexico for something that never happened? And this is only because you made a promise ages ago and then forgot about it until now."

"How can you be so sure it didn't happen?"

"And how can you be so sure it did?"

"You were the only one who never believed the story. What would it hurt you to help an old man with his last wish?"

Don Celestino stood up when he saw both of them looking at him, waiting for a response. "Who knows, maybe one of these days we can go," he said, hoping this would satisfy the old man until he forgot about it, as he usually did with most things.

"One of these days?" He flicked his wrist and turned toward the window. "You say it like I have so many left."

"Why don't we talk about something else, eh?"

Don Celestino glanced at his watch, then over at Socorro, but she seemed in no hurry to leave.

"Your room is quiet," Socorro said. "It must be good when you need to rest."

"Only when this neighbor of mine isn't yelling in his sleep."

"Every night that way?"

"No, but still last night it was hard because I had to go four times to make water." He held up the appropriate number of fingers to show her. "Four — I counted. And then another because I thought it was time to make number two." He held up a pair of fingers on the other hand.

"Fidencio, nobody wants to talk about being sick. Please find something more pleasant to talk about?"

"She was the one who asked me. And anyway, that's how it happens when people get old — nothing works anymore and then one day they wake up dead."

"Ya, stop talking like that."

"Why not, if it's only the truth?"

"Nobody wants to think about getting old and dying," Don Celestino said.

"Bah, and just because you don't want to think about getting old, you think this will make it go away?" The old man sat back. "Maybe I should stop thinking about being constipated."

"You know what I mean."

"And now I can't talk about my own health?"

"Sometimes my mother goes the whole night without sleeping," Socorro said.

"But when I was finally able to rest, I had a dream that I was working again, delivering the mail. Imagine going to sleep and all you do is walk from house to house."

"Still, after so many years?"

"This one is the same dream over and over," Don Celestino said. "He keeps delivering the mail, even if they don't pay him anymore."

"Yes, but this time nobody had mailboxes."

"How do you mean, no mailboxes?"

"No mailboxes, no mailboxes, how much more simple do you want it? Houses with no mailboxes. Like pants with no pockets."

"And where were they?"

"Somebody took them."

"All of them?" Socorro asked.

"Why should that surprise you? We live in a town where people steal whatever they can — cars, lawn mowers, dogs out of the backyard. The other day some idiota walked into a store and tried to steal a stereo by putting it inside his pants."

"And then what else?"

He stayed looking at her for a few seconds.

"With the mailboxes?" she said.

"Yes, so there were no mailboxes," he said. "If I had found them, maybe I would have slept better. But no, I had to keep walking all over town for someplace to put my letters. The sun was hot and my bag felt like it was full of bricks.

"At first I didn't know what to do with so many letters and no mailboxes, but then I knocked and a young boy answered. He must have been nine or ten years old. He had hair down to his shoulders and eyes like a chinito. I asked for his mother or father, but he said they were gone, that it was just him. Then I asked him, 'What happened to all the mailboxes?' But he just shook his head like I was a crazy man. I asked him if he wanted the letter, maybe it was for his mother and father. But he said no, for me to keep it."

"But to do what with it?" she asked.

"That, he didn't tell me. I guess I was just supposed to keep carrying all the letters but for no reason."

"And then?"

"And then nothing. I woke up and stayed there in bed, waiting until it was time to go for my breakfast."

There was a knock at the door and they all turned to see The One With The Flat Face leaning halfway into the room. "Mr. Rosales, you need to get ready for lunch," she said before she continued down the hall.

Socorro glanced at her watch and it was only a couple of minutes past eleven.

"What else is there to do here?" Don Fidencio said. "It takes time to get all these old people into one room and ready to eat."

It seemed as though he wanted to say more but then was unsure what that might be. He gazed out at the archway where The Turtle With The Fedora was being lowered from the special van used to transport the residents to their doctor's appointments. The lift had stalled and he was waiting to see if her wheelchair might roll forward.

The point was, he had talked to his brother and the girl enough already. He had to go eat his lunch now; this was where he lived and slept and took his meals. His brother and the girl were nice to come visit him. It was nice of the girl to ask him questions like she was interested in his life. Tomorrow it might be different. Tomorrow they might not be coming around. Taking time out of their busy days to come visit an old man who couldn't remember the half of what he knew. And really, he wondered if he could blame them.

17

This was Saturday, according to the calendar hanging in the kitchen. Only the fourth day of the month, but by now Don Celestino had marked several of the dates with appointments to see one doctor or another — for his annual exam with his cardiologist, for a follow-up with the urologist, for his bimonthly visit to the podiatrist so one of the nurses could trim his toenails (a precaution his regular doctor had urged him to take because of his diabetes). Other dates on the calendar reminded him of when to change the oil in the car or when he was due for his next haircut, though he tended to go more by what he saw in the mirror than by what was on the calendar. Socorro's name took up the same square every week, not because he thought he would forget but just to have something to make the week appear not as long. His scribbled notes spilled across other squares, making it seem as if these days and weeks were actually one long day that wound down at the bottom of the page, only to begin anew on the next calendar page. In fact, since practically every square noted some activity, today's blank square looked that much more blank. Compared to the surrounding dates, the square appeared pristine, absent of the usual mundane tasks that might occupy his time or at least make it seem that he had more to do than he actually did. It was almost as if he had set aside the day for some special event, only now he had no idea what it might be. He checked the other dates to see if there was something planned for later in the month that he might be able to move up to today. It was only ten o'clock in the morning. He knew from experience that a day like this could drag on and the only thing he would have to look forward to was for it to get dark so he could go to sleep and wait for tomorrow to come around. The car looked fairly clean, and taking out the bucket and rags to wash it seemed unnecessary. His shoes he had polished only two days ago, after having spent most of the morning shopping for a new set of laces. The Wellness Center was closed on the weekends, and walking inside the mall had never interested him — much less if he had to deal with the weekend crowds. When the King Mart was still open, he and Dora used to sometimes go to the little café to drink coffee and read the paper. There was usually another married couple sitting there and they would often strike up a conversation that took up most of the morning. Doing this alone wasn't as easy, though, and now if he talked to anyone it was usually to some other widower looking for a way to pass the time.

After flipping through the thirty or so channels and not finding anything that caught his attention, he walked out to the driveway to get the newspaper. By now he knew to breathe with his mouth to avoid the bad smell drifting through the yard. The smell occurred most mornings and disappeared by noontime, but by then the day was too hot to do much of anything outside. Even the tap water had a lingering odor and taste to it, enough that he had taken to buying purified water. He figured the smell had to be coming from either one of the drying resacas or the sewer plant a couple of miles away. Tamez worked as if he were immune to it. He waved from across the street, where he was mowing a neighbor's yard. Don Celestino did his part and waved back before he started for the front door. Tamez probably thought they were on good terms, that Don Celestino had appreciated his offer to take care of the yard for a reduced rate, as he did for several of his other elderly neighbors. "Not now," Don Celestino had answered, and left it at that. Though what he had really wanted to say was, "Not anytime soon, cabrón." Or better: "Not until after I die and they put me in a hole in the ground and the yard belongs to somebody else." Did he see him walking around with a cane or a walker? Did he have a handicapped tag hanging from his rearview mirror? Had they built a ramp for him to roll his wheelchair up to the front door? If anything, he felt he had more energy than ever to dedicate to his responsibilities around the house. Just a few days earlier, he had spent part of his late afternoon trimming the grass all along the sidewalk leading from the front steps to the street, and he had done this with a fifteen-inch knife that cut an edge as straight as he used to do when trimming one of his customers' sideburns. After he finished with the sidewalk, he took the small piece of carpet that he kneeled on and placed it along the curb so he could trim the grass near the street. Tamez did the same work at the other houses, but always with one of those weed-trimming machines that Don Celestino had no idea about how to operate. No one needed to ask who did a better job, he or Tamez, just as no one needed to ask if an electric shaver did as good a job as a straight razor.

Back inside the house, he sat in his recliner to read the paper, scanning the first couple of pages for anything that he hadn't seen on the news at five that morning. He managed to get through only half of an article about the city commissioners' meeting before his eyes grew faint and he nodded off. Less than a minute later he woke up, upset with himself for not having stayed more alert; it wasn't noon and here he was dozing off. He tossed the paper aside and walked to the kitchen. He ran the water until it was hot enough to rinse the one plate he'd used earlier. The orange grease of the chorizo streaked its way down to the sink and into the drain. He squirted a generous amount of dishwashing liquid onto the sponge before wiping the plate clean on both sides, then repeating the process. His coffee cup could get by with a simple rinse and wipe, but he preferred scrubbing inside and out, around the handle, too, where some coffee might have dribbled down.

The clock on the stove read 10:56. It was still too early to eat his lunch or tune in again to the weather report on the television. He opened the refrigerator so he could pour himself a glass of water. With the pitcher less than full, he walked back to the counter for the jug of purified water. The old jugs used to be the five-gallon size, but one day he saw Socorro struggling to lift the plastic container and he rushed over to help her, something an old man would've never been able to do. Then later that afternoon, just to make it easier on her, he had gone ahead and replaced the five-gallon with the three-gallon size. Now he kept two smaller jugs and made a trip to buy more water whenever he noticed one of them getting low.

The first water station he passed was spray-painted with EL NOE Y LA ROSA on its side and along the metal counter where people set their jugs to retrieve water. Farther down the same street, he passed a station that charged a nickel less, but it meant driving across a parking lot riddled with potholes and broken glass. Some of the grocery stores also sold water, only these outlets were located near the entrance of the building, and he would have to find a parking spot, then walk over to buy the water, then use a shopping cart to bring the filled jugs to wherever he left the car. Socorro had mentioned to him the filter systems she'd seen in some of the other houses she cleaned. He told her he would think about it, but he had trouble believing these machines did as good a job as the water stations. Besides, if he bought the filter, he wouldn't need to go buy water a couple of times a week, and that would be one less thing to occupy his time during the day.

He pulled the car into the small parking lot of the San Juan Water Station. The station had an outlet on either side, but he preferred the left since it was on the driver's side and shaded by a row of Sabal palms that stood at the far end of the lot. A palm from one of the trees had fallen overnight and now lay withering across the dark asphalt. He placed the first jug on the counter and lowered the retractable spigot so it rested less than an inch above the mouth of the jug. After he fed the three quarters into the slot, he pressed the three-gallon button and waited as the water shot out with the force of an open fire hydrant.

He was capping the jug and was about to place it in the backseat when he heard a car honking from the street. An elderly man in a motorized wheelchair was driving halfway on the shoulder and halfway in the right lane, forcing traffic to either slow down or go around him. Some drivers might have missed him were it not for the small U.S. flag fluttering on an antenna high above the chair. He was dressed in a blue-striped Western shirt, khakis, short black boots, and a straw cowboy hat, all of which appeared exceedingly large for him, as if he had shrunk since putting on his clothes that morning. On his lap he held an empty three-gallon jug.

Don Celestino stepped around to the other side of the station to ask the old man if he needed help getting his water, but the man only mumbled something to himself as if he hadn't seen another person nearby. A strip of spittle had dried at the corner of his mouth, caking itself onto his two-day-old stubble. He grabbed the wooden cane hooked on the backrest of his chair and positioned it between his legs as he stood up. Once he had set the jug on the counter, he pulled out a long black billfold with a fighting cock embroidered on its side and then fumbled through a stash of lottery tickets until he finally located his money.

"That machine can be difficult sometimes," Don Celestino said when he noticed that George Washington's face was as worn and tattered as the old man's.

"Eh?" He tried to remove his money from the tray but managed to snatch only a corner before it tore off in his hand. "Then why the hell do they have it here, just to steal my money?"

He stared at the spigot, waiting for his water to come out. A few seconds passed before the tray expelled the torn bill and the service panel began to flash: PLEASE TAKE YOUR MONEY. Then it darkened before it flashed again: POR FAVOR RETIRE SU DINERO.

"The other side works better," Don Celestino said.

"And why would I give them more of my money?" He grabbed the jug off the counter. "It would be better if I just drank the dirty water I have at home." He sat down in the wheelchair, muttering something else to himself, and finally whipped around the station to the other counter. There he looked through his billfold again, but the only dollar he found was more wrinkled than the first one.

"Here," Don Celestino said, and from his own wallet handed him a crisp dollar bill.

The old man held the jug under the rushing water. Afterward he paid Don Celestino with one of his own wrinkled dollars. "I appreciate the help," he said, extending his hand. "Pano Garcia."

"Celestino Rosales."

The old man cocked back his hat. "The one who was a barber?"

Don Celestino nodded as he tried to recognize the other man's face.

"I thought you had died." He lowered himself back down into the chair.

"That must have been somebody else."

"They said you had problems with your heart or something."

"It must have been somebody else, maybe my older brother Fidencio."

"No, I am almost sure it was Celestino Rosales that they told me had died. This was two or three years ago."

"Maybe because of my diabetes."

"No, not because of your diabetes." He looked at the ground and spit, then wiped his mouth on his shoulder. "Why would somebody waste their time telling me that you had diabetes? Tell me who doesn't have that."

"Two years ago was when I sold my business."

"Maybe that was it. Not that you died, but just that you sold the barbershop. Maybe that was what they meant to say."

"People like to talk," Don Celestino said. "Even when they have no idea what they're saying."

"I can tell you don't remember me." The old man laughed to himself. "But how, after so many years? You used to cut hair in a barbershop near Washington Park. I would cut my hair with the one named Lalo, who was my uncle."

"That was back when I was starting out, before I opened my business."

"See? I remember. At least the mind still works." The old man tapped his finger to his temple.

"You look good still," he said, though really he had no recollection of the man.

"I never took care of myself and now I have so many problems with my health. Twice a week they take me to clean my blood." He raised a shirtsleeve to show him his bandaged forearm. "This leg isn't mine." His left shin made a hollow sound when he rapped on it with his cane. "I have some good days, but more than anything I spend the time waiting for God to take me."

"At least you can still get around." Don Celestino handed him the jug of water.

"Maybe you are one of those who likes to kneel down and be giving thanks, but not me. Most of it hasn't been so good." He fiddled with the control stick and moved the wheelchair side to side. Then he cocked back his head and looked up as if he had remembered something. "I can see you have been a lucky one to stay healthy, but just wait and see."

"For what?"

"Just wait." He held up his hand as if cautioning him from coming any closer to the edge of a cliff.

"What will I see?" Don Celestino asked.

But the old man had already spun the wheelchair around and zipped forward. A moment later he was out of the parking lot and back on the boulevard, his tiny flag flickering against a strong headwind.

The traffic was heavier now and he braked for a yellow light he could have easily made. The driver in the truck behind him laid on the horn, which normally would have caused him to return the gesture, but today he simply ignored the sound. He drove a little slower once he was in the neighborhood and closer to the house. When he saw his front yard, he couldn't help thinking about the ambulance pulling up and how Socorro had watched them load him in the back. What must she have been thinking when she saw him so weak and helpless? Then again, his condition that morning had been because of the diabetes, which could've happened to him regardless of his age. He was older, yes, but he was not old. A little old man, un anciano, would be falling asleep in his chair while the rest of the people in the room continued with their conversation as if the unconscious man were a faulty table lamp that at any moment might twinkle back to life. He wanted to believe that the difference in his and Socorro's ages was less dramatic than what the actual years would make a person think. It wasn't as if the thirty years or so that stood between them were suddenly going to widen from one day to the next. If anything, from now on his aging would be gradual, less noticeable: he was an older man, after all; Socorro was the one still holding on to some of her youth.

"Sometimes you sound like your brother," she'd said on the drive home from the nursing home. Now he couldn't recall what it was he had said that had prompted her comment, probably since he was more surprised with her response and how such a thing could have occurred to her: Sometimes you sound like your brother. She seemed disappointed when he turned down his brother's idea to take a trip into Mexico, as if he naturally would be in agreement with such a plan. Sometimes you sound like your brother. Had she realized, as he had during the visit, that he was much closer in age to his brother, an elderly man living in a nursing home, than he was to her? What other similarities did she notice between him and his ninety-one-year-old brother? Was she now only waiting for the day when he would go on with his own stories about Indians kidnapping children and riding through the night? Would she be surprised?

He pulled into the carport and stayed there after turning off the engine. He wondered whether he should be proud of how well he had maintained his health all these years or be worried that the years would eventually catch up to him, and not at a measured rate, as most men experienced, but in his case it would happen in one cruel and sudden push. The former seemed a false and limiting prospect, since he knew he couldn't hold on to his good health forever, while the latter felt self-defeating and no different from the outlook of the old man at the water station.

He stepped out of the car, using the door frame to help pull himself up and out. The easiest way to carry the water jug was by holding the neck in one hand and gripping the plastic handle in the other hand, but just the other day at his doctor's office he had seen a deliveryman hoisting a water jug onto his shoulder like nothing, like he was putting on a shirt. Don Celestino spread his legs in the same way now, evening his stance before gripping the plastic handle. He staggered a little under the extra weight, then caught his balance and headed into the house.

18

Don Fidencio hobbles along the shore, making sure his cane doesn't sink too far into the sand. The strange part is that Amalia is a little girl again, while he is still an old man. Even Petra is only in her thirties, so beautiful and happy. He can see Amalia is wearing the bathing suit they bought for her at the Kress, while her mother has her blue jeans rolled up to her knees and is wearing one of his mail-carrier shirts, with the tails tied into a knot. Neither one seems to notice that he is old and using a wooden cane. That, and he is wearing only his boxers, held up by his trusty suspenders. There are other children there now, running and playing in the water. It must be late summer, the time of year when he usually took the family to Boca Chica. The truck is parked at the southern tip of the beach, near the mouth of the river. Petra walks to the back and, on the tailgate, makes chicken-salad sandwiches for the family. Only he sees her hands are much larger than he remembers, thick and burly, like the hands of a man from Oklahoma that he bunked next to when he was working in the CCC camps. He remembers how the man used to pick up a railroad tie and walk off like nothing. More than sixty years have passed since he has seen hands like this. Where could Petra have gotten these hands? What happened to her young, delicate hands? No wonder she's not wearing her wedding ring. How, with those breakfast sausages for fingers? He asks her if she would like help making the sandwiches. It seems an unusual offer to make, considering that in all the years they were married he never helped her with these sorts of things. And suddenly he wants to help her make sandwiches? What could be next? Making the bed? Scrubbing the toilet? But really, he asks only because he is worried about what kind of job she will do with those hands of hers. He imagines her leaving a big thumbprint in the middle of the white bread and he knows that as tasty as the sandwich might be he won't like that. Who wants to eat a sandwich disfigured in this way? But when he offers to help she doesn't hear him or maybe just ignores him, and goes on. The children have waded into the mouth of the river. The distance to the Mexican side is maybe thirty feet and the wa-

ter barely reaches their chests. He sits in the lawn chair to keep an eye on them, but when he looks down again the lawn chair has large wheels attached to its sides. One of the little boys is giving Amalia a piggyback ride in the water and after they reach the other side she turns and in Spanish shouts, "We're in Mexico, Daddy! We're in Mexico!" He waves and, as usual, yells, "Tell them I said hello and that your father is puro Mexicano!" The children beg him to come over to the other side, and after much persuading, he tries to stand but finds his legs have finally given out on him. He tries repeatedly and keeps falling back into the seat. Finally he rolls the chair closer to the shore, until the wheels begin to sink in the marshy sand. In the weightlessness of the water the old man feels his body young again. He lifts his feet as he floats on his back. He sways along with the river's current, keeping his eyes shut and feeling the water lap against his renewed body. In the distance he can hear the laughter of the children, but when he opens his eyes he's now in the community pool in Amalia's subdivision. Of all places to be. He was there years and years ago when he went up to Houston to visit her and go watch a baseball game. Several families are gathered around the patio tables and some men are grilling shish kebabs. From all the decorations it looks like the Fourth of July. It seems cloudier here than a second ago when he was floating in the river. He is happy to be the only one in the pool. No one seems to notice an old man floating on his back, his underwear now clinging to him in an unflattering manner. The people carry on with their conversations, but with his head halfway in the water he hears only muffled voices. He can barely make out the metal sign hanging from the fence. But how come? But how come? he remembers her asking him the one time he took her to the public swimming pool. What did the words on the sign say? Why did the man tell us we couldn't go inside, Daddy? Just because. But how come, if they let all the other people? What did the sign say, Daddy? If he was grateful for anything that day, it was that she was still too young to read what it said about the dogs and Mexicans. But how come, Daddy? How come we have to go home? The water looks dirty, that's how come — now shut your mouth. And that was all. How could he explain it then, if today, after so many years, he still doesn't have the words to answer her question? He thinks if he can remain very still in the water, just floating, maybe not even breathing, they might not notice him. That's all he wants now, for them to leave him alone and just let him float. He figures he can wait until it gets dark and they leave, then get out of the water. And it's working — he hears less and less of their muffled talk. He feels so at ease that he ignores the tingling in his left calf. This is the happiest he has felt since his accident in the yard, however long ago that was. All he wants is to keep floating along, but a few seconds later his leg cramps up so much that he loses his steadiness and goes down. And there, underwater, he realizes the cramp is really someone pulling on his leg. He strains to see who it is, only the pool water is now as murky as the river. But he knows without seeing his face that it has to be The Son Of A Bitch. The old man yells for help: ¡Ayúdenme! ¡Ayúdenme! ¡Me estoy ahogando! These are the loudest words he has ever shouted, but it all happens underwater. The pool is deeper than he ever imagined. The people keep laughing and having a good time at their barbecue. And he begins to swallow water.

19

The mattress sloped to one side as if the bed might be sinking into the cement floor. The room remained dim, the sun not yet passing through the fabric she had tacked to the window frame. If it were any day other than Sunday, she would already be struggling to get up and prepare breakfast, then rush to get ready for her workday. Socorro could hear the rickety whir of the fan and what sounded like muffled voices coming from the street. When she turned onto her right side, toward the wall, the sheet slid off her leg as if it were caught on something.

"It looks like she wants to wake up."

"I remember when she was a little girl, I would have to carry her to the bathroom so she could get ready for school."

"Mamí?" Socorro squinted until she could make out the figures in the room. "Is something wrong?"

"We just want to talk to you," her aunt said.

"Now, at this hour?"

"I lost my sleep again," her mother answered, "and then your tía woke up."

"Can we talk in the morning?"

"We want to talk now, mi'ja, when your mind isn't so mixed up with other ideas."

Socorro reached for the lamp behind her.

"No, leave it off," her mother said.

"But why?"

"Leave it," she repeated. "We want you to listen to our words."

Socorro sat up so she could at least talk to them more comfortably. She strained to see the outline of her mother's wheelchair angled toward the bed. With her short dark hair slicked back, it looked as though she had just come in from swimming. What little light there was shimmered off the bulbous shape of her forehead. Her aunt sat on the edge of the bed with her legs dangling off the side. She was wearing a thin nightgown, sheer enough to reveal the thick black brassiere that she removed only to bathe. At night she undid her long dark braid and let the ends reach the small of her back.

"A mother only wants her daughter to be happy." She rolled the wheelchair closer in order to pat Socorro's leg.

"Good, because I found somebody who makes me happy."

"And later?"

"What about later?"

"These relationships look nice at first, but then later is when it comes out, that he only wanted a younger woman so he could take advantage of her. And I know because that's the way it happened to the daughter of a woman who used to help at the church, the girl was staying after she did the cleaning, with hopes that there would be more, someday more, someday more than washing his underwear, and cleaning his toilet, and the rest of whatever she did for him, the things he wanted her to do in the bed. And you know what else she got? Nothing, because he was like this one you found for yourself, already with one foot in the ground."

"Celestino is healthier than most men half his age."

"Like the men your own age," her aunt said.

"And that, what difference does it make?"

"What difference?" her mother said, almost whispering as she pulled up even closer to the bed. "Those are the men you are supposed to marry, not their grandfathers."

"Who said anything about marriage?"

"And then?"

"We're just friends."

"Such good friends, but you cannot bring him here for us to meet him? You prefer that your little friend stop the car across the street instead of bringing him inside to meet your family, like you are embarrassed for him to meet us."

"Or maybe for us to meet him?" the aunt offered.

"Bring him here so you can criticize?"

"Friends who are the same age get married."

"Yes, that's why I ended up alone," Socorro snapped, maybe louder than she would have if the lights were on.

"Now you're talking about more than fifteen years ago," her mother said. "How are you going to find a man more young and healthy if you keep thinking about something that happened so long ago? You think that they are all the same, but you would know different if you gave them a chance."

"The men my age have not changed — they only got older."

"No man is perfect," her aunt said.

"And how would you know?" Socorro couldn't believe this was coming from a woman who'd never so much as had a male friend.

"I was just saying, from what I hear."

"Why do you have to keep defending him? You talk about Rogelio like I was the one who made everything go bad."

Her mother leaned forward. "I only want you to see what you're doing, if you go with this other one, the little old man."

"He has a name," she said.

"And that's all you are going to have when he dies," her mother said. "Do you really want people to say, 'There goes the widow of Don Celestino'?"

"They said it once about me, at least this time they would be saying it for more sincere reasons."

"So you do want to marry him?"

"You two were the ones who brought it up."

"Then he hasn't?"

"No, already he was married for more than fifty years, and he has his own family."

"And you, what do you say?" her mother asked.

"I spent six years married, that was enough."

"Hmm," her aunt let out. "She wants us to believe she hasn't thought about it."

"Believe what you want." Socorro pulled more of the blanket up to her chest.

Her mother rolled backward in a half circle. "Later you will see that we were telling you the truth."

"You worry because you think I would go away."

"Bah, now she thinks we cannot live without her." Her aunt laughed.

"You act that way."

The wheelchair squeaked as her mother adjusted herself. "You think your poor tía hasn't sacrificed to be here with us?"

"And where else was she going to go?" Socorro said. "If before this she was living with her mother?"

"Taking care of her." Her aunt stepped off the bed and went to stand behind the wheelchair. "Until God needed her."

"Very nice," her mother said. "Talking that way to your poor tía."

"Sorry."

"We just want to help you, right?"

Her aunt only nodded from behind the chair.

"It would be better if you stopped seeing him," her mother said, "found yourself another house to clean, just so you can get away from him."

"You say it like I was a young girl and I need for my mother to tell me who I can spend time with."

"A mother knows."

"You tell me the same answer for everything, that you know better than I do."

"When you get to fifty, he will already be at eighty-five," her aunt said. "When you are sixty, he will be ninety-five."

Her mother laughed. "As if the man is really going to reach that age."

Socorro clutched her pillow a little tighter and curled up on her side until they left the room, then she shut the door and crawled back into bed. Since when had the differences in people's ages become so important? Her tío Felix had married a girl who was half his age when he was in his sixties, and nobody said anything. No, they congratulated him like he'd won a color television in a raffle at the church.

She lifted the pillow and turned from the wall. Why was she wasting her time arguing with them? Rogelio hadn't wanted her. He'd shown her with his body what he couldn't say to her face. He could've had babies with half the women in Matamoros, and her mother still would have thought they needed to stay married. Maybe in some way, all of it — the ugly woman he found, the baby he left her with, even the drowning — had been a blessing. By now she would have suffered so many years with him. But then maybe she had also given up too soon, before God might have fixed her body. What if her body hadn't changed simply because she had lost faith that it ever would? Maybe this was her biggest mistake.

The first light of day was peeking through the window. A chattering newscaster had replaced the voices in the other room. She could hear her aunt moving around the kitchen, the sound of the kettle on the stove. After a while the scent of cinnamon wafted throughout the house. She knew she hadn't heard the last from her mother and aunt. If this was the only sincere man she had found after all these years of believing she would be alone, who were they to protest? And then it occurred to her that she still hadn't reached the age when her body was supposed to have started changing. How, after giving up on Rogelio and then her own body, could she give up on this new man? Maybe Celestino was the type she should have met years earlier, maybe from the very start. A man who already had his children and didn't care to have any more. A man who simply wanted her for her.

20

Don Fidencio knocked, then waited a minute and knocked a second time, only harder. It was better than opening the door and finding The One With The Hole In His Back asleep on the pot — again. When he didn't get a response, he walked in and searched under the sink, around the toilet, and in the space behind the door.

He hobbled back to the closet for another look. With one hand against the wall, he steadied himself as if he were walking down the aisle of a bus pulling away from its last stop. His five shoe boxes, all of them covered up and in order with their appropriate numbers facing outward, sat on the top shelf where they had been earlier. His three shirts and pants hung where the attendant had left them. For all he knew, they had taken his canes to the flea market and sold them to some other old man with a bad leg. He couldn't believe the lack of respect these women showed him. If they had taken the time to ask, he would have told them that the wooden cane was the one he used when he was out in public. Who knows what else these women would have taken if he hadn't complained at the nurses' station? And then to make matters worse, they laughed when he reported that someone had been stealing his chocolates or that he was missing his lighter or one of his government-issue pens. Then a few days later The One With The Flat Face would come knocking on the door and say that the yardman had found his missing lighter on the patio, under one of the stone benches out by the back fence, or that an attendant had recovered his pocketknife from one of the trays coming out of the dishwasher. Always some excuse. Always some reason to blame him and make it seem like he didn't know where he left things. Look, here comes The One Who Loses Everything.

He set his baseball cap on the nightstand and pushed the chair next to the bed. Once he was sitting, he grabbed hold of the bed railing and with much sacrifice slowly lowered himself so both knees could gently touch the floor. Still holding on to the railing, he bowed all the way down. One of his government-issue pens lay under the center of the bed, for sure tossed there by some careless aide who didn't have the good manners to return the pen to its proper place after using it. He tried several times to grab hold of it, but his hand came up short each time. If he'd had one of his canes with him, this wouldn't have been a problem. The pen would have to wait for later so he could find something else to help him reach it. Off in the corner, near the headboard, lay a diaper, still folded up and unused ("Thanks be to God," he whispered to himself), that must have been meant for the last old man to occupy the bed, because it sure as hell wasn't his (again, "Thanks be to God").

No, they were afraid of him, that was what was going on here. They'd seen how much improvement he had made with his therapy and now they were scared that one of these days he would slip out and this time they wouldn't be able to catch up to him. One good, sturdy cane was all it would take. And soon, not even that. In the evenings he was still sweeping the floors with the dust mop, but now once he was out of sight of the nurses' station, he would lean the mop against the wall and continue on his own, staying close to the wooden railing, just in case. They probably thought he would never get anywhere without the walker. But that showed how much they knew Fidencio Rosales.

After he was convinced he wasn't going to find anything under the bed, it took still more effort to pull himself back into the chair. Then he glanced at his wristwatch and realized his brother and the girl would be coming by in twenty minutes to take him out to lunch. He'd resisted giving her a name like he had done with these people in the prison, but this also made it more difficult to now remember the real name that went with her face. Already he had met her five or six times, however many it was, and he couldn't think of her as more than the girl. It wasn't like The Turtles, so many to keep track of. There was only one of her, whatever her name was. They had taken him to dinner the other day, and the whole time he hadn't been able to remember her name until his brother happened to say it in passing.

From the closet he pulled out the #3 and #4 shoe boxes before he thought to open the #2 box. As soon as they had brought him back to his room, he had written her name in one of his old address books. Which one, though? He had two bundles of the little books, each bound with thick rubber bands. He started with a red one and found the name Julio Betancourt, which meant nothing to him, as did Martin Colunga. This last name had been underlined several times, as if it had some particular importance, but still nothing came to him. Under *M*, he located the name Jimmy Udall, which made sense only because he had MECHANIC written next to it, something he wished he had done with the other names: NEIGHBOR, OLD FRIEND, OLD FRIEND NOT WORTH TALKING TO ANYMORE, WORK FRIEND, NEPHEW WHO DOESN'T CALL ANYMORE, etc. Scattered throughout several of the address books, he found only the initials — DLN or LG or JM or SFL — of women he'd had relations with, or tried to anyway, but he wasn't about to write down their actual names so Petra could find them. The phone numbers themselves were written in a special inverted code that he'd had trouble deciphering at times.

He stopped turning pages when he saw Chano Gonzalez's name. They had been good friends for years at work, but more so whenever it was that Petra left the house to live wherever it was she went. He and Chano would get together Saturday nights to watch the boxing matches on television. Then Chano's eyes started going bad because of his diabetes, which he took care of about as well as Don Fidencio did, only Don Fidencio didn't have diabetes and could eat and drink whatever the hell he wanted. So he started going for him in the car and bringing him back to the house, but it wasn't the same anymore because Chano could barely make out the television and Don Fidencio had to spend the whole time telling him who was winning and how. Later Chano had something go wrong with one of his feet and they had to cut his toes. And after that he only got worse: more toes, more parts of his leg, and finally his woman wouldn't let him out of the house, which was how he stayed until he died a few years later.

DEAD FRIEND, he wrote next to his name. He wrote the same thing next to every name, even ones who might have still been alive.

Under *R*, he found his brother's name, the only other Rosales listed in this particular book. He checked the cover to see if there was a date that might indicate when it became just the two of them left behind. In the end, though, he had to settle for finding the girl's name, written right next to his brother's name. The problem was, he couldn't read his own writing, as tiny and chicken-scratched as it had always been, only now also with this constant tremor that made it seem as if he had written it with the pen held upright between his corn-ridden toes. The *S* he could see, but the rest was a mystery to him. All those years of figuring out mailing addresses, and this is what he had to show for it. Sonia, Sulema, Severa, Sofia, Sylvia, Solidad — none of them sounded right. He could tell now he should've written the name in the same large block letters he had just used to write next to his friends' names. Don Fidencio shut his eyes and concentrated, concentrated, concentrated, the whole time hissing the first letter of her name until it sounded like he was releasing the air from a tire.

When he opened his eyes, he gazed at the letters until he managed to untangle them one by one. There was the *o* that looked more like a lopsided egg, and the *c* and the *q* mixed up with the second *o,* which looked like a cracked egg because it was too close to the first *r,* which swallowed up the second *r* and third *r* or a *p,* but then there was still another *o* that did actually look like an *o.* S-O-C-Q-O-R-P-O, he wrote at the top of the page. It was one thing to not be able to write and another to not know how to spell. He stared at this for a minute or so before he crossed out the *Q*, then the *P.* S-O-C-O-R-O. Now it was so clear to him. Of course, Socorro. That was her name — Socorro. He used both hands to grab ahold of his walker and stand up. "Socorro . . . Socorro . . . Socorro," he said, shuffling out of the room.

They had taken a booth near the back of the little restaurant, where they would still be able to talk if someone put money in the jukebox. Steam billowed out each time the kitchen door swung open and one of the waitresses came out with a plate of food. The place was only half full. A teenage couple in hooded jackets sat in a corner booth where the owner couldn't see them sneaking kisses while they shared the plate they had ordered. At the next table three men in cowboy hats sipped their coffees while the older one of the group did most of the talking. A pair of Border Patrol agents sat close to the door, one of them keeping an eye on the kitchen workers, the other more interested in the carne guisada he had on his plate in front of him.

The food was already on the table by the time Don Celestino came back from the restroom, where he'd checked his sugar level. He had ordered the enchiladas verdes, Socorro the taquitos, and Don Fidencio the menudo. Once the old man started eating, he barely looked up from his bowl. Now and then he stopped between slurping his soup to take a deep breath and chew a tougher piece of tripe. His few remaining teeth clicked in a staccato manner as he gnawed at the meat until he could swallow it.

"Do you remember the last time you ate menudo?" Socorro asked.

He raised his hand to indicate she had caught him in midchew.

"Sometimes they serve it there," he answered finally, "but never with enough spices because people would be burping all night."

"Maybe it's better that way, so you can sleep."

"I barely sleep anyway, at least that way I would have a good reason," Don Fidencio said, and spooned up some hominy. "Last night I spent it lying there, staring at the ceiling.

I would sleep for twenty or thirty minutes, then wake up and just be there. It came and went like that until the early morning, when I remembered something more from our grandfather's story and couldn't sleep anymore. And finally, after another hour, they served breakfast."

"You should write it down," she said, "so it stays with you."

He looked up at her and then at his brother.

"It was nothing that important, just something about when the Indians were attacking them." He slurped up another spoonful. "And anyway, nobody wants to know what an old man remembers."

"Come on and say it," Don Celestino told him. "We've been waiting to hear what you would come up with for the next chapter."

"So you can make fun? No, I prefer to stay with my mouth shut."

"Go on, we want to hear what more you remember."

"I prefer to keep it to myself." He stirred his soup without looking up.

"And if you forget it later?" she asked.

He hadn't considered this. The girl had a point: so much had slipped away from him once. What's to say it wouldn't happen again? This afternoon he could lie down for his nap and wake up to find his memory had been erased completely or smeared to the point of being indistinguishable, like some of the names in his address book. At least if he told it to the girl — Socorro — she could hold on to it for him and tell him later, if he couldn't remember it himself.

"He told me a circus had already traveled through most of Mexico when it arrived in the north and stopped in Linares, before they planned to travel over to this side of the river. All of the families from around there went to see this circus. None of them had ever in their lives seen a bear or an elephant or whatever else they had brought in the circus. It wasn't like those fancy circuses they have today. This one was just a man who came to town with a few wagons full of animals nobody had ever seen. He stopped the wagons in an open field close to a river that passed through one side of town. I think it was in the fall when this took place, but it could've also been the spring, or the summer. But maybe not the spring because they would have been busy in the fields." He stopped to rub the back of his neck, then shook his head. "He told me when it was that it happened, only I forgot that part even before my mind turned to cheese. What I remember was, the circus man had brought out the bear tied to a thick rope, but with so many people crowded around and Papá Grande only seven years old, he could barely see what the animal was doing. His brother was younger and could see even less, but then their father had the good idea to put Papá Grande up on his back so he could be higher. And their uncle did the same with the little brother. Now that he was higher, Papá Grande could see the bear standing on a block of wood and then standing on one paw, then on the other. The bear did more tricks, but by then Papá Grande didn't see them because something had caught his eye. Off in the distance, past the field and away from the river, he could see some horses. They were still more than half a mile away when he spotted them. At first he thought they were just horses, but when they got closer, he could see men on the horses and that these men were Indians."

The old man scratched at the crown of his head. "He never said exactly how many of them — but I guess maybe twenty or more, enough that he should have told his father or his uncle. Maybe he thought the Indians and horses were part of the circus, because he only kept watching them get closer and closer without opening his mouth. If he had, maybe it would have turned out different."

"Maybe he was scared," Socorro said.

"Not as much as when they grabbed his uncle, the one they scalped — it could have been his uncle they scalped first or maybe it was the circus man — I have trouble remembering which one they got hold of first. But it was with all the confusion that he got separated from his mother and his little brother, since she must have been trying to hide him somewhere. Then Papá Grande saw when the first arrow hit his father. That was the other part I remembered, how they killed him." The old man stopped to point down to exactly where. "Right to the bladder was where the arrow got him and how he bled to death. This is the man who would be our great-grandfather."

The waitress refilled Don Fidencio's coffee cup, and he took his time adding the Sweet'N Low and then the creamer. Though his brother and Socorro had finished with their meals, he was only halfway through his bowl of menudo.

"So then to the bladder?" Don Celestino asked.

"Yes, down there to the bladder."

"And you are sure he said it was there, nowhere else?"

"That was the way Papá Grande remembered it, to the bladder." The old man used his butter knife to show him where again.

His brother only halfway nodded.

"What?"

"No, nothing."

"No, nothing what?"

"It just seems like a curious place for the arrow to hit him, that's all."

"And what is so curious about it? The bladder is a part of the body, every man has one. The Indian could have hit him anywhere — in the stomach, in the heart, in the kidneys — but he hit him in the bladder, like I just said."

"Not the appendix?"

Don Fidencio set the butter knife back on the table. "Already I told you what I remembered, the way he told it to me that last time. When I was there, not you."

"I think you might be confused with that one part," Don Celestino said. "How would he know where exactly the arrow got him, that it was exactly in the bladder, if he was only seven years old? At that age, what could he know about a man's bladder?"

"He knew enough just seeing where the arrow was sticking out of his father."

"And that was the only arrow that got him?"

"Maybe it wasn't the only arrow," Don Fidencio said. "I said an arrow to the bladder killed him — that's all I said.

Who cares how many or where the others went? You think Papá Grande sat there counting the arrows that were sticking out of his father, writing it down, so that later you might believe the story?"

"I was only saying it seemed strange that the arrow would hit him right there."

"Go talk to the Indians about that — they were the ones who did it."

"Which Indians?"

"The Indians that attacked the circus," the old man snapped. "Now who is the one that can't remember things?"

"He means what kind," Socorro said.

"Just Indians, the kind that ride horses and shoot arrows, what more do you want me to tell you? All I know is the army had been trying to kill them off or send them to the north, but over here they were also trying to get rid of them. Nobody wanted them around."

"But which ones? Comanche, Apache . . ." Don Celestino tried to remember others, but they weren't coming to him right then. "How can you say, 'Just Indians'?"

"I can say whatever I want." He took a sip of his coffee. "The thing is, you're always against me. Only because I know more about our grandfather and where he came from, more than some people."

"Yes, Fidencio Rosales, the one who knows everything there is to know, even how much I cared about our grandfather."

"If for real you cared, you would at least take me to see the ranchito. It wouldn't matter that you refused to believe what happened, you would still take me."

"Again with your ideas?" Don Celestino leaned back against the booth.

"You said we could go one of these days, you said it, that I remember."

"And tell me how you expect to go in your condition?"

"You make more out of it than it is," he said, and kicked at the walker. "I use this thing only because those women stole my canes. If not, I would be walking fine, same as always, same as I did for forty-two years, and then they couldn't keep me locked up. Against my wishes, they have me there."

"And if you get tired?"

"Then I rest, like I do now. Being tired is not going to kill me. Ya, I would've been dead for years if that was all it took. And anyway, this is just for a couple of days. We could leave in the morning and be there by the afternoon and start looking for the ranchito. And only for a day if you wanted, coming back the next day or the one after that, if we needed to rest."

"If you needed to rest, not me," his brother said.

"What I mean to say is that however it turns out, it wouldn't take so long. Just for a few days to go there and back, so that way you could get back to your house."

Don Celestino thought about how he had just flipped the calendar to a new month, March, then reviewed each day, comparing it to February and January, and tried to fill in as many squares as possible—*take trash can out to curb, buy groceries, pay utility bill, check air-conditioner filter.* He looked at his brother and for just a second he imagined what the calendar might look like with a big *X* across at least a couple of those days.

"But still, all that way to see a ranchito?"

"I checked and it was only four or five hours by bus," Socorro said. "If it was me, I would think it was a short trip. And then on the way back maybe you and your brother would have one less thing to argue about."

Don Celestino turned as if he'd forgotten she was sitting next to him in the booth.

"You wanted to go?"

"Maybe, if somebody invited me."

21

The trip, as it turned out, was shorter than any of them had imagined. At dinnertime Don Fidencio happened to mention it to The Gringo With The Ugly Finger and The One With The Worried Face, who in turn mentioned it to The One With The Flat Face, who in turn mentioned it to The One With The Big Ones, who in turn mentioned it over the phone to Amalia, who then called her father to say she wasn't going to let him take a trip to someplace that probably didn't exist anymore, if it ever did. She reminded him several times, as if he might have forgotten, that she was his legal guardian now.

And it didn't matter how much he complained or who he wanted to call a son of a bitch or who he wanted to say was to blame for all this — the fact that he was being taken care of as if he were an invalid, the fact that they kept making him take so many pills, the fact that they thought he needed more assistance when he needed less, less, less, the fact that they had stolen his canes only to make it look like he did need more assistance, the fact that because of all this she was now claiming that he was too weak to be going anywhere — because he still wasn't going anywhere. Don Fidencio tried to explain that the trip wouldn't take so long, a couple of days at most, but she wasn't listening. No was no. He finally slammed the phone down, then called her back two more times, but only so he could do it again.

Later he called his brother and this time went ahead and left the news on his answering machine (calling back three times because the woman on the recording kept cutting him off before he could spit out all the details). And no, there was no reason to call him back. What was there to talk about? She said it herself, he was too old to be going on trips. She left word with the people in charge of the prison. "The One Already Halfway Dead does not have permission to leave the building, not even for just a couple of days." For nothing.

He spent the rest of that day and the next morning in his room, taking his meals in bed, and came out the next afternoon only when he needed to go outside to smoke. Four of The Turtles had gathered near the large window inside the recreation room, hoping to see the grackles that poked around in the grass. The Turtle With The Fedora knocked on the window to get his attention. When he turned, she motioned for him to move away, find someplace else for his vices, not in the one area reserved for the poor little birds. Don Fidencio stared back at The Turtle With The Fedora with the same lifeless stare he had given the grackles. Then he stood up, steadying his hunched-over body, and without using his walker shuffled over to the window. He reached into his pocket for his cigarettes, drew one out, tapped the end of it on the back of his splotchy hand, then steadily guided it to his waiting lips. It took a few clicks on the lighter before he could make his thumb hold down the tiny lever that kept the flame going. The Turtle With The Fedora looked over her shoulder and said something to The Turtles gathered around her, all of whom shook their heads in unison. She was turning back toward the window when the old man blew a cloud of smoke toward her face.

The Turtles filed out in their wheelchairs, one by one, just as Don Celestino walked through the recreation room to get to the patio. Near the corner of the back fence, one of the male grackles had hopped onto a rotting stump and was using its beak to poke around inside, as if it had found something to eat, a termite or some other insect. Two of the other grackles came to investigate, but the larger one scared them off by flapping its wings.

"They let you smoke out here?" Don Celestino asked.

His brother shrugged, then scooted over to one side of the stone bench. "And why not?"

"You need to take care of your health."

"For what, if this is where they send you when you are ready to die?"

"Just because she said no this time doesn't mean anything. Maybe later she could change her mind."

"You mean when I get a little older?" Don Fidencio drew from his cigarette and cocked his head back to exhale. "No, she just wants me to stay here with all the other strangers who are waiting for their next home." He used his chin to motion toward the ground in case there was any doubt in his brother's mind where this next place might be.

Don Fidencio tapped his cigarette, and the ashes floated onto the patio and then off into the yard. A one-legged grackle was hopping in lopsided circles, carelessly drawing itself closer and closer to the bench, as if it sensed that the old man was preoccupied at the moment.

"What if we went somewhere else that was closer?" Don Celestino asked. "I was thinking we could drive over to Reynosa, see where you went for your first haircut, maybe the shop is still there."

"Ya, I told you that she said no!" he said, then kicked the ashtray canister and sent it rolling into the grass. The gimpy bird hopped along until it was able to lift off and flutter to the top of the wooden fence.

"You should just go and leave me here."

"So you can say that I left you behind?"

"No, so you won't visit me just because you feel guilty."

"Who said anything about feeling guilty?"

"Why else would you be coming around here?"

The one-legged grackle landed back in the grass, just beyond the ashtray canister that lay on its side. The bird pecked at something in the grass but didn't seem to find what it was searching for. A couple of pecks later it looked at the old man, as if it were asking permission to come closer.

"Maybe if I called and explained to her about the trip," Don Celestino said, "maybe she would listen to me."

"You go," he answered. "You and the girl go on the trip."

"Fidencio."

"I told you to go already, just leave me here." His voice started to crack, and he had to twist around in the other direction before his brother finally got the message and stood up.

The old man turned as his brother was walking inside. The Turtle With The Fedora had come to check on the little birds. He could see her saying something to his brother and then they both looked outside toward the patio. When Don Fidencio turned the other way, the one-legged bird was standing on the next bench, gazing back at him.

22

In the early light of day, he found the orange crumbs on his pillow and pajama top. He looked for the rest of the package in the nightstand and then in the #2 shoe box, but found no sign of his last two crackers. After a while he went back to the closet and checked the other four shoe boxes. He figured one of the aides must have come while he was sleeping. The ones on the night shift were the worst, always lurking around in the shadows, waiting for the first chance to go through a sleeping man's things.

The hall was clear all the way to the nurses' station. No Turtles, no hampers, no food carts stacked with trays. This was the best part of the day to be moving around; the others, if they were awake, would need help getting dressed and into their wheelchairs before they made it out of their rooms.

"Good morning to you, Mr. Rosales," said The One With A Beak For A Nose.

With both hands still on the walker, he raised two fingers to acknowledge her but otherwise kept moving.

"Are you feeling better today, sir?"

Don Fidencio gave her only a half shrug. He was alive and her job was safe for another day. What more did she want from him?

The Turtle With The Fedora was parking her wheelchair across from the nurses' station. She tried rolling forward a bit, as if she might block his path, but he scuttled up enough to the right to miss her. "No, this one has no time to say hello like a decent man," she said. "He wakes up only so he can go make life hard for the poor little birds. For that he's good — nothing else. See how he goes as if he were already late to church, but this is only so he can upset the poor birds."

He turned the walker toward the recreation room and came upon an attendant pushing a broom in his direction. The woman didn't look up or try to exchange pleasantries, and for this he was grateful.

"Buenos días," a voice called out from the far end of the hall. Don Fidencio didn't need to turn around to know who it was. Every morning with his "Buenos días," as if anyone believed he really knew how to speak the language.

"¡Buenos días, Mr. Rosales!" The One With The Big Ones repeated. "Looks like you're doing better today. Like I was sharing with your daughter, 'Just give your father some time, and he'll get to liking things here at Amigoland.' " The voice faded only after Don Fidencio turned the walker toward the patio door.

The three or four grackles on the grass fluttered away when they heard the familiar sound of the walker banging against the glass door. With slow measured steps he moved toward the stone bench. A thin layer of fog shrouded the early-morning sun rising in the distance.

One cigarette. That was all he had to last him until these people served their oatmeal and warmed-over biscuit. He lit the cigarette and took a short draw from it. The tiny ember shone brighter than the muted sun and the faint lights coming from the kitchen. The yardman had left the ashtray canister too far for him to reach without standing. He could feel some of his hunger waning now and he realized it was by pure luck that he had this one cigarette to hold him over. He still wanted to blame the aides for taking his package of crackers, though really it was Amalia who had caused all this. As upset as he had been with her, he knew he shouldn't have stayed in bed so long, most of it lost in one restless dream or another. There was one of these he wanted to recall, but the more he tried to remember, he wasn't sure if it was last night that he'd had it or some other night or if he wasn't getting the pieces all mixed up or if what he thought he dreamed might have been someone else's dream that was told to him. He was with his grandfather, that he knew. His grandfather was a little boy, though. He had never seen a photo of his grandfather as a little boy, but he knew this was who it was. Only instead of also being a little boy in the dream, Don Fidencio was as old as he was when he fell asleep. And still, somehow he was able to stay on the horse that the Indian had him on. He clung to the animal's mane while the Indian sat behind him, holding the reins. Another Indian had his grandfather on the horse next to them. He remembered looking over and the little boy cocking back his head, the same as his grandfather used to do when they were off on some adventure, just the two of them. A perfect crescent moon illuminated the plain that eventually stretched out into the darkness before them. At one point Don Fidencio slipped to one side, so much so that he was underneath the horse, but then somehow spun back around to the top. And when he came back up, he was a little boy. He spun around twice more and kept coming up as a little boy. Then he looked over and noticed that the little boy who was his grandfather had disappeared. The Indian began to speak to him in words that he had never heard before, words that sounded as if he were speaking underwater, words that seemed to come from someplace other than his mouth. Beneath him he could hear the gallop of the horses' hooves upon the barren earth. But the longer the Indian spoke, the more Don Fidencio began to hear the Indian's words in his own Spanish. He tried to ask him a question, but the Indian told him to be quiet, to listen. You need to be ready when the sun comes up, the Indian said. Be ready for what? he asked. Just be ready. What about my grandfather? I know where he is. I need to find him, my grandfather. Just be ready. The horses seemed to be moving in slow motion now. Don Fidencio kept asking questions, but the Indian's voice had trailed off.

He had woken up more achy and tired, as if he really had been riding a horse all night. From then on his sleep came and went, until he woke up for good and finally stepped outside for his morning cigarette. He was playing with the lighter — turning it on, turning it off, turning it on, turning it off, counting how many tries it took to make his thumb do what he wanted — when he heard a noise behind him. He figured it was probably the grackles rooting around the stump again, looking for their own breakfast. But the second time it was more of a metallic sound, like the yardman clicking open the back gate. It was too early for this, though. With the fog still heavy, the first rays of sun had barely reached the patio, and dew clung to the weeds and spots of grass. He tried to turn, but his stiff body helped him only so much.

"Fidencio."

How curious, he thought, the yardman calling me by my first name. They had met once, but this had been months ago, and without exchanging names. Since then it had been a friendly wave or a nod, and usually with Don Fidencio standing at the window because the man tended to do his work during the middle of the afternoon when it was too hot to be sitting outside. Even stranger was that he'd whispered his name. What good reason could one man possibly have for whispering another man's name?

"Fidencio," the voice called out, this time with more urgency.

When he finally turned, his brother was standing at the back gate, leaning in so only his white hair floated there like some apparition. Then his brother motioned for him to come closer. The old man held on to the walker in order to stand and see what this was all about.

"Andale, Fidencio."

"Andale to where?" the old man said, though still not sure why they were speaking in hushed voices. He stamped out what was left of his cigarette.

"Over here, so we can go already."

"To where?" Don Fidencio asked. "Was the front door locked?"

"Over here, just hurry."

"They still need to serve the breakfast. Here, they take their time, like old people don't have stomachs anymore."

Don Celestino glanced over his brother's shoulder at the recreation room. He thought he saw someone in a wheelchair at the window.

"It doesn't matter, just get over here."

"Yes, for you with your stomach happy and full, what does it matter, but for me . . ."

"I came to take you with me." Don Celestino reached for his shoulder. "Do you understand?"

Don Fidencio stared back at his brother, trying to make sense of it all.

"Remember I called you last night?" he said. "I told you we were taking the trip to the other side, to Linares. The way Papá Grande wanted you to, remember?"

The old man held on to him as he stepped out from behind the walker.

"You have to bring it with you, Fidencio."

"Ya, I never want to see that thing again."

"Lower your voice," he said. "For now you need it. Later we can find you something else."

Don Fidencio shook his head and set the walker back in front of him. His brother pushed open the gate until it was wide enough for him to make it through. The taxi was idling at the curb, pointed out toward the main road.

PART IV

23

They drove up just as Socorro was crossing the street in front of the bridge; she waved back before she realized Don Celestino and his brother were sitting in a taxi.

"She changed her mind, then?"

"A man should be able to take a trip if he wants." He had come around the car to kiss her on the cheek and open the door, but she wasn't responding to either gesture.

"Celestino." She stayed where she was on the sidewalk and a man pulling a mini–shopping cart had to step into the grass to avoid bumping into her. "You talked with her, yes or no?"

"So she could tell me no?"

"She got that from her mother," Don Fidencio called out from the backseat. "The both of them were born with heads as hard as that pavement."

"Then what, Celestino?" she asked. "You stole him?"

"How could I steal him?" he said. "If he came on his own, that's not stealing."

Down the street the traffic had just stopped at the light and a moment later a patrol car eased up behind the other cars.

"You took an old man without permission."

"Why when I call him an old man, you say he's my brother, and now I help him, and you say he's an old man?"

"You know what I mean, Celestino."

"You were the one who said we should take the trip."

"For all of us to go together, yes — not for you to steal him!"

"Please stop saying it that way and just get in the taxi."

"For what?" she said. "So they can take us all to jail?"

"Nothing's going to happen," he said, and tried not to flinch when he heard what he thought were sirens. The traffic at the light was pulling to one side.

"Answer me," Socorro said. "How could you, knowing the problems you were going to cause?"

"He promised he would go back," Don Celestino said. "Just for a couple of days. We take him to see the ranchito and after that we can come home."

He had more to say about this, but he was watching the patrol car turn the corner that led away from the bridge, back in the direction they had come from earlier.

Socorro walked away, toward the front of the taxi, as if she might suddenly turn and cross the bridge. Most of the other cleaning women had either caught their rides or taken the bus. When she glanced back, the old man was in the backseat, fiddling with his suspenders, causing his shirt to untuck. He had buttoned his shirt the wrong way and it looked as if one shoulder was higher than the other. They must have stopped along the way to eat something because crumbs and grease stains blotched the front of his clothes. Beneath his cap, the sleep had stayed crusted to the corner of his left eye.

"And the medicines?" she asked.

"The medicines?" Don Celestino said.

"Please tell me you weren't going to take him without his medicines."

"No, no, of course not," he said. "I was going to buy them for him. How could we go without the medicines?"

"So, then?"

"Maybe your friend that works at the pharmacy can help us."

"No, no more medicines," the old man said, and wagged his finger at them.

"Please, Don Fidencio, this is so you can go on your trip."

"Ya, I have taken enough pills!" He was still motioning with his finger. "No more, I tell you. At least that, at least let me live like a normal man."

Don Celestino squatted down next to the rear door of the taxi. "Look, you want to go on this trip or you want us to drive you back?"

"You already said you would take me."

"Not if you were going to get sick on us. So you can end up in the hospital? Is that what you want, to be sick in another bed?"

This seemed to quiet the old man. He shook his head a little longer before he swung open his door for Socorro.

"Stay where you are, Don Fidencio."

"No," he said, "so you and your man can be together in the backseat."

He planted his feet squarely on the curb but kept rocking back and forth, not quite making it off the seat, until his brother gave him a hand. After he was finally standing on the sidewalk, Socorro brushed off the crumbs and then redid the buttons on his shirt while he stood there looking like a man being measured for a new suit.

24

This early in the morning there was hardly any traffic on the bridge going to the other side. The driver paid the toll, and less than a minute later they had crossed over. On the other bridge, headed in the opposite direction, two rows of cars and trucks inched along toward the U.S. checkpoint. The pedestrian line that Socorro had used to cross over only a few minutes earlier now extended the full length of the bridge.

Up ahead, the taxi driver slowed down for the speed bumps leading to the mini–traffic light in front of the customs building. Red meant you had to pull over for one of the inspectors to look in your trunk before permitting you to drive on; green meant you were free to move forward.

"But these men need their papers to travel," Socorro said, as the driver continued on.

"That, they can do at the bus station, and much faster, with no lines."

Don Celestino patted her hand. "The man knows — he takes people to the bus station all the time, right?"

"Only for the last seventeen years," he said, glancing in the rearview mirror.

Away from the bridge the city buses swelled with people's arms and faces in the open windows. The more hopeful of the street vendors were setting up for that occasional tourist who might wander over this early in the day. The homemade-candy vendors stood guard over their glass stands, shooing away the incessant flies and bees. A young man with tire shanks for knees crawled between the cars, hustling along the pavement to catch up to an arm reaching out with a few pesos. A barefoot boy, hunched over as he carried a three-foot-high crucifix on his back, searched for his next customer among the idling traffic. On this side of the street, a city worker in green coveralls was raising a small dust storm with her thatched broom. Next to a taxi stand, a driver in a yellow muscle shirt was haggling with a sunburned tourist, while his equally sunburned wife and kids waited on the sidewalk, trying not to touch anything. A skinny woman, holding two nylon-woven bags teeming with groceries, berated her three kids as she crammed them into a packed Maxi-Taxi van. Farther down a campesino rode atop his wooden cart as his burro clomped along, both of them scornful of the honking cars and trucks behind them.

After the second block they were able to get beyond some of the congestion and speed the rest of the way down Calle Obregón, passing the restaurants, the bars, the discos, the curio shops, the occasional boutique or doctor's office or dentist's office, and several pharmacies other than the one they were looking for. The driver, a slight man with reddish-brown skin and a smallish head, had to keep pushing his oversize aviator glasses back up his thin nose. Once he was closer to the center of town he turned on his radio so everyone on the street could hear the cumbia playing over the sound of his muffler. He especially wanted to impress the young mother pushing the stroller near Plaza Hidalgo, but the girl paid as much attention to him as she did to the babbling coming from her baby.

Don Fidencio rolled down his window to get some air. Later it would rain; he didn't need a weatherman to tell him this, he felt it in his knees, especially the weaker of the two. Across the street he could make out the cathedral's conical spires rising higher and higher into the grayish sky like a pair of matching dunce caps. If they weren't in such a rush, he would tell the driver to pull over so he could get his shoes shined at one of the stands in the plaza. These black-rubber-soled shoes weren't the kind one would normally think to shine, but at the same time it was a good idea to make sure they were presentable before arriving in Linares. Not that anybody would've paid attention to what an old man had to say. If they hadn't listened to him about the pills, what chance was there that they would stop now? Pills for his heart. Pills for his blood pressure. Pills for his cholesterol. Pills for his kidneys. Pills for his heartburn. Pills for the pain in his legs. Pills for him to make cacas. Pills for him to sleep. Pills for this pill or that other pill not to make him sick. Everybody wanted to give him a pill, whether he wanted it or not. Breakfast, lunch, dinner, they always had a pill for him. Like he might die if they didn't force another pill down his throat before he finished his meal. The One With The White Pants used to push his cart through the mess hall like it was a hot summer day and he was selling paletas to all the kids who had been only waiting for him to ring his bell and now they were going to chase him down the street with money in their hands. *Please, sir, give me just one more for my heartburn — I can feel the meat loaf coming up already. No, me first, me first. I need one for the terrible pain in my big toe. I want one for my arthritis. Me first, sir, me first. Me, me, me!!! Give me one of those big pills you would not feed to a horse! Please, sir, me first!*

25

Chayo raised her glasses, holding them up close to her face, then removed them altogether since they were really only reading glasses and at the moment she didn't have anything in front of her to read, not a prescription, not a label off an old vial, not the name of a medicine scribbled in English on a piece of paper that she could then look up in her big red book with all the proper medications listed in Spanish. The glasses were attached to a silver-beaded necklace that she was knotting up between her fingers until she finally let it rest against the front of her blue smock. Then she and Socorro moved to one end of the counter while the two men lingered at the other end: Don Fidencio, near a small rack of sunglasses, trying on the various styles; Don Celestino, next to a plastic display, where he was sniffing an open tube of brilliantine.

"You can pretend the medicines are for my mother," Socorro said, reaching out for her hand.

"Your mother, I have known for many years," Chayo replied.

"But remember that first time, how I came here and you hadn't met her?"

"That was different. By then your mother had been to many doctors. You showed me what they had given her."

"Don Fidencio has been to the doctor many times."

"Yes, but who can say what they prescribed for him?" She let go of Socorro's hand. "Here you have me in the dark. All you can tell me is that he needs medicines for his blood pressure and cholesterol, so he will not urinate so frequently, and because he had a stroke not that long ago, and the rest only God knows. Like that, you want me to guess, like I was his doctor."

"Only enough for a little while, for a few days, until we get back from the trip."

"At a great risk, and not just for him — for you, for me," Chayo said. "Tell me what you are going to do if he gets sick anyway or if I give him the wrong medicines and they do him harm. Then what?"

They both turned when the door chimed. The security guard smiled briefly as he held open the door for a young pregnant woman with two young children, then he went back to crossing his arms over his flak jacket. Chayo excused herself to attend to some of the other customers that had entered the small pharmacy. She left Socorro waiting at the end of the counter near the display of mentholated lozenges and the long glass case containing various brands of condoms and contact solutions. A string of Telmex phone cards, each wrapped in plastic, dangled from the register inside a Plexiglas booth. The cashier girl counted off the colorful bills in front of her, arranging them into disheveled stacks. At one point she looked up at Socorro and gave her the passive smile of someone who isn't paid enough to be genuinely pleasant. Then she entered an amount into an office calculator and waited for the machine to produce a receipt before sticking it and two of the stacks of bills into a metal box beneath the register. The pregnant woman was now lingering near the booth, holding one child in the cradle of her right arm and carrying another in a stroller. She wanted to know what size diapers she should buy if she needed one that fit both a seven-month-old and an eighteen-month-old. Chayo told her that, unfortunately, she would have to buy different sizes, but today she would make her a special price on the Pampers.

Once she had taken care of her customer, she and Socorro walked to the counter where she kept the pharmaceutical book.

"Just tell me how you want me to feel doing something like this?"

"If we have to, we can find a doctor," Socorro said.

"The doctor you should have found before you brought him here. Before, not later. That's how it is supposed to happen. These medicines are not for taking chances."

"And if he goes with no medicines?"

Chayo turned toward the center of the store as the old man was trying on a pair of dark sunglasses and crouching to see himself in the tiny mirror. The squared frames were the kind his doctor had given him years ago after removing his cataracts. He held them against his brow, then stared up at the fluorescent lights as if he were staring into the sun. When he looked back down, he lost his balance and staggered forward, in the direction of the sunglass rack, but at the last second grabbed hold of the walker to correct himself.

"Only so you can go for a few days," Chayo said, shaking her head, "and nothing too strong. After that you have to promise to take him to a doctor, with someone who can prescribe some real medicine. A man his age and in that condition needs special care."

She reached for the beaded necklace that held her glasses, sliding her fingers down it as if she were counting off each bead on a rosary. Then she walked around to the other side of the counter and opened the big red book.

The old man clung to his brother's arms as he made his way down the three steps from the pharmacy. The security guard was kind enough to carry the walker and open it again on the sidewalk.

They were about to walk back to the taxi when Don Fidencio noticed an old india sitting in the shade near the bottom step, her cupped and pleading hand stretched out in their direction. The frayed rebozo draped the edges of her withered face and then stretched out to cover what at first appeared to be a child but was only the swollen curve of her back. He reached into his pocket for some change, but all he found was his lighter.

"Here," Don Celestino said, and handed him the change from the medicines.

The old man dropped a few pesos into the india's hand and she hid the coins somewhere under her rebozo. Then she nodded and, raising the same hand, said, "May God bless you with a long life."

The old man stared at her, wondering if he shouldn't take his money back or at least ask for a more useful blessing. He was about to say something to her, but he could feel his brother tugging at his arm.

26

Now he sat in a plastic chair with a Carta Blanca beer logo against the backrest. His brother and the girl had helped him get to the little café and bought him a bottle of water so he could take his medicines while they went to buy the tickets. Don Fidencio's job was to keep an eye on his plastic bag with the medicines and his brother's leather pouch that had his insulin, making sure nobody ran off with them.

Dust swirled through the open doors at either end of the central station. Down the middle of the lobby, a young man, maybe only as tall as his dust broom, plowed the never-ending trash, which included receipts, cigarette butts, and candy wrappers that people preferred to toss on the floor rather than into one of the nearby trash cans. Where the old man sat, the space was lined with a tiny convenience store that appeared to sell only frozen treats and sex magazines, a pharmacy offering minor travel remedies along with an assortment of salty snacks, an open-sided café serving quick meals already under the heat lamps, and, just beyond the front doors, a counter where a porter would store luggage for a small hourly fee. On the opposite side, the eight bus counters, each with its own set of uniformed attendants, stretched the length of the lobby. So far his brother and the girl had stopped at three of the counters.

When he turned back, a barefoot little boy was standing next to the table. Several dime-size patches blotted his thick crew cut. A smear of yellowed mocos had dried under his nose.

"Buy my Chiclets, sir," the boy said, extending a grubby hand with several packets of fluorescent-colored gum.

"No," the old man answered.

"Buy my Chiclets, please, sir." He tilted his head to one side.

Don Fidencio lifted a finger and wagged it at the boy.

"Come on, sir, buy my Chiclets."

"I don't want any Chiclets."

Don Fidencio looked back across the lobby. His brother and the girl were talking to an attendant behind one of the counters.

"Buy my Chiclets, sir."

"Are you one of those little deaf boys? I told you, 'No Chiclets.'"

The little boy stared back for a second. "Are you blind?"

"Do I look blind to you?"

"You wear those dark glasses," the little boy replied. "The same as Macario The Blind Man wears."

"I'm not blind. Now go, leave me alone."

"People say Macario is not blind, but they still call him Macario The Blind Man, and the other people who don't know give him money."

"These are called sunglasses," Don Fidencio said.

"But we're inside, where the sun never comes out."

"Leave me alone already."

"Buy my Chiclets."

"I have no money."

"But, sir, the Chiclets cost nothing, only four pesos."

"Go away."

"Then I will give them to you for two pesos."

"Already I said no."

"But why?"

"Finally," Don Celestino said, walking up to the table. "None of them have direct service to Linares. We had to buy tickets to Ciudad Victoria, and from there we can make the connection."

Don Fidencio spread his legs so he could begin to stand up. "I was thinking I was going to spend the day here, sleeping in this bus station."

"You made a friend?" Socorro said.

"Please, lady, buy my Chiclets." The boy tilted his head to one side.

"Ignore him. If not, he'll follow us all over Mexico," said Don Fidencio.

"What flavors do you have?" She bent down to look at the packets.

"All the best ones," the little boy answered, opening his carton the whole way.

She plucked out four packets, two white and two purple, then handed him the money. The little boy thanked her and ran off.

Don Fidencio shook his head. "I never would have bought from that boy."

"I know," Socorro replied, "but you got your Chiclets anyway." She pulled open his shirt pocket and deposited the four packets.

Don Celestino helped him get to his feet before grabbing the plastic bag and his pouch. They were halfway to the terminal when Socorro stopped to look back.

"Your walker, Don Fidencio."

His brother rushed over to get it for him.

"Leave it," the old man said. "I can make my way without it." He continued to hobble along, his body leaning forward as if the walker were still in front of him.

"And if you fall?" Don Celestino moved the frame toward him.

"How's that going to happen, sitting inside a bus station?" he said. "You two are worse than those women at the prison. I could walk fine before they left me with this thing."

"What if you use the walker just for now and later I go buy you a new cane?" Socorro said.

"And where are you going to find a cane?"

"Anywhere, on the street or at the mercado, then you can have a brand-new one."

The old man considered the girl's words.

"Then I can use just the cane and no more walker?"

"Yes, just the cane, no more with the walker," Don Celestino said.

"And how do I know you won't make me use it again later?"

"We can give it to somebody or throw it away if you want."

The old man leaned his weight back on the walker. "This better not be a lie," he said, "just to fool an old man."

Don Celestino held open the glass door, and his brother shuffled down the narrow hallway. A large glassed-in bulletin board covered the section of the wall that travelers were most likely to see upon arriving at this northern border. Pushing the walker in a straight line required too much of the old man's attention for him to read any of the notices or catch a glimpse of the black-and-white photos of dead bodies strewn across the scrubland, one revealing only her face inside the unzipped body bag. Up ahead he could make out a sign directing them to their next stop, INMIGRACIÓN.

A digital clock was blinking in one corner of the small, dark office. Through a missing section of the blinds, Don Celestino could make out the desk and chair where somebody should have been sitting.

"The security guard says they have different hours every day," Socorro said as she walked up. "That we need to wait a few minutes, but if they left for lunch, it could also be later this afternoon."

"And our papers to travel?"

Socorro answered with only a shrug.

Don Fidencio used the walker to steady himself as he stood up from one of the plastic chairs in the terminal. "I can just imagine if when I was still working we had opened the post office only when we felt like it."

"Where are you going?" his brother asked.

"I need to go make water, or do I need to ask your permission?" He pushed the walker ahead of him, taking one heavy step after another, as though he had one more acre to plow before the sun went down.

Don Celestino caught up with him as he was parking the walker to one side of the stairs. "You're going to kill yourself going up there."

"And tell me what choice I have," Don Fidencio answered, then pointed back in the direction of the corded-off elevator. "You want me to have an accident?"

He took a deep breath and, with his brother at his side, started climbing. There were eight steps between the ground floor and the first landing, and from there the staircase turned right and there was no telling how many more steps there were to the second floor. In between, a framed portrait of the Virgen de Guadalupe, adorned with a cluster of flickering candles and a display of plastic flowers set on a metal shelf, hung from the wall just above the landing. Below the shelf, a rusty padlock secured the collection box. Normally people about to travel to a nearby ranchito or as far away as Tuxtla Gutiérrez would stop to ask the Virgen for providence on their journey, to keep their ailing mother alive until they were able to arrive, to keep the bus driver awake and alert, to keep any bandits from trying to stop the bus in the middle of the night, or just to keep the porters from searching through their modest packages for any valuables. But Don Fidencio asked her only to provide him with enough strength to make it up the remaining three steps to the landing, then the next flight, all of this without losing his balance and toppling backward down the steps, particularly because he could see himself getting entangled with his guide, who would most likely land on top of him, and then for sure he would crack open his old melon.

"That wasn't so bad," Don Celestino said as they reached the landing.

The old man looked at him and then up at the Virgen's compassionate eyes. If he hadn't already asked her for so much, he would beg her to find something else for his brother to do; if he was going to fall, he preferred to do this unaccompanied. Instead, he leaned against the railing with both hands and tried to gather the strength he needed for the remaining eight steps.

After more than a minute of standing there and people having to step around them, Don Celestino grabbed him by the elbow. "Ready?"

The old man yanked his arm away, again counted the steps leading to the second floor, and began climbing. He took the first three steps without thinking about them too much, simply lifting his right leg, pulling up his weaker leg to the same step, then repeating. His brother followed closely behind, ready to help should he need it. This time Don Fidencio kept his head down and focused on the motion of his legs and feet. He gripped the railing tighter when a young boy chased his sister up the stairs and they both brushed up against him. It was only a matter of time before he fell over: if his legs didn't give out on him, it would be on account of these people allowing their children to run loose like farm animals.

When they reached the second floor, Don Fidencio pushed open the glass door and then paused. He looked at his brother, standing next to him now. He knew there had to be a reason they had climbed all the way up the stairs. The girl, they had left downstairs, with the walker and the plastic bag full of medicines. The concession stand was downstairs. The guards were downstairs. The immigration office with no immigration officer was downstairs. He remembered it was urgent, whatever it was that had forced him up here. Why else risk his life climbing the stairs? A young man with white jeans and matching cowboy boots was walking toward him. He flapped his hands, then patted them dry on the sides of his jeans.

"And now what are you waiting for?" Don Celestino asked.

"I was just catching my breath."

"You want me to go the rest of the way with you?"

"So I can use the toilet?" he said. "No, I can go alone."

"Are you sure?" He was still holding him by the arm.

"For what, you want to take it out for me?"

His brother released him, and the old man continued down the hall. If he knew anything about his body, the urge to relieve himself would return momentarily; it always did. That merciless pecan or peach seed, whatever it was, would see to it.

A middle-aged woman wearing a green smock sat on a bar stool just behind the turnstile that led into the men's and women's restrooms. Her dark bangs hung in an uneven line that reached almost low enough to hide her furrowed brow. From her expression, it seemed something bitter had lodged itself between her molars. On the turnstile sat a cigar box where she kept her large bills, some of which stuck out along the edges. In front of the box stood a set of tiny columns made up of centavos and a few smaller pesos that a sly hand would be less likely to want to make off with. Hanging from the turnstile, a cardboard sign announced the DOS PESOS entry fee.

"Buenos días," Don Fidencio said.

"Buenas tardes," the woman corrected him.

He glanced at his watch and smiled at her.

"You wanted to use the services?"

"Only to freshen up a little before the long bus ride."

She tapped on the cardboard sign.

"Even to go in and just to turn around and come back out?" He twirled a finger in the air to show her how quick he would be.

"If all you want to do is turn around, that you can do right here, for free."

"But to go inside?"

Again, she pointed to the sign. "Maybe you can't see with those glasses."

A short, tubby man in a dark tie brushed up against him.

"Go ahead." She dropped the pesos into the slot, and the man pushed through the turnstile.

"And him?"

"He works downstairs," she said. "Are you just going to stand there, in everyone's way?"

Don Fidencio swayed a bit as he tried to keep his balance.

"I have a need to be here."

"And tell me, who doesn't have a need to be here?"

After looking at her for a few seconds and realizing he would have to irrigate the front of the turnstile before this sour woman would allow him to pass, he turned to go back and borrow some money from his brother.

Socorro was waiting at the bottom of the stairs when they finally made it back down. She held on to the walker and had set the plastic bag and leather pouch inside the wire basket.

"We need to hurry. Already they started boarding."

"And the papers?" Don Celestino asked.

"The guard says you can get them when the bus stops at the first checkpoint."

Don Celestino took his pouch from the basket and they walked toward the security post that led out to the buses. The same clean-shaven guard Socorro had spoken to earlier signaled for them to move on through security since they had no real luggage to speak of. The driver stood near the bus door, waiting for the last few passengers. The dark shade of his suit and tie matched the blazer and short skirt worn by the young attendant. She tore Don Celestino's tickets in half and handed him three small plastic bags, each filled with a snack and a bottle of purified water. Socorro packed everything into her own bag as she boarded the bus.

Don Fidencio was still trying to figure out how to get the walker through the narrow entrance. He had tried twice and each time the frame collided with the sides.

"That, we need to fold up and store down below, with the luggage," Don Celestino said. "Give it to me so I can hand it to the boy." The porter was squatting near the middle of the bus, rearranging the last packages to go into the luggage compartment.

Don Fidencio ignored him, though, as if by his waiting a little longer, the entrance might widen or the walker shrink in size.

His brother tapped him on the shoulder. "You should go find your seat, and I'll take care of storing it."

"I can give it to him by myself," the old man snapped. "You think I need your help for everything, like a little baby? Leave me and go sit with the girl."

Don Celestino stared at his brother for a moment, then boarded the bus. A tall man, holding a briefcase in one hand and a large pillow in the other, sat in the front seat. Behind him, a younger man with a long blondish ponytail sat in the aisle seat, while his guitar case sat upright in the window seat. A couple of rows back, an elderly woman held her granddaughter, who was resting her head on the old woman's lap. Across from them, a gaunt man kept his hand on his wife's very pregnant belly. None of these people or any of the other passengers so much as looked up as Don Celestino was making his way toward the middle of the bus.

"And your brother?" Socorro asked.

"He was giving his walker to the boy so he could store it underneath."

"They already closed the space," she said, leaning over again to glance out the window.

They both turned when they heard the driver let out a moan as he removed his jacket and placed it on a wire hanger inside his compartment. Once he was seated, he spent a few seconds stroking the bristles of his mustache in the rearview mirror, then pulled the lever to close the door. Don Celestino started for the front of the bus, but he had to slow down for a woman in the aisle who was stuffing her bag into the luggage rack.

"Wait," Socorro called out. "I see him now."

Don Fidencio was walking toward the front, steadying himself with one hand against the side of the bus. The driver opened the door and stood up to help him climb the three high steps, each one more arduous than the last. Once at the top, the old man grabbed hold of the luggage rack and staggered forward until he reached his seat.

Don Celestino turned to look over his seat back. "I thought you were giving it to the boy. What took you so long?"

"Nothing," he answered. "Why do I have to give you a report?"

The driver closed the door again. After he had cleaned his yellow-tinted aviator glasses, he inserted a videocassette into the VCR, and several monitors dropped down from the luggage rack. A pretty female attendant, dressed the same as the real-life attendant outside, only this one with light-brown hair and with not as dark a complexion, appeared on the screen to explain all the luxury features on Omnibuses de México, including a quiet and relaxing ride, roomy seats that reclined to the passengers' comfort, a wide selection of feature films that were sure to entertain, and, of course, the cleanest restrooms. The image of the pretty attendant segued to footage of the bus coasting through the Mexican countryside.

When the video ended, the driver took a final look at the instrument panel and crossed himself, then dug a finger into his tight collar and pulled out a thin gold necklace with a San Cristóbal pendant, which he gently kissed before stuffing it back in his shirt. The porter squeegeed the windshield one last time, then signaled thumbs-up when he was done, but the driver was more interested in waving good-bye to the young attendant. After she gave him the same cursory smile she gave to every other driver of Omnibuses de México, he slid the gearshift into reverse. The bus glided backward only a couple of inches before the back wheels lurched up and then down again with a harsh grinding sound. The driver slammed on the brakes, jerking all the passengers forward and then back into their seats. A few seconds later the porter dragged out a flattened metal frame with three plastic wheels still dangling from it, the fourth rolling aimlessly through the parking lot. Socorro and Don Celestino glanced over their seats, but the old man was already leaning back with his eyes closed, about to take his first peaceful nap in some time.

27

When they had passed the last of the grocery stores and car dealerships and tire-repair shops and fried-chicken restaurants and Pemex stations, the road narrowed from a bustling four-lane, with lush plants and shrubs growing along the median, to a narrow two-lane, with only a pair of white stripes that served as the shoulders. The ranch-style houses, mixed in with cinder-block houses, were set several feet from the road, leaving a dirt path on either side for those traveling by foot or hoof.

Near the edge of town, the driver stopped for a young man wearing a muscle shirt and baggy shorts, and on his shoulder carrying a wicker basket. His bellows of "¡Tortas! ¡Tortas!" roused Don Fidencio from his nap. He looked up in time to see the vendor had passed him and stopped to sell his food to one of the other passengers.

"Give me some money, before he comes back," the old man said, leaning forward.

"Why do you want to waste money?" Don Celestino handed him one of the plastic bags the attendant had given them. "We have your lunch right here, already paid for with the ticket."

He opened the bag and found two triangle halves of a sandwich and a small bag of Japanese peanuts. "Is this what you're going to feed me for the whole trip? A ham-and-cheese sandwich?"

"It's the same as the tortas."

"At least those are hot."

"That was all they put in the bags, Fidencio."

When his brother didn't take it back, he tossed the plastic bag onto the seat next to him. The bus driver stopped to drop off the torta vendor and then reached over to insert another videocassette. The old man was about to fall back to sleep when the bus filled with Hindu music from the feature film, translated into Spanish as *The Evil Within Both of Us*. A large group of men and women were singing and dancing across an outdoor platform. It seemed to be some sort of family gathering, with children and adults seated at tables around the edges of the stage. When the music reached its climax, the gathering was suddenly disrupted by the arrival of several armed and hooded men. The fathers stood up to defend their families and were gunned down at once, leaving only the women to guard their children. Bodies flew through the air in slow motion, women and children crawled under tables, but the performers continued their singing and dancing. After a few minutes, the old man had trouble following what was happening on the screen. As hard as he tried, he couldn't keep up with the dubbed-over story line, and finally he turned toward the window. Standing in the center of a small plot of land half cleared of the surrounding brush, a shirtless man holding a machete at his side had paused from working. He stared at the bus as if he could make out the old man looking at him through the tinted window. Farther along, the few plots of land made room for the mesquite and huisache and granejo and paloverde, and eventually the vast sea of scrubland broken up only occasionally by a white cross and an arrangement of plastic flowers that marked the last site of an unlucky traveler on this road.

Don Fidencio had his eyes closed for only a few minutes before he felt someone tapping his shoulder.

The old man blinked his eyes open. "Why are you bothering me?"

"We're almost at the checkpoint," Don Celestino said. "I need your driver's license or something with your photo and name so I can get our papers to travel."

"I left all that in my wallet."

"And now tell me how you thought you could go on a trip without your wallet."

"It stayed back there inside my shoe boxes," he said. "The ones you didn't let me bring."

The bus vibrated unsteadily as it rolled across the grated lines on the road and came to a smooth stop under the open-sided checkpoint. The highway continued south and north from this point, but with no other sign of life as far as they could see in either direction. An officer dressed in green pants and khaki shirt approached the bus with a clipboard in hand. Don Celestino reached the front of the bus just as the driver was opening the door to shake hands with the official.

"Excuse me," Don Celestino said, "but the immigration office was closed at the bus station and they told me that I could get our visas here."

"Over there." The official pointed to a single metal office that stood directly across the other lane used for smaller vehicles. "Go knock, see if today you find him in a good mood."

"And hurry," the driver added, "or you'll have to take the next bus."

The men were still laughing as he waited for a large white truck with Texas plates to pass so he could make it across the lane. He found the office door open and an older woman in a long gingham apron mopping the tiled floor. "Is this where I can get a visa?"

"I only clean the office for the one who sits at the desk," the woman replied.

A short pile of blank visa forms lay on the surface of the otherwise bare desk.

"You know when he's supposed to be back?"

"He comes back whenever he feels like it, any more you have to ask him. I just clean the floor."

He stepped to one side of the entrance to let her pour the water onto a patch of weeds, then carry away the bucket and mop. Back at the bus, the driver was already on the first step, leaning down to shake hands one last time with the official.

"You got everything you needed?" the official asked.

Don Celestino nodded and held up the two forms, folded in half, before he tucked them into the top pocket of his guayabera.

A few minutes later, as the bus was pulling back onto the road, Socorro asked him the same question but got a different response.

"And later if somebody asks, what are we going to do?" she said. "You never stop to think about how things might turn out. You think I can help you if the two of you get in trouble?"

"I was asleep," Don Fidencio said, now sitting back up and leaning forward to hear a little better. "And anyway, if I was born on this side, for what do I need papers?"

"You still need them to be in either country."

"So I'm not supposed to be here, but now I can't get back over there? Is that what you want to tell me? Not here and not there?"

His brother looked at him and then at Socorro. "Just give me time and I'll figure something out," he said, and leaned back in his seat.

"Sure," Don Fidencio said, "sure you will."

The bus barreled through an open stretch of highway, slowing down only when the red light above the driver buzzed, indicating that he had again exceeded the one-hundred-kilometers-per-hour speed limit. The buzzer, which was actually more of a high-pitched squeal, was interfering with the passengers' movie, as well as the cassette tape he was playing up front for his own pleasure. The combination of the Norteño music, the squealing buzzer, and the Hindu music from the movie forced him to ease his foot off the accelerator. The only other time he reduced his speed was when he found himself stuck behind a car or trailer with a driver who didn't extend him the courtesy of moving off to the shoulder. On the tighter curves, he slowed down to a sluggish eighty kilometers per hour.

After feeling what seemed to be each and every pebble the bus had rolled over, the old man opened his eyes. Three more crosses marked the curve up ahead. A woman was pulling the weeds growing around the last of these shrines, each of them no bigger than a doghouse. Off in the distance he made out a teetering windmill still spinning, though only one of its blades remained in place. Halfway up a small hill, he thought he spotted a thicket of palo amarillo, the kind his grandfather used to search for when he wasn't feeling well and needed to brew another batch of the stems. Together they would venture out into the monte without any clear direction, but turning this way and that way, down along a creek or up some gravelly hillside, as his grandfather picked up a trace of the vanilla-scented flowers. A moment later Don Fidencio grabbed the seat in front of him to pull himself up.

"I need to make water," he announced to anyone interested in knowing.

"You went at the bus station," Don Celestino said back over his shoulder.

"This time I can make it there without your help."

"Yes, yes, without my help — and then if you have an accident and fall?"

"So then what, you want me to stay here and do it in the plastic bag?"

Socorro kept her eyes closed, pretending to be asleep, while the two brothers continued arguing between the seats: something about a pecan, then a guava; something about shoe boxes; something about sacrifices; something about knowing better. Two days ago she'd wanted to come along on the trip, if only to spend more time with Don Celestino. She knew it was silly, but she imagined the trip would somehow make things between them more real. If they were away from home for a while, people would see them together out in public, like a normal couple, and it would continue when they got back. She had been trying to think of the best way of telling her mother, but then Don Celestino said they weren't going after all. She was disappointed at first, though later that night she realized the trip would have been difficult for Don Fidencio. The man needed more care than they had considered before agreeing to take him. Those times they'd gone out to eat, he had refused to wear anything on his collar to protect his clothes. Afterward she'd tried to help him wipe off some of the stains, but they almost always had to return him to the nursing home with various wet splotches across his shirt and pants. Of course, the old man cared little about how he looked; she was the one who worried what people would think, especially the nurses and aides. And none of this was taking into account how he seemed to be losing a little more strength every day. It was difficult helping him get in and out of the car as it was. And now a bus? She had seen how the nurse's aides struggled to get these poor old people in and out of their wheelchairs, their beds, their restrooms. What if one day he couldn't go to the toilet on his own or bathe himself? What if they bought him the cane he insisted on using but then saw that he needed the walker? Though she had gone to bed feeling sorry for him, by the morning she had woken up thankful that his daughter had put an end to the whole thing. She didn't know what to think when she first saw the two men sitting in the taxi at the bridge. What was going through his head, believing he could steal his ninety-one-year-old brother and run away to Mexico? This wasn't going to make the man's life any better. If anything, from now on they probably wouldn't allow him to leave the nursing home even for a short while to eat lunch somewhere. And then one final thought had crossed her mind: What if the old man gets sick on the trip?

Maybe it was her fault for encouraging them to take the trip. Maybe even her fault for insisting that he introduce her to his family. If they hadn't met, Don Fidencio might not have continued telling his grandfather's story as much as he did. What did it matter if she met his family anyway? Or he met hers? She had met his brother, and it wasn't as if anything had changed. Wasn't it enough that she had found someone? Was she imagining this thing between them was more than what it was? The only thing she knew for certain was that she had more questions than answers, and sometimes only questions.

It sounded as if they'd stopped arguing. Then she felt Don Celestino standing up to follow his brother to the lavatory. She opened her eyes just as the bus climbed a low hill that opened up into a new valley. The blossoming white flowers of the yucca spotted the distant hills, and farther to the west, the huisache splashed orange-and-yellow hues along the horizon. A few cinder-block houses with thatched roofs stood at the end of a winding path extending out from the highway. When the bus reached the bottom of the hill, a young boy was standing by himself near the shoulder. He held a falcon tethered to his forearm, which was padded with the remains of what looked like a quilted blanket. A large wire cage stood next to him as he waited for his next customer to pull over. There was nothing around him except for more and more open range. The gust of wind and dirt from a passing truck caused the bird to flap its sizable wings and the vendor boy to extend his padded arm to avoid being swatted. As the bus zoomed by, the boy was still struggling to pull down on the tether with his other hand. Socorro turned in her seat until she finally lost him in the unforgiving scrubland.

28

The engine lights start flashing, but with no sign that there is trouble with the engine. He has no idea what has become of the driver, or why, of all people, an old man who has never driven a bus, and much less through Mexico, would be the one at the wheel. He tries, for the fourth time, to eject the video from the VCR, and again, like so many other things in his remaining days, it refuses to cooperate with him. He has listened to enough of this strange music in some tongue he has never heard but feels compelled to hum along to. What he needs to do is find a safe place to pull over somewhere on this mountain road and add water to the overheated engine. Because of the dense clouds he has trouble seeing beyond the solid white line at the shoulder, but he imagines the drop is severe and not something any of them would survive if he were to miscalculate one of these curves when the front end of the bus swept over the edge. He eases up on the accelerator as he approaches a group of men walking single file in the opposite direction. But when he gets closer he sees that he is one of these men, only younger, just as he was the only other time he traveled so far into Mexico. The old man desperately wants to slide open the little window and speak to this younger version of himself, tell him how it all turns out, that he makes it back home alive — hungry, but alive — and that from then on he'll take work only when they travel up north, where it will be less likely for these men to accuse him of not belonging where he is and forcing him to go somewhere else, and that later he will find a good job, but one that over many, many years will require him to walk farther than he is walking now, no matter how difficult that might be to imagine. When the road opens up he decides to pull over, only he notices that he has no brakes. There is a gas pedal and then a wide-open space to the left. He sees the highway flashing just beneath him. Of all the buses to be put in charge of, they gave him one without so much as a brake pedal. And the accelerator he thought he was controlling turns out to not change in the slightest when he takes his foot off it completely or stomps on it all the way to the floor. The bus simply continues at the same pace, regardless of what he does or doesn't do, whether going downhill or up an incline. He lifts his hands from the steering wheel and it turns smoothly with each curve. Then he stands, watching the bus continue the same as when he was driving, or thought he was. What he wants more than anything is to get back to his own seat and fall back to sleep, as he was doing before he was put in charge of driving a bus that needs no driver. He holds on to the backrests to guide himself past the other passengers, who don't so much as thank him for his efforts. But what else should he expect from someone like The Turtle With The Fedora or The Turtle With The Orange Gloves or The One Who Cries Like A Dying Calf *or The Gringo With The Ugly Finger? "I pretty much stopped taking buses when I joined up with Pan Am. Then it was nothing but blue, blue skies for yours truly. My little accident wasn't going to keep me grounded, no sir." They're all here, in the seats where the other passengers were earlier. The One With The Hole In His Back balances his withered body across several rows so his wound can get some air from the open window. He has left his darkened parts exposed only so that he can keep hold of his cowboy hat in the bustling wind. "*I CAN FEEL IT GETTING SMALLER NOW. ALREADY I HAD TOLD THEM TO LEAVE IT, THAT IT JUST NEEDED SOME FRESH AIR AND IT WOULD HEAL BY ITSELF. BUT DID THEY LISTEN?*" The lack of empty spaces sends him shuffling back to the driver's seat. At least they're past the mountains and hills and are on a level highway. Everything is so much flatter now. The narrow road has two ample lanes* *going in the same direction and, across a narrow median, another two lanes going in the opposite direction. Something about this feels familiar. He tries to remember the stretch of road from the other time he was here, but he realizes how pointless this is for him, trying to remember something he experienced a lifetime ago. The needle has fallen off the compass. Who knows where they may be headed? "¡Teléfono!" The bus has slowed down and is traveling through a busy street. No more mountains, no more checkpoints, no more buzzer going off. Still there is something he wants to recall about being here. They're driving straight into the sun, and then up ahead he sees what looks like a long line of cars, all heading toward a bridge.*

29

Most of the passengers were still asleep when the bus pulled over. The driver pressed a button on the console and muted the video.

"You need to wake up," Socorro said.

"Are we there?" Don Celestino sat up and rubbed the sleep from his eyes.

"Look for yourself," she answered, turning to rouse his brother.

Three soldiers were boarding the bus. One stayed up front; the other two walked down the aisle to check everyone's papers. They wore flak jackets over their dark-green fatigues, and the one at the front carried a submachine gun strapped to his shoulder. Don Celestino pulled his seat back to the upright position when the first soldier walked by him.

"I told you something like this would happen," Socorro whispered. "But what do I know?"

"Nothing's going to happen." He caressed her hand.

"You say it like I have something to worry about," she said. "You and your brother are the ones."

The younger of two soldiers was now at the rear of the bus, making his way toward the middle. His partner had stopped in front of the long-haired musician and nudged him until he sat up.

"I bought two tickets," the passenger stammered in his broken Spanish. "Two tickets," he repeated, pointing to the guitar case in the next seat and then holding up two fingers.

The soldier shook his head. "Identification," he said. "Visa."

He stood there, waiting for the man to produce the documents. After searching through his front and back pockets, the traveler located the papers in the side pocket of his cargo pants.

"Citizens?"

Don Celestino and Don Fidencio turned to see the other soldier standing in the aisle between their seats. Socorro nodded first, and then the two men.

"Identification?"

She handed him the ID card she had been holding since the bus pulled over. The soldier glanced at it, then handed it back. He held his position as Don Celestino searched his pockets for the missing card. Don Fidencio was rummaging through the plastic bag with the medicines.

"We just got married," Socorro announced, as she placed her hand on Celestino's leg.

"Married?" The soldier took a closer look at the groom.

Don Celestino looked up at her for a second and then turned to smile at the soldier. "Yes, but with all the celebrating I think I forgot my wallet."

"And when was it that you said you were married?" he asked Socorro.

"A few hours ago, just this morning," she answered.

"A morning wedding then?"

"Yes, so everyone could still get to their work."

The soldier tilted back his helmet and regarded the one ring that she owned and that only a minute earlier she had switched over from the other hand. The soldier looked over the seat at the old man traveling with them, then turned when his partner walked up.

"These two say they were married today."

"Married?" The second soldier leaned back to look at the newlyweds.

"That's what she said, 'married,'" the first soldier confirmed. Then, turning back to the bride, he asked, "Where was this that you say you got married to this man?"

"Matamoros. It was a simple ceremony. Only my father and aunt. My brothers couldn't come."

"I thought you said there was a lot of celebrating," the soldier said, then checked to see if the old man behind them had anything to add.

"For the family, yes," Don Celestino clarified. "They were all very excited to see us get married."

"So this was a few hours ago that you say the two of you were married?" the second one asked, also taking time to glance over the seat at the other passenger.

"Already I know what you must be thinking," Don Fidencio interrupted, leaning forward. "Now imagine my reaction when I heard my only daughter wanted to marry a man almost the same age as her father."

"Nobody's talking to you," Don Celestino snapped into the tiny space between the seats.

"Listen to how my new son-in-law speaks to me. Listen, listen to him and tell me what I can expect later on, if today is only the first day."

"This man is your father?" the first soldier asked.

She looked over the seat back at Don Fidencio, then smiled and nodded.

"Only because she had no place to leave me, for that reason she brought me on this trip. '*To celebrate, to celebrate, we have to celebrate!*' Who knows where they'll put me to sleep tonight and what will go on between them — in what ways they will be celebrating! Can you imagine? I thank God that He took her mother and she's not here to experience such things."

The second soldier looked at the first one and motioned to him that they had wasted enough time. Another bus was pulling into the checkpoint.

Don Celestino waited until they were off the bus before he turned around in his seat. "No more from you."

"You should be thanking me," his brother said.

"For insulting and embarrassing me?"

"He saved us," Socorro said. "What does it matter what he said?"

They quieted after this, but the incident kept stirring inside her, especially Don Celestino's reaction when she first told the soldier about the wedding. It was the same face he had made that time she'd added too much salt to the rice.

30

The lush mountains of the Sierra Madre Oriental, their tops covered in the dark and stirring clouds, formed a striking backdrop to the rather plain northern city of Ciudad Victoria. Though it was still late afternoon, the streetlights had turned on early due to the overcast sky. The station served as a stopping point for those traveling south into the interior — San Luis Potosí, Aguascalientes, Querétaro — and those continuing north toward the border. It was the other road, the one headed northwest, that led to Linares.

The old man sat in the café and sipped his coffee as he watched the flow of travelers move from the entrance to the terminal, and a few minutes later watched a new flow of travelers go in the opposite direction. Most of the people moved too quickly, particularly the porters with their hand trucks, for him to take any real notice of them. Closer, though, a gringo with short, spiky hair leaned his bicycle against one of the stone benches. He wore tight black shorts and a bright-yellow shirt that clung to his body. His tennies had cleats that clicked each time he walked around the bicycle. The old man noticed that the gringo's legs were smooth-smooth-smooth, like a woman's shaved legs. Personally, he had never cared if his women shaved their legs or not, though he wasn't about to complain if they were already in bed when he made this discovery. One of them, he thought it might have been a woman who worked in a fabric shop downtown, used to shave them and then ask him to feel them. So he felt them. Yes, they were smooth. Did she want a prize for this? Okay then . . . first prize for the smoothest legs at the Rio Motel, room sixteen, or whatever it was that afternoon. What he didn't like was one afternoon for her legs to be smooth and the next to be rough like he was rubbing up against a shrimper's face. If they were going to be smooth one day, then they needed to stay nice and smooth the next time. A man should be able to expect certain things.

Before he knew it, the gringo was standing before him, leaning over the cord that separated the café from the rest of the lobby. He spoke in broken Spanish, stopping to look through a tattered phrase book, but none of it was making any sense to the old man until he said the word boleto and pointed at the ticket counter. He considered telling the poor gringo that he spoke English, if only to stop him from further mangling the language. Yes, yes, the old man finally nodded; he would watch his bicycle while he went to buy a ticket. It was then that he realized he had somehow become the watchman for people with better things to do than sit around and make sure no one stole their belongings. After his brother and the girl had helped him off the bus and into the terminal, they had gone off to buy the tickets for the final leg of the trip; the leather pouch and the plastic bag with their water and snacks lay on the table before him. His own plastic bag with the pill dispenser sat on his lap so he wouldn't forget it. As if they would ever let this happen.

He opened a newspaper someone had left behind on the next chair. In the photos on the second page, a dead teenage girl, her torso draped in what looked like a black plastic trash bag, lay on a small dune. Another photo showed her wearing a formal dress and tiara. He began to read about the tragedy, a strangulation, and about the young girl's distraught mother, then about the possible suspects. But after the first few lines, he remembered how reading long passages in Spanish, or English for that matter, had become a chore to him. He had to read one sentence, then the next, then start over at the beginning, this time hoping to keep the information straight in his head by the time he reached the end of the paragraph. With the morning obituaries, he cared about only three things: name, age, place of death. The name was easy enough to spot. The age was usually the only number in the paragraph, unless instead of the actual age they put the deceased's date of birth, which meant he had to do the math, and this, too, was work for him. If there was somewhere that he could jot down the dates, he might go ahead and subtract the numbers, but if he was on the pot, then forget it — they died when they died. And the place of death concerned him only in that he wanted to know if it was somebody down the hall from him, one of The Turtles or some other somebody. This, he had learned, was the only way to find out, because the girls who worked there weren't going to say anything. By his way of thinking, they should have posted the news up on the bulletin board, not some other useless information like the schedule for the next sing-along with The Jesus Christ Loves Everybody Women. And who really cared to read the forecast by looking to see if the aides had posted the smiley sun made with bright-yellow construction paper or the dark rain clouds made with cotton balls on black construction paper? They hardly went outside to begin with.

Another group of passengers arrived in the terminal lobby. Two teenage boys with bright-blue soccer jerseys were the first to make it through with their backpacks. Next came a man dragging an oversize suitcase, while his wife carried the baby and pulled along another boy. But then an elderly couple, each using a wooden cane and holding on to each other, held back the flow of passengers, forcing them to pause while the seniors found their way through the lobby. A young man who appeared to be their grandson carried a valise and a nylon woven bag. The old man and woman turned in the direction of the café, until the grandson redirected them toward the exit.

"Buy my Chiclets."

Don Fidencio turned to look at the little boy, making sure he wasn't the same one from before. This one seemed to have longer hair, but it was matted and crusty, with a greenish stain just below his left ear. His T-shirt was tattered along the collar and it looked as though he had dripped mustard across the front. He was standing on his left foot while his right leg formed a triangle against his other leg.

"Buy my Chiclets."

"No, go away."

"But why?"

"Go ask your brother."

"I only have sisters." He held up his grubby fingers. "Five of them, all of them bigger."

"Doesn't matter, I still don't want your candies."

"But Chiclets are gum, not candy." He held out the small carton, balanced on the palm of his hand, as evidence of what he said.

"I don't like gum."

"Buy some Chiclets and you can give them to your friends."

"Friends?" He laughed. "I have no friends anymore."

"But why?"

"Your friends go away when you get old, that's why."

"To where do they go?"

"On vacation."

"On a bus, like you?"

"Yes, but the bus only goes one way."

The little boy thought about this before he gave a little shrug.

"Then buy my Chiclets and that way you make new friends."

"Ya, leave me alone."

"Don't be mean, sir. Buy my Chiclets." He turned his face to one side and blinked his big doe eyes at him. The old man knew this must have been something they trained all of them to do before sending them out with their first box of Chiclets.

"I have no money."

"And that?" The boy pointed toward some coins the girl had left behind after she bought the coffee. His brother had also given him a couple of small bills, but those he was smart enough to stuff in his pocket.

"That's not my money. It belongs to a friend."

"You said you had no friends."

The old man glanced around to see where the hell the girl and his brother might be. When he turned back, the security guard had the little boy by the arm, forcing him to stand on both legs and drop a purple packet from his carton.

"He was going to buy my Chiclets," the boy said. "Right, sir?"

"Was he bothering you?" the guard asked. "Already I had told him to not be bothering the passengers. But they keep coming, like the flies. You chase them out one door and they come in through the other one. They don't understand anything about rules, no matter how many times you explain the way things work around here."

"He said he was going to buy lots of them, but he couldn't decide which ones he liked more — right, sir?" The boy reached for the old man's arm, but the guard pulled him back. "I told him, 'Pick the green ones, my favorites' — right, sir? Right, you said you wanted to buy?"

Don Fidencio looked at the boy and then up at the guard.

"Come on," the guard said, yanking on the boy's arm. "You come here only to tell me more lies, so you can do what you want. Maybe someday you can learn the rules and how to respect other people."

"But he said he wanted to, I heard him." The little boy was dragging his feet, making his body go limp.

"Yes, like the man and woman you were bothering earlier." The guard pulled harder now. "Everybody, everybody wants to buy your gum."

"Wait," the old man called out.

"What is it?" The guard had the boy halfway out of the café.

"I told you he wanted to buy, I told you," the young one responded.

"How much did you say they were, the green ones?" He gestured for the boy to come closer.

"Only one peso, sir, that way you buy lots of them and give them to all your new friends. You will see how many friends you can make with the Chiclets."

Don Fidencio gazed at the coins on the table, unsure what denominations they might be. There was a larger goldish-looking coin with an eagle on it, then a copper coin with the image of a man, an indio, it looked like, and finally several smaller coins with what looked like wreaths of some sort. "This," the old man said, "whatever this will buy." He slid the coins across the table as though he had more important things to do than to be counting dirty coins in a bus station.

"All of it?" The boy was back to standing on one leg.

"Some for now, and the others I can save." He waited for him to take the coins.

"Yes or no?" the guard demanded. "We're not going to stand here all day, selling your Chiclets."

After the boy added up all the money, he looked back at his carton and started counting the packets, but then stopped suddenly and placed the whole carton on the table. "You see?" he said to the guard. "He wanted to buy all of them."

"Now at least say 'thank you' to the man."

"Thank you, sir," the boy said, and scurried off from the table and the guard.

The old man bent over to recover the packet that had fallen earlier. He was returning it to the carton when his brother and the girl walked up.

"I thought you didn't like Chiclets," she said.

"I bought them just to pass the time."

"Well, now you have more time," his brother said. "The next bus leaves in an hour but doesn't get to Linares until after dark. We should just find a hotel so we can rest, then leave early in the morning."

31

After staring at the grimy keypad for a couple of minutes, Socorro finally took out a pen and, on the palm of her hand, jotted down her mother's number. She was standing on the corner outside their hotel, which had fifty channels on the television but no phone in the room. The noise from the traffic and the nearby torta stand was loud enough that she wondered if she shouldn't have walked an extra block to the plaza and found another pay phone. Before this, she had gone to the pharmacy so she could buy the calling card she was now inserting into the card reader. The number on her palm still looked strange to her, like she was off a digit, but she couldn't say which. She blamed her forgetfulness on all the traveling they had done that day. Who wouldn't be a little disoriented so far from home?

As the phone rang, she imagined, as she had most of the day, how exactly she would go about telling them where she was. It was still too early for her mother or her aunt to be missing her. She had thought she would ask her mother about her day, how she was feeling, if the swelling in her feet had gone away, if she had taken her afternoon nap and remembered to keep her feet elevated. There was no need to rush into the news about the trip. It would be like peeling an onion, layer by layer, and slowly revealing what had occurred and how, so her mother could see that the sudden trip actually wasn't so sudden. There was the news of Celestino's brother, the poor man living in a home filled with the elderly and infirm. There was the news of their grandfather and how he was kidnapped as a child by the Indians and taken from his ranchito in Mexico to the United States. There was the news of the terrible things that had happened to the other people in their family. There was the news of Don Fidencio's promise to his grandfather to someday return to the ranchito in his place. There was the news of his need to fulfill this promise but also the unfortunate condition of his health (something her mother would surely be able to understand), and how if the poor old man were going to make the trip, he would need help. There was more, but with these details she thought her mother would accept the rest of what she needed to tell her. And perhaps her plan would have worked if she hadn't blurted the whole thing out as soon as her mother answered the phone.

"And then, what do you want from me?" her mother said, only after what seemed like an interminable pause. "What did you call here for? Not to ask for my advice, not to see if this was a good idea."

"Just to let you know, that's all." Across the street a taxi driver blasted his horn at another driver who'd tried to cut him off. "So you wouldn't be worried about me."

"And now you want us to relax, knowing you ran off with two little old men?"

"We didn't plan it this way," she said, then repeated herself over the traffic and the flush of heat she could feel spreading across her chest.

"You also never said anything about taking a trip," her mother said. "What you want is to go have your fun, leave us here, and then come back whenever you feel like it because here you always have a bed."

"Are you saying not to come back?" The remaining minutes on her calling card were counting down on the digital screen above the keypad, and she was glad she bought only enough for a five-minute call.

"Not if you are going to act like a woman who any man can take to sleep wherever he decides you will lie down, and you run off with him."

She rubbed the nape of her neck and could feel a feverish sweat soaking through her hair. "Celestino is not just any man."

"He is to me, he is to your tía. We only know him from looking through the window when he drops you off across the street. For us, he is *any* man."

"Like bringing him to the house would change things, after the way the two of you talk about him."

"At least then we would know who you ran away with."

"Maybe later I will bring him to the house."

"And when will that be, when you come to tell us that already you married him?"

"I never said we were getting married, that things were that serious."

"Not serious for getting married, but serious for other things," her mother said. "And if he gets you in trouble?"

"Trouble how?"

"Trouble the way old men can get young women in trouble."

"You know if that was even possible for me, it would have happened years ago."

"With a little faith, it would have."

"I had faith."

"If you had waited."

"I did wait," she said. "He was the one who didn't wait, remember?"

"You never stop blaming the poor man, dead so many years." Her mother had more to say on this matter, but by now the automated voice had announced that only a few seconds remained on the calling card. Socorro thought about going back to the pharmacy to buy another card so they could finish their conversation, then realized they'd been having the same conversation for years and would probably continue to do so. Now she only had to wait for the seconds to tick away.

32

The restaurant at Hotel de los Monteros overlooked the plaza and a corner of the church. Since it was barely five o'clock, the hour Don Fidencio normally ate his dinner, they were the only customers in the place. The waiter had sat them at a table near the large picture window, smudged from people stopping to peer through the tinted glass. The old man was sitting closest to the window and next to the new shopping bags that sat on the extra chair.

They were still looking out the window when the waiter came around to their table. His gaunt and slouched posture made him appear to be much shorter than he actually was. He was dressed in a white shirt, black pants and vest, and a faded bow tie that tilted upward like a broken weather vane.

"Would you care to order something to drink — coffee, maybe a drink from the bar?"

"A mineral water," Socorro said.

"For me, a coffee," Don Celestino answered.

"And something for the gentleman?"

Don Fidencio looked up from the menu and then turned around to make sure he was talking to him.

"Bring me a Carta Blanca."

The waiter nodded and walked into the back.

"Are you sure you should be drinking?" Socorro asked.

"What's so wrong with drinking one beer?"

"Because of your medicines," Don Celestino said. "All the trouble of going to the pharmacy, and now you want to be drinking?"

The old man placed a hand on either corner of the table. "In the first place, it was your idea to buy a bagful of medicines, not mine. And in the second place, it has been forty years that I've been taking medicines and it never stopped me from having a beer."

"Before you weren't ninety-one or living in a nursing home."

"So far you've told me all the reasons that I should be drinking."

"Say what you want, Fidencio, but you need to take care of yourself, at least for this trip."

"What you want is for me to stop living," he responded. "If I keep taking the medicines that you bought me, what does it matter? Just let me take care of the rest."

The waiter returned with the order and made a display of pouring the beer into the small glass. He set a tiny bowl of limes to one side of the drink.

When the waiter left, Socorro reached over to the extra chair and set the three shopping bags on the table. "Don't you want to open them?"

"You found everything?" the old man asked.

"Almost," she said. "We had to go to two different stores for the toothbrushes and the deodorant and the shavers."

Don Fidencio glanced again at the three medium-size shopping bags propped up in front of him. "And the other thing?"

"Look inside the bag," his brother replied.

"Unless you bought one for a baby, I don't know where you could have put it."

Socorro opened one of the bags and handed him a clear plastic package, a little bigger than a manila envelope. He turned it over several times. "And this?"

"Open it."

He tried to undo the snap buttons at one corner, but his fingers weren't cooperating and she finally had to pull it open for him. The three aluminum bars, zigzagging end over end, reminded him of the security grille they used at night to close the post office. He wondered what he was supposed to do with a mangled cane. But then she quickly extended the three parts and the handle into a full cane. "See if you like it."

"And if it comes apart?"

"I tried it in the store."

"For you, a young girl, but just imagine a grown man." He leaned the cane against the table. "I try it, I fall, I break my hip, my leg, my head, something, and from there I go back to that place."

"You're not going to fall," Don Celestino said.

"Then let me see you who knows so much. Try it, see if it doesn't give out on you."

"I don't need to try it."

"Only because you're afraid," Don Fidencio said. "That, I can see from here."

"If I can walk without a cane, why would I be afraid of falling?"

"Not afraid of falling, afraid that people will see you with a cane, like a little old man."

Don Celestino flicked his wrist at this idea. "Believe me, I'll use a cane if that day ever comes, and I'll use it without so many protests, like somebody I know."

The old man took a sip of his beer. "Then don't expect me to be the first one to try that thing."

Don Celestino turned to Socorro, but she was already looking at him, waiting. Finally he stood up and tossed his napkin on the chair; he didn't know how it was he let himself get talked into so much. He jiggled the cane in front of him as if it were a divining rod. As he took his first steps, he tried to remember if he had ever needed any help walking. With the exception of the diabetes, he had been healthy all his life, which made using the cane all the more ridiculous to him.

What would they want him to do next? Go to the restroom every hour?

"You walk like it was a rake and not like a cane in your hand," his brother called out, loud enough to be heard across the room. "At least put some weight on it."

Don Celestino spread his legs now, so his stance would be similar to his brother's. Then he leaned forward some, like a man looking for his keys in the grass. He tightened his grip to make sure his hand didn't slip when he leaned on the handle. The lights had been dimmed around the other half of the restaurant, so he took his time maneuvering around the table and chairs in his way. The waiter had left a tray stand in the narrow aisle, and Don Celestino considered taking another route but then managed to get through the narrow gap. With the tip of the cane, he flicked away a cigarette butt. He imagined that if someday he did have to use a cane, he would walk as normally as he had without it, using it more as a precaution than anything else. His brother liked to exaggerate things. The walker probably wasn't as bad as he had made it out to be.

When he reached the far end of the restaurant, near the doors to the kitchen, he turned around. Socorro waved to him while his brother only motioned for him to come back.

"I knew he would try to make it look so easy," Don Fidencio said. "What does he know about needing it to go everywhere?"

"He was just trying to help," she said.

"To make it look like there was no reason for me to be worried and that anybody could do it. Watch him, how he pretends to know how."

He was walking back in the same crouched manner and paused when one of the kitchen doors swung open. A different waiter walked out carrying a broom and dustpan but stopped and held the door when he noticed someone nearby. Then he rushed over to assist the older gentleman with the cane, obviously lost to be off in this dark corner of the restaurant.

When Don Fidencio had finished off the last bit of his enchiladas verdes, the waiter removed all the plates from the table.

"Can I offer the travelers a dessert?"

"Nothing for me," Socorro answered.

"Coffees for the gentlemen?"

Don Celestino shook his head. "Just the check, please."

"And for me, another Carta Blanca," the old man said, ignoring his brother's gaze. "I want to make a toast."

"We don't need to be making toasts, Fidencio."

"Me, not you," he replied.

The waiter returned with the beer, poured it with the same flair as earlier, and left again. Don Fidencio raised his glass and waited for his brother and the girl to do the same. "To Celestino," he said, "the brave one who kept his word about the trip and this morning rescued his brother."

His brother and the girl raised their glasses and drank.

"There's more." He kept his glass in the air. "May he live a long and happy life with such a lovely companion by his side."

Socorro reached for Don Celestino's hand.

"And at last, I raise my glass to my little brother for finally believing our grandfather's story and for helping me to keep my promise to him." Then he leaned back and swilled the drink.

"Because I said I would take you there doesn't mean I believed it," his brother responded.

"Then what?"

"That I would take you, that was all. Why does it always have to be more with you?"

"It sounds like you're taking a child, only to amuse him."

"What does it matter why I said yes?"

"It matters," the old man said. "I was going to tell you what else I remembered today on the bus."

"Tell us tomorrow on the way to the station," Don Celestino argued. "I want to get some rest."

"At seven o'clock?"

"I woke up early to go get you, and I wasn't the one who slept most of the way on the bus."

"Bah, now you want to blame me for being able to sleep. If tonight is like most nights, I'll be lucky to sleep a few hours."

"Go on and tell us, and after that we can go rest for tomorrow," Socorro said.

The old man looked at his brother and then over at the girl.

"I'm only telling it for you," he said. "Whoever else can listen if he wants."

He took another swig of his beer and then poured the rest of the bottle into his glass. "Papá Grande had only ever been on an old mule that belonged to his uncle. La Chueca, they called it, because it walked with a limp. You can imagine how slow the poor animal must have walked?" He jounced about on his wooden chair to demonstrate to her how it might have been to ride the gimpy mule. "And now here he was, this little boy on a real horse, being taken by the one who had killed his father."

"With the arrow?" she said.

"Exactly, and already you know where." He checked to see if his brother was listening. "But that wasn't all of it, because he had also seen almost everybody at the circus killed, even his mother, who had been hit across the face with the back of a small ax. Then there was the midget that they scalped. And not just scalped, because this one was still alive when they peeled back the top of his head."

"And so now he's a midget?" Don Celestino asked.

"He was always a midget, that's the way he was born."

"All the other times it was Papá Grande's uncle or just a man in the circus, nobody else."

"So now I remember the circus man had a midget with him. Somebody had to help him with the bear. What difference does it make?"

"It sounds like you're making up the story as you go."

"Why would I say he was little if he wasn't little? This is only what Papá Grande told me."

"Maybe he remembered wrong — maybe you remembered wrong." He looked at Socorro but found no support. "Before, you said the circus man came alone. You never mentioned anybody else. Now you made it the helper and maybe one of our uncles who got scalped. Next you're going to tell us that it was our uncle who was the midget."

"Then tell me how you remember it."

"I don't remember any midget, that I do know."

"By then they had killed and skinned a small bear that was in a cage."

"Now the poor bear?" Don Celestino glanced up at the ceiling. "What more, a lion?"

"He never said anything about a lion, just a small black bear." Don Fidencio stared at his brother a moment longer before turning back to the girl. "And after that they rode away as fast as the horses would go, crossing fields and small riverbeds and valleys. All night they rode this way. Papá Grande had never been any farther than Linares, and now they were taking him from everything he knew. Already he had some idea that this would be the last time he'd see his home and that there was no one left. But still he couldn't help looking back, wondering if anybody was following them. The sun had gone down, and the world around him had started to grow dark." He paused to sip his beer.

"The Indians kept going and only stopped for the horses to drink water. There were times when Papá Grande thought he was going to fall asleep on the horse. He felt weak because since that morning he hadn't eaten and only chewed on some kind of beans that the Indian had given him from a tree they passed. It was when they were climbing a large hill that they saw what looked like twenty soldiers following their trail, maybe only a mile behind them. This gave Papá Grande a little bit of hope, but they were still so far away." Don Fidencio noticed his brother wanting to interrupt. "Now that I think about it, I remember he told me that it was just before dark that they saw the soldiers. How else would they be able to see so far?" He took a sip, then wiped the edge of his mouth with his cuff. "But whatever time it happened, it was right then that one of the other children, a little girl, she thought it would be a good idea to scream so the soldiers could hear them. And without thinking about it, the Indian she was with reached around and cut her throat, from one ear to the other. The screaming ended right there. No more screaming, just the horses running. The Indian tossed her body to one side without slowing down. And what could they do now but stay quiet-quiet and pray that the soldiers would catch up? Papá Grande said those Indians knew about horses better than most men, probably better than the soldiers."

"I thought you said he had never been on a real horse," Don Celestino said.

"I knew you wouldn't stay quiet forever." The old man used the interruption as an opportunity to take another drink. "Papá Grande knew they were good because he was there, on the horse, and saw how they controlled the horses, how they rode them."

"Yes, but how could he know they were better than most men if he had never climbed onto a horse?"

"I thought you were sleepy?"

"Until you kept me up with your story."

"The way I remember it, they rode through the night," Don Fidencio replied, surprised his brother didn't object. "The Indians stopped only two times to water the horses, but they wouldn't let the children get down, maybe because they were afraid one of them might escape."

"Those poor children, all that time without eating or sleeping?" Socorro turned toward Don Celestino, but he was staring out the window as if they were still on the bus.

"The worst of it was that, after a while, he felt like he had to make water, but there was no way for him to tell this to the Indian, not that he would have stopped anyway." The old man shook his head. "The whole night that way. Not until they crossed the river did they let him go free."

"Only him?"

"The way Papá Grande told me, only him. The rest of the children, they took with them to the north. Maybe they thought leaving one little boy would force the soldiers to stop or that they would be satisfied with only that one child. But who knows, why him and not the others?"

"He was lucky, no?" Socorro said.

"Lucky that they freed him, but not so lucky with what had happened earlier." He took the last sip of his beer.

The waiter, who had been standing off to the side and halfway listening, stepped up now. "Another cold beer for the gentleman?"

"No, just the bill," Don Celestino said before his brother had a chance to answer.

After paying, they walked out of the restaurant and through the lobby. Don Fidencio kept testing his new cane by stabbing it into various splotches and cigarette burns on the carpet. Don Celestino had rented two rooms, his brother's located on the ground floor, and a bigger room upstairs for him and Socorro. They agreed to meet for coffee and a quick breakfast at seven and try to be in the taxi by seven thirty. If they were still hungry, they could buy a snack at one of the stores inside the terminal or wait until they arrived at their destination. It was only a two-hour bus ride to Linares.

33

The same waiter unlocked the doors early the next morning. His shirt was still untucked and he held the tail ends together as if they were part of his bathrobe. Don Celestino pulled a chair out for Socorro. As it had been the evening before, they were the only customers in the restaurant.

A few minutes later the waiter brought out some coffee for Don Celestino and an orange juice for Socorro. He placed a basket of fresh bolillos on the table, turning back one corner of the checkered cloth they were wrapped in.

"I knew this would happen," Don Celestino said. It was now quarter after seven.

"It must take him longer to get dressed," she said.

"Then he should get up earlier."

A man not quite as old but using a cane walked into the restaurant. He wore a black guayabera and a pair of gray pants with sharp creases. He surveyed the surroundings until he saw the waiter motioning that his table was ready. When he arrived at the table, he hooked his cane on the backrest of one of the chairs and then tugged on it to make sure it was secure.

"Maybe he couldn't sleep," Socorro said.

"He can sleep more on the bus if that's the problem." Don Celestino glanced at his watch again.

"What if something happened? Maybe we did wrong in leaving him alone in his own room, not even on the same floor."

"Where else did you want him?" he asked. "Sleeping between us there in the bed?"

"If you want, I can go check on him."

"No, you wait for us here." He pushed away from the table and stood up.

"Remember his age, Celestino."

"You think I might forget?"

A cleaning girl in bleached jeans and T-shirt was emptying an ashtray container down the hall from the room. She didn't seem to notice or care when Don Celestino pressed up against the door. The room was silent as far as he could tell. No television. No shower. As he had suspected, the old man was probably still asleep or barely getting ready, maybe sitting on the toilet.

He stayed listening for a few seconds before he knocked.

"Fidencio?"

He knocked harder the second time and then tried the doorknob.

"Fidencio, are you asleep?"

The third knock was loud enough to hear in the bathroom, if that's where he was. Don Celestino told himself there were plenty of reasons why he might not be opening the door, though he couldn't see why he wouldn't at least answer, let him know that he had heard him knocking.

When it was clear that his brother wasn't going to open the door, Don Celestino asked the cleaning girl for help. She walked over, dragging a plastic trash bag as if someone might take off with it when she had her back turned. Her dark hair, still wet from her shower that morning, was pulled back into a high ponytail.

"And your key?" she asked.

"I have my key." He dangled it from the wooden slat with his upstairs room number written on it. "But my brother's not answering his door."

"Maybe because he doesn't want to come out or wants you to leave him alone." Her slew of keys hung off a large metal ring like a jailer might carry.

"Yes, but he's an older man."

The girl stared at him for a moment, as if she were attempting to do the math in her head. "I shouldn't be doing this," she said as she inserted the key. "The manager is the one you should go tell."

She knocked as she was turning the knob, and then into the door frame called out, "Hello? Cleaning!"

She pushed open the door less than an inch before the security chain pulled taut and then someone pushed back from the other side. "I knew this was a mistake," she said, and moved over.

"Fidencio," his brother said into the tiny crack between the door and the door frame. "Open the door already."

"Go away!" the old man shouted from somewhere inside the room.

"What happened to breakfast, like we said?"

"Nothing, leave me alone."

"What do you mean, leave you alone?" Don Celestino was now talking down at the doorknob as if it were some type of transmitter. "We need to catch a bus, remember, to Linares?"

"Go yourself!"

"Are you sick?"

"Ya, I told you to leave me alone!"

The door to the next room opened and a bare-chested man peered down the hall. He cocked back his head as if to ask what exactly the problem was at 7:23 in the morning. The cleaning girl waved hello to him.

"Now let's see if he doesn't call the manager and they run me off," she muttered after the man had gone back inside.

Socorro walked up as Don Celestino was pressing his shoulder against the door. It took some convincing that he was going to hurt himself before he backed away and finally agreed to go wait in the restaurant. Maybe she could get the old man to open the door. The cleaning girl returned to her work down the hall but kept looking back every so often.

Socorro leaned into the closed door. "But you don't feel sick, right?"

"No, you can go and leave me, there's nothing wrong."

"And you took your medicines again today?"

"Yes, all of them," Don Fidencio said, tired of all the questions. "Just like yesterday."

"You slept good?"

"All night, like a baby."

"Then?"

"Please, just leave me."

"Take as long as you want, but I'm not going anywhere."

"And then what, you think you're just going to be there, standing in the hall?"

"I can sit if I get tired," she said.

"How will that look, a young lady sitting on the floor outside a hotel room?"

"If you can stay in there, I can stay where I am."

Don Fidencio considered what she was saying. He was sitting in a plastic chair against the far wall, as he had been doing since four that morning, when he woke up in bed with his clothes still on. It was now close to eight. When he ducked his head, he could see the very edges of her sandals under the door.

"And my brother?"

"He went back to the restaurant, but I know he's worried."

After a while he leaned on his cane until he could push himself up. He was wearing an undershirt and a bath towel, which he was doing his best to keep knotted. A trace of light from under the door helped guide him. He shuffled in her direction, using the cane to clear a path, first pushing his shoes to one side and then the pile of clothes to the other.

"Wait until I tell you when," he said, then unchained the door and shuffled back to the plastic chair. "Ya."

Socorro edged open the door as if he might have suddenly fallen back to sleep and she didn't want to wake him. The bathroom light was on and added to the sliver of daylight pouring in from between the curtains. The old man was sitting with an extra towel on his lap, where he kept the plastic bag with his medicines. Once she shut the door, he leaned back so he could adjust the position of the bag. Then the curtains blew open and the air in the room seemed to change.

"I better close the window," she said.

"No."

"Something smells bad."

"But not from outside."

She noticed then that the bed was stripped bare and the sheets were lying near the entrance to the bathroom. A dark stain spread out from the center of the mattress, fading as it made its way toward the edges. She held her place as she glanced around the dim space, trying to avoid the mattress and then understanding that the only other direction for her to look was toward the old man.

"Don't go telling him," he said.

"He worries about you."

"Say whatever you want, just not this."

"You want me to lie to your brother?"

"It matters more to me than it does to him," he said. "He only cares that I'm still alive."

When she finally nodded, Don Fidencio thought about making her swear to this, but he let it pass when she pulled up a chair and sat next to him.

"You should have called us."

"For what, if it was too late?"

"It was an accident," she said. "People have accidents."

"But how many times?" he opened his hands to ask. "Old people who are supposed to be in nursing homes, those are the ones who have the accidents." He paused as he glanced at the bed. "He never should have taken me out of that place. He should have left me to die there with the rest of them."

"Please, stop saying those things." She tried to reach out to him, but he pulled away.

"And why not, if this is only the truth — my body is useless, the same as I am. So young, what do you know about these things, about your body not doing what you wanted it to do, what it was supposed to do?"

Socorro looked the other way, then down at her lap. She wanted to say something to him, offer some words of hope or a way to restore his faith that things would get better, but instead they stayed like this, each of them realizing there was nothing left to say.

"Let me help you," she said, kneeling beside him.

He raised the sleeve of the undershirt to wipe at his nose. "I want to stay alone, without any help."

"We can't leave you here," she said.

"So that he can take me back there, leave me like they did already once, this time for good?"

"Nobody's going to take you back," she said, now standing next to him. "Your brother promised to take you to Linares."

"How, then?" he said, and with his chin he motioned toward the pile of clothes.

"Leave it," she said. "Just clean yourself, and I can go buy you new pants and a shirt to wear, like if it was another trip."

"And if it happens to me again?"

"It won't," she said.

"And still, if it happens?"

"It won't, I told you."

"Now you sound like me when I was trying to convince Amalia and her husband."

"Maybe I do." She helped him stand up. "Maybe you were right to call him that ugly name you like to call him."

"The Son Of A Bitch?"

"That one."

They ended up staying an extra day in Ciudad Victoria. Socorro explained to Don Celestino how his brother had been sick during the night, probably from something he ate at the bus station, and was in no condition to be traveling. He hadn't opened the door because he'd been embarrassed for anyone to see him that way.

She spent the rest of the morning shopping for the clothes the old man would need for the next couple of days. By the time she returned to the hotel, she found that Don Fidencio had used one of the plastic chairs to sit in the shower while he cleaned himself. And meanwhile, Don Celestino had gone out for a walk and, as she discovered later that afternoon, located a pharmacy that sold those little blue vitamins he was so fond of.

34

Two men, both short and dark, stood alongside the lonely highway. They wore straw cowboy hats, the bands soiled a dark hue as evidence of their labor. Earlier it had drizzled, and their bright long-sleeve shirts, one yellow and the other red, were still dripping from the cuffs. Next to them stood a nylon sack thick with bristling ears of corn. Empty soda bottles of various colors, potato-chip wrappers, and cigarette butts littered the gravel patch where they had come to wait for their ride.

Don Fidencio leaned back against the headrest as the driver edged the bus onto the shoulder. This would be no less than the tenth stop he'd made in the last two hours since leaving the station. They had missed the first-class bus earlier that morning and, in order to not waste any more time, his brother insisted they take the next direct bus, which, as it turned out, was direct but not nonstop.

Behind the two men, the shoulder dipped and then farther on extended toward what appeared to be a grove of some sort. One of the men turned and called to someone behind them. A moment later, as the dust and empty wrappers were still settling back to the ground, two young women emerged from where the earth dropped off. The same man held out his hand to a woman carrying a baby swaddled in a pink blanket; the second woman carried a wet tarp and a pair of plastic shopping bags filled with groceries. The four adults boarded the bus with the sleeping baby and the nylon sack. Once the bus pulled back onto the road, the old man yawned and turned toward the window again. The bus slowed for a curve in the road and then accelerated again on the straightaway. A wet goat stood tethered to a metal stake near the shoulder. Across the dense countryside there was no sign of a house or a farm or so much as a dirt path leading to the metal stake. Just a goat getting sprayed with the rainwater still on the highway.

They crossed a truss bridge with only two lanes and a while later passed a sign that read, BIENVENIDO A NUEVO LEÓN. At least they were getting closer; the next sign indicated that it was thirty kilometers to Linares. The clouds from earlier had lifted, and what remained of them was covering the very tops of the mountains to the west. The blossoming huisache roused the countryside with alternating splotches of green and a yellowish-orange. Less frequent were the yuccas' lush white flowers blossoming high above the rest of the scrubland. Even an old man with poor eyesight could tell the land had changed the farther from the border they ventured. He wondered if his grandfather had ridden past these same thickets when he was taken from his home. This thought sat with him for several kilometers until he tried to recall the last thing he had seen of his own house, but he moved on when he realized that all he could recall was the dank hotel room he had been in the last two nights, which he was trying his best to forget. They hadn't arrived yet and he was asking himself what the point of it was. All this way to wake up dirty in his own bed? It didn't matter how far they traveled because this wasn't going to change his condition. Tomorrow or the day after tomorrow or the day after, the same thing might happen again, and if not that, then something worse. How far could he be from another stroke or from having to be fed and refed because he couldn't so much as remember to swallow? And more unbearable things, those that he had heard happening down the hall — he could only imagine what the shouts and gurgles and sobbing were all about. If anything, the worst of it was probably more likely to happen than not happen. And so the shame he felt that early morning in the hotel had since been replaced with the simple and irrefutable truth that this was where his life was headed now; he had escaped one prison only to discover that there was no way of escaping his own failing body.

The old man had fallen asleep by the time the baby started crying. Only with the hum of the tires on the road and the soundtrack to the most recent romantic comedy did he manage to sleep through the wails.

The baby was still sobbing when Socorro caught the infant's attention by opening her eyes and mouth wider than he had seen anyone do in his short life. He seemed confused now, not sure if he should return to crying or pay more attention to the lady with the curious face.

"Did you hear me?" Don Celestino asked.

She ducked just below the seat back and then peeked over the top, which caused the baby to giggle and hide in his mother's shoulder before they started the game all over again.

"Socorro?"

"Why don't we talk about it later?" This time she peeked around the side of the seat and sent the baby into a fit of laughter. "I think we are almost there."

"Because already it's been two days since we left."

"I called her once, she knows where I am. What more do you want?"

The baby's mother turned to see what was so funny and then stared at Socorro until she sat back in her seat. The mother placed the baby against her other shoulder, which did little to calm him. Finally she rearranged the blanket to cover the child and give him her full breast.

"She's going to think I wouldn't let you call."

"Why are you so worried?"

"You ask me that question when you know the woman doesn't like me?"

"And you think a phone call is going to change that?"

"Maybe one of these days she'll change her mind about us being together."

"Let me worry about my mother, and you worry about your brother."

Don Celestino turned away, as if he were gazing out the opposite window at something he had spotted on the countryside.

"I don't know why you want to make it worse," he said when he turned back.

"And I don't know why you always have to worry about how things look to everybody else."

He glanced over his shoulder, as if he might need to go to the lavatory. Then he turned back toward the seats in front of him. At least his brother was snoring loud enough that he had little chance of hearing them.

"Sometimes it seems like you're afraid," she said.

"What is there to be afraid of?"

"Nothing." And now it was Socorro who turned away. They were passing in front of a brick schoolhouse, long and narrow, with a chain-link fence surrounding it. Schoolgirls dressed in gray skirts and white knit shirts gathered in a large circle near one corner of the yard, while the boys, in their darker pants and white shirts, chased a soccer ball at the other end.

"How can you say I'm afraid?"

"Then tell me why it all has to be a secret with us."

"How much of a secret can it be, if your mother knows and my brother is here with us?"

"And the rest?"

"We're together," he said. "Going places, seeing things together, like a couple. What does it matter, the rest of them?"

He was still searching for a way to make her understand when they pulled into the central station. They waited for everyone to exit before he helped his brother to stand up and make it down the aisle and off the bus.

Don Celestino carried their change of clothes and the toiletries in a small backpack they had bought the day before. He would have put his brother's medicines in there as well, but the old man said he didn't want to arrive in town with his hands empty, like some trampa. They walked in halting steps as they avoided the direct path of the travelers exiting the terminal and the candy vendors who were waiting for them with wicker baskets balanced atop their heads. As they entered the building, two little boys wearing identical red-checked shirts raced around the rows and under the seats, neither one paying much attention to their mother, who was yelling for them to come sit down. The bus driver, his tie loosened, entered the small, sparsely lit café at the far end of the terminal. Most of the turquoise-colored seats in the sitting area were filled with travelers waiting for their destination to be announced. Three bus lines operated out of Linares, but only two of these counters were open. According to the schedules listed on the wall behind the counters, each of the companies offered service back to Ciudad Victoria at least once every hour. If they were lucky, Don Celestino thought, they might be able to head back north as early as tomorrow afternoon.

Socorro held his hand while he kept a close eye on Don

Fidencio ambling forward with his cane. They had barely arrived at the exit before a couple of taxi drivers began jockeying for their business, each offering to carry their bags for them. Outside, a row of six taxis stretched the length of the building. The drivers let their conversations trail off when they noticed the possibility of a new fare. Don Celestino led them toward a small green-and-white taxi with spoked hubcaps. The driver, a young man no more than twenty-five, wore baggy blue jeans and a white T-shirt underneath his Chicago Bulls jersey. He was sitting on the edge of his open trunk, talking to another driver leaning against the hood of his car.

Before they reached the taxi, though, the old man stopped suddenly and looked around. "I say we should go with another one."

"For what, if they're all the same?" Don Celestino tugged on Socorro's hand, but his brother had already pulled away and was walking to the end of the line.

"That's not how it works here," the young driver complained. "The first one in line goes before the rest."

But Don Fidencio had no interest in what he or the other drivers were saying or in stopping to respond. With the rubber tip of his cane he knocked on the door of a faded red taxi. The driver was an older man who had been napping in the front passenger seat. He quickly opened the back door and trunk before he realized his new customers had no real luggage.

When they were all situated, he swung the car around the

long row of taxis, ignoring the shouts from the other drivers. "And to where can I take you?"

"You know this town?" Don Fidencio was sitting up front with his cane hooked on the seat; he still hadn't learned how to fold it up, so it was best to leave the thing as it was.

"You ask if I know this town?" The driver took hold of the steering wheel with both hands, then shook his head and rolled his eyes up toward the material drooping from the ceiling. "I have spent all my years in this one place. Nobody knows Linares better than me. Nobody, nobody — that I can guarantee you."

Don Fidencio made sure to glance over his shoulder at his brother.

"Those other boys with their new cars don't know the half of what I have up here." He pointed to the side of his head. "Now tell me, with what can I be of service?"

"We came to look for a ranchito that's supposed to be somewhere around Linares," Don Celestino said.

"Of those we have no shortage," the driver replied. "Which ranchito is it?"

"Fidencio?" his brother said.

"Eh?"

"The name of the ranchito?"

"Wait so it can come to me," Don Fidencio said. "I heard it so many times, every time he wanted to tell me the story."

"Then you should know it."

"It had a funny sound to it."

"Yes, but tell him the name."

"You want me to remember every last detail?" the old man said. "Like if it wasn't enough that I can still tell you what happened to our grandfather." He rubbed at the back of his neck for a few seconds, then ran his fingers across the stubble on his chin.

"If all you were going to remember was the story, we should have gone to some other place that was closer."

"Maybe if he heard or saw the name," Socorro said.

"Excuse me," Don Celestino said, "but is there someplace where they have all the names of the ranchitos?"

The driver glanced into the cracked mirror, but he had to adjust it to find the passenger's face. "At the municipal building, there they would have the records and names of the ranchitos, if that's what you are looking for."

"Then to the municipal building."

On this command the driver turned sharply to the right and drove several blocks before he slapped the steering wheel. "Only that today is Saturday, and Saturday is one of the days when the municipal building is closed. If you had come yesterday, Friday, then they were open all day. Now they don't open until Monday. Closed Saturday and Sunday, open on Monday. That's how they do it here."

"One more day is nothing," Socorro said.

"You mean two days — today and Sunday." Don Celestino counted them off on his fingers. "And then another day to travel back."

"If all of you would be quiet, allow for a man to think," Don Fidencio said.

The driver pulled over next to an open-sided furniture store that faced the street. A salesgirl came to the front and waited for her first customers of the afternoon. She was standing next to a brand-new bedroom set. Lamps, nightstand, and a queen-size bed with a carved headboard of an eagle in flight. She smiled at the old man in an inviting sort of way. Her lavender skirt accentuated her dark legs as far up as he could see. She'd either forgotten to button her shirt all the way or the poor button at the top had simply busted from all the strain. He finally had to force himself to shut his eyes so he could concentrate. Then he tapped his hand on his knee just to make sure he didn't doze off while trying to recall what he had been told. He went over it from beginning to end — the news of a circus arriving in town . . . the trip into town on the limping mule . . . the muzzled bear in its cage and the midget man who went around collecting money from everyone . . . Papá Grande first hanging on from his uncle's back and later from his father's back, and seeing more because his father was taller, but also seeing the horses so far away and up on the bluff . . . then not seeing the horses on the bluff, but having a sense he would see the horses again . . . and not knowing what to say to his father, especially since the horses were gone and the bear was standing on its hind legs and following the midget in a circle . . . everyone laughing and laughing, and then screaming because the horses had finally arrived, but not alone . . . dropping down from his father's back and hiding under a wagon . . . but then pulling away in time to see them kill the bear, and scalp the midget and then his uncle, and finally shoot his father down below, and him lying in the dirt, bleeding to death . . . and then the Indians gathering all the children, and his mother fighting to stop the one that had grabbed him, and then her front being covered in blood . . . and then they were riding away, faster and faster, from the only place he had known — all of what he thought he remembered from his grandfather's story.

"It was either El Rancho Papote or El Rancho Capote."

"That first one, Papote, isn't even a word," the driver said. "And the second one, if it is a ranchito, I never heard of it." He looked into the backseat for some indication of what they wanted to do. "What if I drive around some more and see if it comes to him?"

They crossed through the middle of town, along the way passing the municipal offices. An army jeep rumbled off in the opposite direction as one of the three soldiers stood in the back of the vehicle, holding on to the roll bar with one hand and his Uzi with the other. The taxi driver had just passed a Pemex station when he slowed down and pointed to a street that rose as it approached a small bridge. "Over there is where we have the festival every year. If you want, I can show you where."

"I want to see it," Socorro said.

Don Celestino was staring out the window and didn't seem to care one way or another about the festival grounds. His brother had his eyes closed again and was hoping he would fall asleep so the name of the ranchito might come to him in a dream.

The driver turned left and slowed down for the first of many speed bumps that awaited them every few hundred feet. The brick and cinder-block houses were set close to the street, each with its own fence of unpainted pickets or metal bars that had chicken wire near the bottom. The one or two larger houses had stone walls with shards of green and brown glass mortared along the top. Here and there bright-eyed bougainvilleas peered over the shorter fences. The smell of masa wafted through the car as they passed a tortillería every few blocks. In between were tiny family-run stores where men gathered outside to talk about their work or lack of it. The driver honked at a man in a cowboy hat who was riding a green bicycle in the opposite direction. Later he tapped the horn at a young woman wearing those blue-jean pants they liked to wear now.

As they crossed the bridge, down below they could see the thatched roofs of several ramshackle houses that edged toward the slow-moving creek. Chickens walked about freely and a hog remained tied to a utility pole. The houses became scarcer as the paved road turned to caliche and later to hardened dirt. They knocked about as the taxi heaved itself in and out of potholes or jerked to one side to avoid a large stone and, in the process, hit a larger one. Finally they came to a clearing where a dozen empty concession stands, painted in bright reds and pinks and yellows, extended across a small valley like a ghost town only recently abandoned. At the far end of the lot stood a small Ferris wheel, one of its top seats rocking back and forth with the light gusts of wind.

"What you see here is for the harvest, so the crops will be good," the driver explained. "Every year for as long as I can remember, they have made the festival in the months of July and August."

They drove over a low-water crossing made of concrete

and wide enough for only one vehicle to pass at a time. On either side of the flat crossing, stones that once lined the creek lay now like dead fish washed upon the shore. From there they climbed up the embankment and found a paved road leading toward a church and then a fountain that appeared as if it had been dry for several years.

"That was about when it happened," Don Fidencio said. "July or August, I remember now."

"What if I drive out to the country like we were going to the dam?" the driver asked, glancing at his fuel gauge. "Maybe then the name will also come to you."

For some time they traveled the same highway the bus had traveled earlier. On the road they passed a peanut field budding with hunched-over workers. The rising sun cast these truncated shadows in the direction of the road and the passing cars. A Ford car dealership gleamed brightly in the distance, followed by a larger farm-implement business displaying various tractors and combines. They reached a crossroads where a tall chain-link fence separated the edge of the road from two large factories, each with its own smokestack pumping grayish clouds into the sky.

"And those?" Socorro asked.

"In one, they make cereal for people to eat in the morning," the driver said, "and in the other one, they have a dairy — the two of them, the cereal and the milk, right next to each other." He pointed back and forth at them. "We only cared that they brought work."

"So they hired many people?"

"The ones who hadn't left already."

Don Fidencio gazed out at the cinder-block houses and small lots, hoping to see something that might stir his memory. One woman appeared to be washing clothes in a white bucket, but then pulled out a goatskin and wrung the discolored water back into the container. At the next house a shiny new truck with Michigan license plates was parked sideways in the front yard. Two men were setting fence posts and looked up when they heard the approaching car. They waved to the old man in the passenger seat, but it seemed more out of curiosity from seeing a taxi so far from town. He was beginning to think he might not ever remember the name of the ranchito, or maybe his grandfather had never actually mentioned it.

The driver coasted around a wide curve and brought them in the direct path of the sun. He pulled on the visor, but it came unhinged before he could put it back in its original spot. "And can I ask why you are looking for this ranchito?"

"We wanted to see where our grandfather was from," Don Fidencio said. "When he was only seven, the Indians came and stole him from his family, took him to the north."

"They used to tell stories like that when I was a young boy."

"After the Indians crossed the river, they left him there, and from then on he lived with another family over on that side. This was back about eighteen fifty, more or less."

"Right around the time when it became the other side."

The driver slowed down when they came upon a man riding in a cart. The wide brim of his straw hat cast a shadow across the hindquarters of the gray mule. When the driver reached the cart, he stopped along its right side, but then had to put the car into reverse when he realized the farmer had no intention of stopping.

"Excuse me," the driver inquired, craning his head out the window, "but would you know where we could find El Rancho . . ."

"Capote," Don Fidencio said.

"El Rancho Capote, sir. These people want to find El Rancho Capote." He was having trouble guiding the car backward in a straight line and not dropping off into the ditch or, on the other side, hitting the mule.

"El Capote?" the farmer repeated without looking down, as if the words had suddenly crossed his mind. He was an older man, with sunken cheeks and a dark mustache that angled out from the corners of his mouth. When he shifted his weight in the cart, his tan pants rode up his leg a bit and revealed ankle-high boots, only recently shined by the looks of them. A young boy sat next to him, dressed almost identically.

"Yes, El Capote."

"Never heard of that one." He shook his head and then so did the little boy.

"Then what about El Rancho Papote?" the driver asked, jerking the wheel to the right when the car hit a pothole.

"Even less." The mule swished its tail as if to agree with the farmer and the little boy. "Tell them they should look for something easier to find."

"These men and the young lady have come from the United States and are looking for the home of their grandfather — the men say that the Indians took their grandfather."

The farmer allowed his vision to drift away from the dirt

road so he could peer into the taxi, the front and then the back, and then the front again.

"You say it was their grandfather who the Indians took?"

"He was a young boy when it happened, only seven," the driver explained.

But the farmer was leaning over at the time, listening to something the little boy was telling him. When he finished, the farmer sat back up and twitched the reins to make the mule go faster. "Why not take these people to the municipal offices, where they know more and could help them?"

"Yes, I told them," the driver replied, "but today is also Saturday."

"What they should have done was come a day earlier." The farmer was now looking only straight ahead. "Who would think to come on a day when people are supposed to be resting?"

The driver parked in the taxi zone and quickly stepped out of the car to unload the luggage, forgetting they had only a backpack and a plastic shopping bag. With little else to do, he came around and helped the old man out of the front seat and up the three marble steps leading to the front desk. Hotel Los Laureles came with the driver's highest recommendations. They would be near the center of town and just across the street from the municipal offices, which they would want to visit first thing Monday morning.

"Here I am bringing you these travelers from the United States," the driver announced with a wink. The clerk had been sleeping in an overstuffed recliner behind the counter and was now using his fingers to comb his hair back into place.

He pushed a clipboard and registration form across the counter. "Your information, please," the clerk said, pausing halfway through so he could yawn.

The hotel lobby was attached to a women's shoe store, which shined brightly through the adjoining entrance. A little boy sat on a purple sofa in the lobby, watching cartoons on a wide-screen television. His younger brother rode a Big Wheel around and around the sofa, changing his direction only when his mother yelled at him from the doorway of the shoe store.

This time Don Celestino made sure the two rooms he reserved were on the ground floor, next to each other. He paid the fare and added an extra twenty pesos for the man's efforts.

"Then I will leave so you can rest," the driver said once they were checked in. "If you need anything else, you can find me around the corner at the taxi stand. Just ask them for Isidro."

After resting from their bus ride and misadventure through the countryside, they headed out to a restaurant the taxi driver had recommended. Socorro walked between the two brothers, holding on to each one by the arm and slowing down enough for Don Fidencio. Along the way they crossed in front of the municipal offices and only glanced toward the darkened windows. A security guard leaned back with his foot against one of the columns outside the two-story redbrick building. He was smoking a cigarette and chatting with a young woman who had stopped as she was walking by with her groceries in hand.

A pair of splayed goats roasted over an open fire in the front window of the restaurant. The hostess showed the lady and two gentlemen to a table in the center of the empty dining room. After having seen the open fire, they decided to share a large order of cabrito, which the waiter later brought out on a hibachi that he set up on a metal stand. Other than a light breakfast and what they had snacked on during the bus ride, this would be their first actual meal of the day.

"Please," the old man answered when Socorro asked if she could serve him. "I don't know how long it has been since I had cabrito. Sometimes me and Petra would go across to the other side to eat."

"I remember you used to go on Saturdays," his brother said.

"It must have been for our anniversaries, when we still celebrated them. We would go to the Matamoros Café because she liked a group that played there. Not that I really liked to dance so much, but you know how it is. That was the last time we went together, when we were still married, before she died on me."

"How long were you married before she passed away?" Socorro asked.

"First she left, then she died years later, but for me she died the day she took her valises from the front door and left. Like that, I thought of her."

"It must have been hard, no?"

Don Fidencio continued chewing the meat until he could swallow. "Maybe it was," he said. "But to tell you the truth, her leaving is one of those things I don't remember so good anymore. Not that I would want to, but that's how it is. God doesn't give me the choice of what I can remember and what to forget. In that way I was lucky, to not remember the things I could never change."

Socorro waited for him to finish eating.

"And of what you can remember, what would you change?"

"Nothing," Don Fidencio said, and set down his fork.

"Not one thing?"

"Only that I wouldn't be here, still alive and giving people trouble."

"Nobody here thinks that way," his brother said.

"And later, when we have to go back across and I have nowhere else to go, you still think I won't be giving people trouble?"

"Maybe when we get back, your daughter will change her mind and take you home," Socorro said.

The old man turned and looked at his brother.

"You never know," Don Celestino said, and shrugged.

But he did know, and so did the girl, and, of course, so did Don Fidencio.

It was still early in the evening, not yet dark, and people were just beginning to arrive in the jardin. An informal group of musicians carried their instruments up the steps of the gazebo. The French-horn player still had on a shirt with grease stains just below his name patch. One of the two female violinists held a toddler on her lap as she opened her case with the other hand.

Don Fidencio sat on one of the metal benches that was close enough for him to watch the musicians. Pigeons of all shapes and colors waddled dangerously close to his feet. They were lucky he had his hands full at the moment. His brother had bought him the ice cream earlier, just before he and the girl went for a stroll. The old man was taking great care in how he placed his warm tongue up against the frozen treat for a second and then slowly drew it back into his mouth. He didn't know what his brother was thinking to bring the ice cream to him in a cone, when he should have asked for it in a paper cup. And not just a cone, but a cone the size of one of his shoes. Most of the ice cream sat inside the cone, but it was the top scoop that teetered about whenever he licked a bit too eagerly, which was the only way he had ever known to eat ice cream.

The cooler weather had brought out the sons and daughters, fathers and mothers, grandfathers and grandmothers, and so on who filled the square and together strolled or sat on the benches. Don Celestino angled his hand up toward his chest and secured her hold on his arm as they walked along with the other couples. In front of them a ranchero clomped along with his woman at his side. She kept her arms crossed over her chest while he rested a firm hand on the shoulder closest to him, as if she might suddenly try to run off. Some of the other couples carried infants in their arms or in strollers. A few paces ahead of them, an elderly couple walked holding hands as the gentleman used a tortoiseshell cane to make his way. His wife was wearing a stylish rebozo wrapped loosely around her neck. When they turned at the corner of the jardin, they stopped and she pointed at something across the street, then leaned over so she could repeat whatever it was she'd said, this time directly into his ear.

"Look," Socorro said, motioning in the same direction.

A large group of well-dressed people had gathered outside the church. Seven or eight mariachis were forming a half circle in order to serenade the bride and groom.

"Do you want to go see?" she asked, pulling a little closer to him.

"For what," Don Celestino said, "if they're all the same?"

"Not all of them. This one looks like it would be fun to watch." The bride and groom were taking their first dance in the courtyard as their guests clapped in rhythm to the music.

"We don't even know them."

"Other people are watching," she said. A small group, including the security guard from earlier, had gathered along the edges of the courtyard.

"Maybe they like to see weddings," he said. "Maybe they haven't seen one with music."

"And if someone invited you to one, you wouldn't go?"

"Maybe, it depends."

"What about for yourself, if you were to get married again someday?"

She had caught him off guard, and he had to think about how to answer her. "If I were to get married, then yes, I guess I would have to go."

"But not because you wanted to?"

"Then for what other reason?" he said. "It would have to be because I wanted to."

She looked at him for a moment, then turned her attention to the celebration across the street. The bride and groom were waving good-bye as they stepped into the backseat of a black sedan adorned with a wreath of flowers across its hood.

"Why don't we just keep walking?" Don Celestino tugged on her hand, but she stayed where she was.

The sun had dipped below the cathedral tower, leaving most of the jardin in the emerging shadow. Don Fidencio reached over and pitched the bottom half of his cone into a trash can. All he wanted now was to go lie down in his room. If he could remember which direction the hotel was, he would head out by himself. The musicians were ready to start their performance, the last strums of the mariachis growing fainter. Only when the jardin lights flickered on was Don Fidencio able to make out his brother and the girl. They were standing a few feet apart, and she had turned her back to him. And around them drifted all the other couples, arm in arm, hand in hand.

35

The next morning Socorro waited outside in the hall while Don Fidencio finished getting dressed and taking his medicines. A few minutes later he opened the door and asked her to please come reassemble the cane; he had been looking at it before going to sleep and had managed to fold it but now couldn't make it extend all the way back to its original setting. A cane two feet tall would be of no use to him.

When they finally made it out of the room and down the hall, his brother was at the front desk, paying for one more night. A young boy, standing on a milk crate, was working the front desk for his father. He smiled when the old man ambled up to the counter.

"You have a message, Señor Rosales," the boy said, holding up the small piece of folded paper as proof. "I wrote it down myself."

"For which Señor Rosales?"

"The man told me it was for the one who couldn't remember where he came from."

Don Fidencio handed the boy the tip he was obviously waiting for and then opened the note.

I found what you were looking for.

— Isidro

They traveled in the same direction as the previous day, passing the furniture store and Pemex station, but once they had left the center of town, the driver veered onto a country road and a mile or so later crossed a wrought-iron bridge. Don Fidencio rolled down his window to get a better look at the low-flowing river. Two enormous Montezuma cypresses, their trunks flared at the base and ending in long horizontal roots, rose from the muddy shore on either side. Farther downstream a rope bridge hung high above the water, with a couple of slats missing and others dangling like loose teeth. The window had been down only a few seconds when Don Fidencio caught a whiff of the putrid water and hurried to roll it back up, but then stopped midway when they were across the bridge and he sensed something else lingering in the air. With his nose wedged in close to the top of the window, the old man took a couple of cautious sniffs before he allowed himself to breathe deeply.

"Oranges?"

"Over there." Isidro pointed to a grove that now bordered the dirt road. Young men leaned forward on rickety ladders that edged up to the trees. "When I was a boy, that was all they grew here."

"I used to have one in my backyard," Don Fidencio replied. "An orange one and a grapefruit tree, but the grapefruit went with the hurricane."

"Those are bad, the hurricanes," Isidro agreed. "What year was this?"

"In the year nineteen sixty-seven, that is one detail I never forget."

The driver was about to ask another question when Don Celestino leaned forward. "And you trust this woman's directions?"

"My tía, the only sister left from my mother's side of the family, was born not so far away from there and only moved closer to town when she married my tío."

"Maybe you should have brought her with you."

"I invited her, but she was already going to mass. No, it was better that way, for you to have more space."

"We could have left my brother behind," Don Fidencio said. "He never believed the story anyway."

"My tía said that she had also heard stories like the one about your grandfather."

"You see, everyone believes the story except for my little brother."

"But that it happened in this place, El Rancho Capote?" Don Celestino asked.

"No, only that there used to be a ranchito by that name, but with time, more and more people left and then they changed the name to El Rancho De La Paz. For that reason, we couldn't find it."

"And these people who left, did she say the Indians took them?"

"No, those ones, the gringos came and took." The driver glanced into the rearview mirror. "You know, to go work on the other side."

The grove ended and the dirt road turned to caliche. They could feel the rocks and pebbles ricocheting off the rusted chassis, at times hitting just below their feet. Don Fidencio placed both hands on the dashboard to keep from bumping against the door every time the driver jerked the car this way or that way to avoid a pothole. He slowed down some when they came across a large pen with a pair of sheepdogs keeping a vigilant watch over a flock of goats. Up the same road, a lone coyote trotted out of the brush and across the way, ducking under a barbwire fence into a cleared field, and then pausing to look over its shoulder at the old man in the passenger seat.

The road ended at the edge of a scorched field that stretched out as far as they could see. To the right a pair of tractor tires formed arches on either side of the dirt road leading toward a dozen or so cinder-block houses. As soon as they crossed into the ranchito, a small pack of dogs of various sizes and mixed breeds rushed toward the taxi. A mangy chow barked at Don Fidencio's door, causing him to reach for his aluminum cane until he realized the window was rolled halfway up.

At the first lot, a skinny woman was hanging her laundry across a clothesline to one side of the house. She stayed looking at the idling taxi, a clothespin dangling from the corner of her mouth.

"Buenos días," the driver called out.

The woman responded to his greeting with a half nod.

He waited to see if she would approach the car or at least call the dogs off, but she stayed put. The clothespin shifted slightly, as if she might be gnawing on its end.

"What a good day to be washing clothes, no?" The driver pointed up at the clear sky. "There's a good breeze. Already I can see the sun will dry your clothes very fast, maybe not even half an hour."

"You want her to wash your socks?" Don Fidencio said.

"I was only trying to be pleasant."

"Be pleasant some other time," the old man said. "For now just ask her if this is the right place."

The driver turned back toward the woman. "These gentlemen and the lady are looking for El Rancho De La Paz."

The clothespin bobbed slightly, which he took to mean *yes*. A black goat was now sniffing about the basket of wet clothes.

"The one that used to be El Rancho Capote?" he called out.

The woman only stared back and, without turning, kicked the goat just as it started chewing the edge of her wicker basket.

"Ask her if there's a family by the name of Rosales."

The driver did, and the woman cocked her head back while using the tip of her clothespin to point somewhere down the road. He waved to her before easing off the brake and coasting away. Most of the remaining cinder-block houses were single-story, each with its own fenced-in lot. After a while the dogs fell back and quieted. At the end of the dirt road, they came upon a two-story house with a corrugated metal roof that was roughly thatched over with dried-out palm fronds. A cypress with a trunk more than half the width of the house filled most of the lot. In its sprawling shadow rested a small gray truck with a rusted-out bed and a front grille guard made of metal pipes. Lying beneath the engine, a German shepherd mix raised its head from the cool dirt and let out the first of many aimless barks. A woman wearing a black skirt and a washed-out Six Flags T-shirt was picking chiles near the front gate.

"Excuse me," said the driver, "these people have come from the United States and are looking for El Rancho De La Paz."

"This is it here," the woman said, clutching the chiles in her apron. "What are they looking for?"

"Just to see it," the driver answered. "They say their family came from here."

She stayed where she was and ducked so she could peer into the front and back seats. "From which family, there are only a few of us that stayed?"

"Rosales," the driver replied. "They say they come from the Rosales family."

"I used to be Rosales many years ago, but I became Rosales de Gomez, by my husband." She stretched her neck as she stood back up. "Only he was one of them that left."

"Can they speak to you?"

"Maybe it would be better if they talked with my grandmother," the woman said. "Let me go see if she can come outside."

They waited for the woman to call off the dog before they opened the doors. After being in the taxi so long, Don Fidencio took a while to unbend his legs and get to his feet.

"Feo!" the woman called out. "Feo, come here!"

On its stiff and bowed legs, the dog finally lumbered over to where she stood. Since the animal had no collar, she grabbed it by the scruff.

"He bites?" the old man asked.

"Not anymore." She pried open the dog's mouth so he could see the gaps between its missing teeth. "Those days have passed."

The old man wasn't so convinced and kept his distance.

"Don't be afraid," the woman said, then took his unsteady hand in hers and together they stroked the dog's head and back. "You see?" The dog sat with one leg curled under and sticking out between the other three legs, and then after a while it let itself drop to the ground and lay in the dirt.

Socorro and Don Celestino sat under the tree on a wooden bench while Don Fidencio sat on a kitchen chair with its front legs wrapped with duct tape. Isidro had stayed in the taxi, where he was now resting. With most of the clouds having drifted, the large tree provided enough shade for them to sit comfortably. The old man gazed at the massive trunk and its horizontal roots that stretched outward from the base like the hoof of some prehistoric creature that had come back to roam the earth.

"But last night you said you would call in the morning," Don Celestino said, continuing their hushed conversation from the car.

"If it was so important, you should've called her."

"She's your mother. She's not related to me, remember?"

"Yes, I know," she answered, though not as hushed.

There was more they both wanted to say, but just then the screen door opened and the woman came out, guiding her grandmother by the arm. The two women shuffled forward in halting steps, as if the grandmother were dragging a heavy load and having to gather her strength between each stride. At first her milky eyes stayed pointed downward, until the left one began drifting over to one side and then up toward the thick branches of the tree. Her silver hair was parted in the middle, and in the back formed into one long braid that reached her waist. The flowery housedress fit loose around her body but stretched out for her sagging arms.

Her granddaughter helped her to sit down in the one remaining chair and then find the first waiting hand. "Socorro De La Peña," her guest said. "Thank you for coming outside to meet us."

"How rare it is for people to come visit our home." The old woman glanced over her shoulder, unaware that she was looking at the tree.

"And your name?" Socorro asked.

"I have been here so long and raised so many children that everyone calls me Mamá Nene." She seemed to want to say more but stopped so she could reach out for a cobweb she had noticed hanging in front of her and then did it again, several more times, gently plucking at each thread of the web, before her granddaughter could take hold of her hand and bring it back down so she could continue greeting her guests.

Don Fidencio looked over at his brother, who was staring back at him. He could already imagine what he would be saying in the taxi, that the whole trip had been a waste of his time, all this way so they could meet an old blind woman who didn't make any sense, especially when there was a building full of them back where they had started the trip.

"We just stopped by to see the ranchito and meet some people," Don Celestino said, "before we have to head back."

"Why rush off so fast, after all the effort it must have taken for you to get here?" the old woman replied, shaking his hand. "Besides, Carmen says that you're a Rosales, like us."

"Yes, Celestino Rosales." He patted her hand before making room for his brother. "This was something we all wanted to do, to come and visit where our family came from."

"And you are right about the effort to get here," Don

Fidencio said as he took his turn shaking her hand, "but I knew we would find it."

"You traveled a far distance, then?" Mamá Nene was still holding on to his hand with both of hers.

"Yes, for me, very far," he answered. "I am not so young anymore to be traveling these long distances. You know how it is, getting on and off these buses, never stopping long enough to rest."

"Then you should sit for a while, no?" she offered. "When Carmen told me there were some people by the name of Rosales, I said to her, 'Since when has a Rosales come this far to visit us?'"

"And to think that at first these two wanted to stay and not come. 'But how can we, Fidencio? Look how far it is, and then at your age!' As if I were already dying. I had to lower my head like a calf they wanted to drag away from its mother. And this I told them from the beginning, that we needed to go, no matter what, that it was important, that I had made a promise to come back. If they'd let me, I would have walked all the way here. In my life I've walked farther than most people will ever know."

Mamá Nene reached out for her granddaughter's hand. "Did you hear him?"

"Yes, what a journey to make, and so far."

"More than two days on the bus," Don Celestino added. "There was no direct service from Matamoros, so then we had to go part of the way on one bus, and without papers because the office was closed, and then stay in a hotel because there were no buses until later that night."

"No, the name, the name." The old woman turned back toward her granddaughter. "I thought you said you were listening?"

"I heard him," Carmen said. "How funny, no?"

"And why funny? You say it like it was just another name, another Rosales."

The granddaughter rubbed her shoulders and smiled at their guests. "These people only stopped by to say hello."

"Of all the places they could have stopped to say hello, and then with such sacrifice to get here?" she answered. "You think I would not recognize the name Fidencio Rosales?"

"Yes, but you are confusing the man with someone else. Remember that the one they took was many, many years ago?"

"Then why did he come back? For what?"

"That was our grandfather, the one you want to remember," Don Celestino tried to explain. "We came to see the place where he was from."

"We never stopped from hoping, always waiting for this day," the old woman said, her voice quivering as if she might not be able to continue. "My father, he always told us that the boy would come back."

"We can leave if this is going to upset her." Socorro was standing near the granddaughter. "We didn't know this would happen."

"She gets confused, but then it usually passes."

"I know who you are." The old woman groped about until Don Fidencio again offered her his hand. "I know, I know."

"No, señora," Don Celestino said. "The boy you are thinking of was our grandfather. My brother was named after him. There are two Fidencios, you understand? The one who went away, and my brother, who is the grandson of that boy. Two different Fidencios, the old one and the young one."

The old woman nodded and smiled but without looking in the direction of the person speaking. "My father was also named after you. That was why he never lost the hope that the uncle he had heard so much about would one day escape and return to this place."

"Forgive her," the granddaughter said. "Sometimes I have trouble changing her mind."

"And you, talking to them like if I wasn't here!" She brushed her granddaughter's hands away from her shoulder. "I know what I'm saying."

Don Celestino stood up first and signaled to his brother that it was time to leave. Socorro grabbed her purse from the back of the chair where it had been hanging.

"We waited," the old woman mumbled. "That I do know, that we waited."

Don Fidencio looked at her for a moment. It did seem such a far distance to travel only to now turn around and head back. They'd been rushing for the last four days. Rushing to leave the nursing home, rushing to pick up the girl, rushing to cross the bridge, rushing to the pharmacy, rushing to the bus station, rushing to get ready in the morning, rushing to find this place. What would it hurt to stay for a while longer and visit? She was still holding his hand.

"How nice to arrive somewhere and know people have been waiting for you," he said.

"We knew that with time you would find your way back. I remember they used to talk about how smart a boy you were."

Don Celestino motioned to his brother, trying to get his attention, but the old man ignored him altogether.

"So many years since the afternoon they took me from my home. It was difficult, a long journey back to this place. But I needed to return before it was too late."

"My grandfather was Magarito, your younger brother — the one they were able to hide when the Indians came. His son was my father. I remember at the end of every day he would look in that direction, to the north." She paused to point off into the distance. "One day I asked my father why, 'Why always that way?' and he told me it was an old habit, from watching his own father do the same thing. He would stand there and wait until it was dark and he could see no more."

"Yes, of course, my little brother. At least he was able to escape." He glanced over at Don Celestino, who was sitting again since it appeared they weren't leaving anytime soon. "But how many were there that died the day they took me from the circus?"

"You mean to say the festival for the harvest?"

"There was a bear, I remember," Don Fidencio said. "A black one they kept on a rope and that did tricks, made the people laugh."

"A stranger, a foreigner that nobody had seen before or

knew from where he came, some said he was a Russian and others said he was French, but it was on the last day that he showed up. My grandfather said he spoke another tongue nobody had heard, and the only way he knew for how to communicate was to pass around his dirty hat. He had brought the animals, but it was for the festival." The old woman tilted her head down toward her dress and held a piece of frayed fabric between her thumb and forefinger.

"And the others?" Don Fidencio asked.

"They tore off the top of tío Osvaldo's head, and when he was still alive, I heard, but from other people, not from my grandfather. There were some things he would not talk about."

"Of what he saw?"

"That, and that your mother had hidden him in the hay that the stranger had brought for the animals. He always felt bad that she'd had time to do this for him and not for you. Maybe both of you would have been safe."

"She did what she could, my mother. She held on to her children the best that she could. I never blamed her or my brother for how things turned out. There was nothing more they could have done."

The old woman smiled. "But tell me, why did it take you so long?"

He looked over to Don Celestino for some idea of how to answer, but his brother only raised his eyebrows, the same as the old woman.

"No, if someone should have felt bad, it was me. I was the one who saw the Indians when they were far away, but for some reason I stayed with my mouth shut. I watched them getting closer and closer until it was too late, and then they took us away. A cousin of my father had moved to the other side, and he was the one who took me in. As far as we knew, nobody had survived the tragedy that day." He paused to shake his head for emphasis, then realized the old woman wouldn't know either way. "And by the time I was old enough to come back, I had already married and made a life for myself. But I never stopped telling the story to my family, to my children, to my grandchildren. Even then I kept wanting to come back, but the years, they got away from me."

The old woman half smiled and made as if she were gazing toward the sky. "Still, late or early, I give thanks to God that He brought you all this way."

Don Celestino stood up and held his hand out for Socorro. "I wish we could stay longer, but we only came for a short visit."

"All this way and so quickly you want to leave again?" the old woman said. "I was thinking you would stay the rest of the day, maybe even spend the night. We have room for all of you. Tell them, Carmen. Take them and show them where they can rest after coming so far." She turned to one side and then the other, as if unsure where she'd left her granddaughter.

Socorro was helping the old man to his feet. "We would stay longer, but now after four days we need to go back."

"And how can you compare your four days to how long ago it was that they took the boy away from here?" The old woman shook her head.

"Why not at least stay for lunch?" Carmen asked. "I can make more nopalitos con papas for everyone."

"That would be nice," Don Celestino said, "except we have a driver who brought us here and he must be in a hurry to get back."

But when they looked toward the road, Isidro had reclined his seat and was sleeping peacefully behind the wheel.

Most of the small kitchen was visible with only the light from the faint bulb above the sink. Carmen lit the gas stove and heated the two covered pans that sat on the burners. With a match she lit a third burner for the comal so she could make the corn tortillas. On the counter sat a molcajete half full with a pulpy chile verde.

"If we had more people come to visit, maybe her mind wouldn't get away from her as much." She handed Socorro one end of a tablecloth so they could spread it over the long wooden table.

"For things that happened so long ago?"

"More because she has trouble remembering what was good."

Together they scooted the table across the cement floor until it was more toward the center of the room.

"But all of us pass through times like that, no?"

"Yes, I suppose, but it gets worse when it feels like all you can remember was what made you sad."

Socorro took care of setting the plates and glasses on the table, and adding a fork and paper napkin from a roll on the counter to each setting. When the food was almost ready, Carmen brought out a pitcher of fresh orange juice from the refrigerator. She was about to call the others when Socorro asked to use her bathroom and then followed her upstairs, taking care with each step since there was no railing or anything to hold on to until the cement stairs reached the beginning of the second level and the door to the bedroom. A brand-new air conditioner, its thick cord lying unplugged to one side, jutted out from one of the windows. On the nightstand sat a portable stereo the size of a small suitcase, and at the foot of the bed two fruit crates held up a brand-new television. The music was turned down on the stereo, but the display panel continued to pulsate with a prism of colors. The only other piece of furniture was a small dresser topped with six or seven framed photos.

"Is this your family?"

"My son and his wife in Chicago, but the baby I still need to meet. And this one over here is my husband from the last time he came here for a few days."

In the photo they were standing outside near the tree and he had his arm wrapped around her shoulder, though neither one of them was smiling for the camera.

"It must be hard to be so far away."

"I had to accept it. Worse was when my sons told me that they wanted to follow him. And what could I do, if already they were men? Sometimes it feels like that's all I do, wait and wait for them to come back." She ran her hand along the edge of a smaller frame.

After she showed her guest the bathroom, Carmen walked back down to finish preparing the meal. Socorro washed her face and neck in the sink and then used a little water to pat down her hair. With the taxi ride and sitting out in the yard she could feel the thin layer of dirt, most of which was gathering into a grayish soapy water in the sink. Before long she heard Carmen calling everyone inside. As much time as it usually took Don Fidencio to eat, she wondered how long they would be here. She thought that later, when they got back to town, she would go ahead and buy a phone card. Her mother would be upset that she hadn't called again, but more just because she had gone on the trip. She wasn't interested in discussing this with her; she was calling only to let her know that they were coming home tomorrow. Later she would have to promise never to do anything like this again. For a few weeks she might have to come home a little earlier, before dark, just to not worry her. She could take care of herself, but her mother must have still been concerned those times she arrived after dark, as she had been doing for the last few months.

She ran her fingers through her hair one last time and was about to use a plastic clip, but then remembered that he preferred her hair down. As soon as she had it down, though, she wanted it up. She brushed it back and for a while tried to find some way to keep her hair up but also down, neither one of which was pleasing to her now.

They sat on long wooden benches that were on either side of the kitchen table. Sunlight now flooded in from the side door, which had stayed open with only the screen to keep the flies out. Carmen served each of the plates with the nopalitos con papas, then pulled the last two tortillas off the comal, wrapped them in a kitchen towel, and placed them at the center of the table. Her grandmother waited patiently for her to explain where everything was on her plate.

"There's no comparing a meal made at home," Socorro said once she had taken her first bite. "All these days we were going to restaurants or buying food to take on the bus."

"Maybe this will convince you to stay longer," Mamá Nene said. "We have waited such a long time for this man to return and you want to take him away again so soon."

"Believe me, I am in no hurry to leave, not after what it took us to get here," Don Fidencio said.

"Then stay the night and you can rest here. Carmen will fix up the other bedroom for you."

He looked to his brother.

"Remember that we need to get back, Fidencio." He motioned toward the side door and the road, where Isidro was still sleeping in the taxi.

"But this afternoon?"

Don Celestino glanced over at Socorro and then finally looked back at his brother. "No, probably not today. But for sure in the morning."

"So you come for him early tomorrow, now that you know how to find the house, and from here you can leave to the bus station." The old woman cuffed the table with the palm of her hand. "That way at least we can hear more of his story."

"There isn't that much to tell really," Don Fidencio said, and continued chewing.

"The Indians take you with them and you come back here so many years later, and there is nothing else to say?"

He tried to stall, think of some way to change the subject, but the old woman was holding her milky gaze on him. He wondered how he thought he could ever get away with pretending he was his grandfather. And then he realized he had just accepted the old woman's offer to spend the night.

"I wish there was more I could still remember, but so many years later." He shrugged with his palms open to everyone else at the table.

"You remembered how to get back here to this place," the old woman said.

And what was he supposed to say to this? He kept chewing his food, hoping that if he took long enough the old woman would forget she'd asked him a question.

"The other day you told us some more of the story," Socorro said. "Maybe you can tell her how you rode on the horse with the army chasing you."

The girl must have thought she was being helpful. He set down his fork and looked toward the door at the light streaming into the room. A moment later he shut his eyes as he began to speak. "They had run the horses most of the night and stopped only two times to let them drink water. I had to ride on a horse with the same Indian who had shot my father with the arrow. This one must have been the leader because he rode in front and told them what to do. I wanted to jump down and run away, hide somewhere in the dark, but a little girl had screamed earlier when she saw that the army was following us. She stopped screaming when they cut her throat and threw her body down. I could hear the other horses trampling over her, how it sounded when her bones were breaking under the hoofs."

"Desgraciados," the old woman said. "For that reason they had wanted to run them off. That, or kill them all. Nobody wanted them around, not here or over on the other side."

"And later when they stopped, maybe because of what happened with the little girl, the rest of the children, they wouldn't let them get down from the horses, not to drink water or just to stand up, for nothing. And what could we do, if none of us spoke their language?" Don Fidencio quieted after this. The others assumed he was trying to recall more details of his story, but after a long pause he opened his eyes.

"And the rest?" the old woman asked.

"Who knows?" he said. "That's all I can remember, after all this time."

"But you said the other part like it happened only yesterday."

She had stopped eating and was facing him again. It was clear to him that she wasn't going to let it pass until she heard everything that happened, whether it actually did or not.

"What I can remember is that as soon as they crossed the river, they left me there and rode off. And from then on, my life was on the other side."

"And the others?"

"Those ones, they took with them to the north. I stood there and watched the dust rise from the horses galloping away. The army crossed the river later, but they were still too far behind."

"But tell me why you, if they had taken so many other children?" she asked, her palms open now as if she were waiting to catch something in her arms. "Why not one of the other boys or girls? You said there had been at least six more."

Don Fidencio rubbed at the stubble on his chin. Now she was asking him questions he had few answers for. It seemed reasonable to want to know and yet he couldn't recall if his grandfather had even told him this part of the story.

"Sometimes God has a plan for us," Socorro offered.

No one disputed this, but as the moment passed so did any of the influence her words might have had.

"Maybe it was so the army would stop to help when they saw a little boy that was left behind?" Don Celestino said. "They couldn't keep chasing after them and just leave him there. At least one or two of the soldiers would have to stop for him."

The old woman crossed her arms. "Maybe so, but it still doesn't answer why this little boy."

"If he was older than the rest, maybe they only wanted to keep the younger ones that were easier to control," Carmen said, though barely loud enough to be heard.

"And tell me, since when has it been so difficult for a man to control a young boy?"

Except for the old woman and Don Fidencio, everyone had managed to eat all of his or her meal. Carmen offered to pick up his plate with the others, and though he could have kept eating, he slid it toward her. What was the point? Without so much as looking in her direction, he could feel the old woman's eyes fixed on him.

"Ya, some more is coming back to me," he said finally, then removed the paper napkin from his shirt collar and again closed his eyes.

"I told you that they wouldn't let us get off the horses. Riding and riding, it must have been more than twelve hours without eating or sleeping or stopping to make water, and that last one was something I had needed to do for a long time. My father had bought me an agua de naranja earlier that day. Imagine how hard this was, and then for me, who before then had never been on a real horse. At first I thought that I could last until we got to wherever they were taking us, but things changed when the sun started coming up." He paused at this point, as if unsure whether to keep going. He could hear dogs barking off in the distance, but otherwise the room was silent, waiting. "I meant for only a little to come out, only to relieve some of the pressure from not making water for so long. But no matter how much I wanted to stop right then, it kept coming, until I could see my pants filling up like a balloon. Maybe it would have passed, but the Indian felt the sides of his legs getting wet. I had wet the horse, too, only it had been running all night and was already sweating. He grabbed me by the hair and yelled at me, telling me something in his words that I would never understand, but I knew it was bad. I thought he was going to hit me or throw me to the ground and I would get trampled like the little girl. How was I to know what he was capable of, and then so angry? We rode this way for at least another hour, with my wet pants stuck to my legs and other places where I could feel my skin rubbing against the sides of the horse. I thought there would be some relief when he reached the river, but it took time because they were looking for a good place to cross. It had rained hard only days before and the river was high. I could see the current was strong, taking with it tree branches and a large black dog that at first looked like it was swimming but then went to one side. With all that water rushing in front of us, I felt that I wanted to go again. From where, I don't know, since they had not given me anything to drink and only an hour earlier I had let go a stream of water, everything inside me. I was afraid of what the Indian might do if it were to happen again. Throw me into the river to drown? I was lucky that before long one of them found a good place to cross and they all turned the horses in that direction. As soon as we entered the water, my pants began to fill up again, only now it was washing away what had happened to me earlier. The Indians were moving through the river slow and with much caution, waiting for the horses to get their footing before making them go forward. The animals were struggling against the current. I remember the Indian wrapped one arm around my chest and held on to me tighter than he had since he had put me on the horse. This man who had killed my family and now he was protecting me. And me, after thinking all night of how I might escape, I was holding on to him as if he were my father, the one who had brought me into this world." He stopped to wipe the corner of his mouth with the back of his hand. "The horses struggled more when we finally reached the other side and they had to climb out of the river. By that time the army was not so far behind. I thought the Indian wouldn't be mad anymore because the river had rinsed everything away, but with the morning sun the smell was still there. Then he grabbed me by the hair and dragged me to the ground, and there he left me."

Don Fidencio sat back and crossed his arms. No one spoke for a long time, unsure if he would remember more.

Finally the old woman dropped her hands to the table. "At least we should give thanks that it turned out in this manner, that they didn't take you away to live with their people."

"Still, the way it happened," he said.

"Some other way and you might never have returned to this place."

He knew he had made up most of what he'd said, but now he wasn't exactly sure which part this was. Maybe his grandfather had told him some of these details. He wondered if he hadn't confused some of his own story with the one he'd heard as a young boy. Or if it wasn't the other way around. If it wasn't really his grandfather's story mixed up with his own, which would mean he might not have had the accident in the yard and then the other one in the hotel room. It was possible, he thought. And why not? Why couldn't he have imagined one for the other, then mixed up which was which? If he had trouble knowing when his dreams weren't real, why couldn't the same happen when he was awake? But then he remembered that one of the accidents led to him being locked up in that place and all because of The Son Of A Bitch, whatever his name was. So no, it had happened to him at least once, that he could clearly remember. But the rest?

No one had said anything for the last minute or so, making the silence and its uneasiness all the more obvious. It seemed the only thing left for him to do now was open his eyes.

36

On the way back to the hotel, Isidro remembered a shorter route that avoided the long loop around town and instead cut through the country, skirting alongside the orange groves that buzzed with workers up in and around the base of the trees. Don Celestino and Socorro held hands but spoke very little along the way. They kept all four windows rolled down in order to stay somewhat cool on what was easily the hottest day of their trip. Then later, when there was another vehicle on the road, usually a truck loaded with oranges, they would quickly roll up the windows on the driver's side until the dust had settled behind them.

Once they were back in town, Isidro took some of the less-busy streets until he pulled up in front of the jardin. Don Celestino paid him for his services, including a little extra for his efforts in locating the ranchito, and reminded him to come around early in the morning. After stopping for dinner in the same restaurant as the first day, they crossed the street and walked to a pharmacy so Socorro could buy a calling card. Back in the jardin, he waited on a bench near the pay phone while she dialed her mother's number. The phone was still ringing when she smiled back at him, then cupped a hand over her other ear and turned away to say hello.

As Don Celestino had missed his afternoon nap, he was having trouble keeping his eyes open. Their visit had lasted much longer than he had imagined it would. The lunch had led to coffee and more talking, mainly between his brother and the old woman. Twice more she invited him to spend the night, forgetting that he had already accepted her offer. Don Celestino finally stood up and excused himself and Socorro, saying they'd be back early tomorrow morning. Now he worried if he had done wrong in leaving his brother out there. If he fell or got sick in the middle of the night, they probably wouldn't have a doctor nearby. Though his brother wouldn't need his medicine again until the morning, Don Celestino would have felt better knowing he hadn't left the pills back at the hotel. They had come all this way with him still healthy, and he could just imagine getting back the next morning and learning that something terrible had happened to him. Then how would he explain it to Amalia? Against your wishes we took your father from the nursing home and went to Mexico, but then left him to spend the night at a ranchito with a confused old woman and her granddaughter, and it just happened that he got sick on us. What did she care about some old promise her father had made to their grandfather a lifetime ago?

"That was fast," he said when she came back. "Was she mad?"

"She wasn't the one who answered," Socorro said, and sat next to him on the bench.

"So you talked with your tía?"

"No, with my brother Marcos. He came to visit the day after we left."

"And he plans to spend some time with your mother?"

"He said two more days," she said, "but that before he leaves he wants to meet you."

37

She hadn't wanted to exactly, but she didn't want to tell him no either. They were supposed to be packing, then checking out of the hotel, then finding the driver, then going for his brother even though they had promised to let him stay the night, and then finally heading to the station so they could take the next bus to Ciudad Victoria. Once they were back in the room, though, he had started with a little kiss on her cheek, followed by an innocent-enough hug, but then another kiss behind her ear and a longer one at the back of her neck, near her shoulders, and finally one on the lips as tender as the first. And once he had so easily undone the metal fasteners, she knew they wouldn't be leaving anytime soon.

Only when the evening light had dimmed and he was holding her from behind did it seem there was time for her to say anything. "But I thought that was why we came back to the room?"

"It was, but you saw how it got late on us."

"You were the one who said it wouldn't take long."

"Yes, but if we leave now, we'll be on the bus all night, then get there tired, and what good will that do us?"

"Then tomorrow, when we get back?"

"Maybe. Remember, I have to take Fidencio across. Who knows what kind of a fight he's going to give me."

"And after that?"

"If it's not too late. You saw how long it took us to get here."

"That was because we left late. If we leave early, there should still be light."

He didn't respond because it didn't seem her comment needed a response. Right now what he wanted was to hold her in his arms. How was he supposed to know when the first bus would pull out of Linares and after so many stops arrive in Ciudad Victoria, only so they could wait around for the next bus to take them the rest of the way to Matamoros? After being intimate, his favorite part was the time when he could relax and be grateful they had found each other and could be together in this way. Was that asking so much, to be able to enjoy this quiet moment?

"Then you don't want to?"

"I didn't say that," he answered, opening his eyes once again. "We go to sleep now, and tomorrow we see how things turn out, that's what I meant."

"Say if you don't want to meet him."

"You were the one who at first didn't want me to meet your family." He pulled away some and turned over onto his back; it was clear that she wasn't going to let him enjoy the moment. She stayed where she was, as if she had failed to notice his retreat or, if she had, that it didn't matter.

"That was before, with my mother and my tía, the way they are. This is different with my brother."

"And how do you want me to know how they do things in your family, when you tell me 'no' and then suddenly you tell me 'yes'? At least I told you how things were from the beginning."

But he did know, and knew that she knew that he knew. So why pretend? She had explained to him how her mother had been against the relationship before she could even invite him to come over to the house. She remembered telling him that maybe someday he'd be welcome, if one of her brothers could change her mother's mind, at least get her to accept him. And now Marcos, her youngest brother, was here, so why was it such a mystery that she would want them to meet? Even more, he knew the reason his children were neither for nor against them was because he had avoided telling them anything for fear of how they would react. So there was nothing to say about the relationship, since for them it didn't exist.

"Tell me what's going to happen with us, Celestino," she said a few minutes later. "After we get back."

Earlier he had turned the other way, onto his side, so now they had their backs to each other. Lying there in the dark and with the drone of the air conditioner, she wanted to believe that he could have somehow dozed off, but she knew better.

38

Don Fidencio woke up early the next day with his arms and legs wrapped around the extra pillow. Though the shades were drawn and only the bathroom light was on, he was pretty sure it was morning. There was no partitioning curtain or another old man in the room; his own bed was missing the rails that the aides raised every night and then had to come back to lower from one side each time he had to trudge over to the toilet. It wasn't until he heard the sound of something clanging atop the stove that he finally recalled where he was. He smiled for only a second before he let go of the pillow and stuck his hand under the covers and reached for his crotch. Then he patted the mattress under him and on either side. The pillow, he remembered, had been between his legs. All of them were dry, though. In his old head he tried again to understand how it was that two accidents could still be considered accidents. He thanked God that the last one had happened away from that place, away from where they would have forced him to start wearing the diapers that the rest of them did, and from there how long would it be before they put him in a wheelchair or started spoon-feeding him at The Table Of Mutes? Since arriving there he'd seen men much younger than himself lose control of their bodies. Their eyes lost all correspondence with the person behind them, not to mention with the person in front of them. Their bowels gave way or simply shut down for good. They had to be fed once, then again because their mouths would open before they chewed the food. And he thanked God even more — lying down and not on his bare knees only because he worried about ever standing up again — that this last accident had happened someplace other than in his daughter's house, where he would have never heard the end of it.

With much sacrifice, he sat up in bed and placed his feet on the floor. As soon as he felt the coolness of the cement, he knew that he'd forgotten to wear the padded socks his doctor had recommended. Wasn't it enough that he could remember to brush his teeth and comb his hair and almost always pull up his zipper and that he wasn't telling the same story over and over like the one who liked to tell everybody about his ugly finger? At least his grandfather's story had been handed down to him and he was only trying to keep it from slipping away, though he never imagined having to retell it with so much detail. His throat still felt raw from talking so much the day before. After his brother and the girl had left, he had made up so many things he couldn't say where the truth ended and the less-truthful parts began, so that with time it all became the same to him.

He grabbed his cigarettes and lighter off the nightstand and shuffled to the bathroom to take care of his morning business. Once he had turned around and backed up some, he pushed his boxers down past his knees and, holding on to the sink, lowered himself onto the pot. As soon as he was comfortable, he lit his first cigarette, making sure to keep his arm extended so the ashes wouldn't fall on his underwear. What could be more pitiful than an old man spending his last days wearing underwear with burn marks on them? These were the new pair the girl had bought for him after his accident. They came with what looked like tiny alligators on them. At least that was what he thought when he first saw them — now he couldn't tell if they were lizards. Carmen had offered to wash his clothes later today. He would have to ask her then — alligators or lizards? A man should know what he has on his underwear. For now he would say they were alligators.

From where he was sitting, he reached into the sink and tapped off the ashes. It seemed years since he had smoked indoors, much less while on the pot. Before it used to be that there was always someone watching. It was a miracle that he had been able to get out through the back gate. Or that he had been outside when his brother came around. If it had been drizzling, as it looked like it might, he would have stayed inside and waited for later. Or even that his accident in the hotel bed hadn't been something worse like another stroke that might have landed him in the hospital and from there back in the nursing home. He realized that it was only by a miracle of God that he was so far away from that place and all those strangers. And really, how many miracles could one old man expect to have?

39

As he had grown used to for this last year, Don Celestino woke up alone the next morning. It took him a few seconds to recall that he hadn't gone to bed alone, though. The lights were still off, but he could make out the shape of his pants on the chair. At first he thought she might be in the bathroom; the door was half shut. It was possible that she'd gotten up to relieve herself and figured it wasn't worth closing the door the whole way. But she was also modest when it came to her body, preferring the room as dark as possible when they were intimate or, if it was during the day, as it usually was at his house, for them to stay under the covers. At least if there were some sound, any little bit, coming from that part of the room. How many minutes had gone by now? Five? Ten? These last few mornings he'd been the one to wake up first, much earlier and more alert. It was still dark outside. The hotel didn't have a restaurant and the lights were off in the lobby. She wouldn't have thought to go out for a walk at this early hour. He had a feeling he should get up to see where she was, but he also sensed that he might be alone for more obvious reasons.

"Socorro," he called out finally.

He did it again a few seconds later, but still with no response. In the harsh light of the bathroom, he found that she had taken her brush and a few toiletries and had left the clutter that was on his side of the bathroom vanity. The area was wiped clean, with no sign that she had ever actually been there. The handwritten note attached to the mirror was all that she had left behind:

> Maybe I should have stayed and not come — only you know what you want.

And that was all. No name at the top, no signature at the bottom. As if the last guest in this room had left the message for the next traveler. He tried to remember their last conversation, if it could actually be called a conversation, with only one of them eager to talk and the other ready for sleep. If this was about meeting her brother, then fine, he would meet him, shake his hand, talk to him for a while, whatever made her happy. Because he didn't want to jump on a bus in the middle of the night was no reason to leave this way.

He dressed and washed his face, barely taking his usual time before the mirror, and then hurried next door to grab the bag with his brother's medicines. Outside the hotel the dim streetlights guided him along the sidewalk that led past the municipal building and to the taxi stand. Two cars were parked, one behind the other, and he found Isidro sleeping soundly in the driver's seat of the first one. The windows were rolled up, with only a tiny crack at the top.

The other driver stepped out of his car with a cigarette in his hand. "Taxi?"

"I arranged yesterday for him to take me," Don Celestino said. He tapped on the window, but the sleeping man only scrunched his nose as if a fly were trying to disturb his sleep.

"With this one, you might be here all day," the young man said. "Let me take you where you need to go."

"Do you know how to get to a ranchito they call De La Paz?"

The driver blew out a trail of smoke. "How hard can it be?"

"We took a long time to find it yesterday."

"Only because you went with Isidro. He can get lost going from the front to the backseat."

Don Celestino glanced at the sleeping man. "I set everything up with him."

"I can make you a special price," the young man said. "The half of whatever my friend said he would charge you."

"That would be good, but he already knows the way."

The driver didn't respond at first, then said, "However you want it."

"Thank you," Don Celestino said, "but I should go with him."

"That's fine." The young man stamped out what was left of his cigarette. "I was only trying to help."

"Yes, but thank you for offering."

The driver nodded as he looked over at the other taxi. Then he reached into his own car and laid on the horn until Isidro jolted up. "Now you can thank me," he said.

The sun had risen by the time they reached the outskirts of town. From there they retraced many of the same dirt roads from the last two days, passing this windmill or crossing that ironwork bridge. At one point the same old man and his grandson in the mule-driven cart waved to them the same way they had when they first arrived in Linares. A short while later Isidro stopped and doubled back, shaking his head as if overnight someone had changed the roads on him. Before they could turn left off the main highway he had to wait for a bus passing in the opposite direction. Don Celestino craned his neck in time to see the blackened and soot-covered back windows as the bus headed eastbound, in the direction of Ciudad Victoria. He turned around to the front before this image had completely faded, then a second later twisted around again, but by now it was gone.

"You would be more lost if you had gone with another driver, believe me."

"No, I wanted to wait for you," Don Celestino said. "This

will only take a few minutes for me to get my brother. And from there you can take us to the bus station."

"And your wife?"

For a second he considered ignoring the question altogether. And then he wondered what Socorro might say if she were the one sitting back here.

"Really, we're only friends."

"Friends?" he said, as if he had heard the word before but not used in this particular context.

"She had to leave early," Don Celestino said, "so she could see her family."

"To tell you the truth, in my mind I had the two of you married."

"Maybe one of these days."

Don Celestino brought his other arm down from the seat back. They were passing the first set of groves, and the workers were only beginning to pull their ladders from the trucks. He blamed himself for not making more of an effort to stay awake. It was one thing for him to accidentally fall asleep and another to will himself to fall asleep so he wouldn't have to talk. But even if he had stayed awake, he wasn't sure he had the words to make her understand his hesitation. Less than a year ago he had promised himself not to remarry, and not because of some loyalty to his deceased wife but simply so he wouldn't have to go through the experience of losing someone again. If the right words had come to him last night, he might have told her that he had resisted getting closer for fear of putting her through the same. Because to meet her family was to get closer to her, and to tell his family was to say that he was serious about this young woman he had met, otherwise why risk telling them something that might hurt them? And to be more serious was to get married and to know that this marriage, as wonderful as it might end up being for both of them, would inevitably end someday. All of this he had done for her.

His logic made less and less sense to him the longer they took to arrive. Did he think he was the only one who understood what was happening? Wasn't this the same woman who had seen them loading him into an ambulance with his eyes glazed over and the oxygen mask covering most of his face? And still she had come to visit him in the hospital later that day. She had met his brother and seen what their future together might look like if she chose to stay with him, which apparently hadn't been much of a choice until earlier this morning. So what exactly was he protecting her from? And what exactly had he convinced himself she was too young to comprehend? And then he realized that she had already been alone herself, and for much longer than he probably ever would.

They crossed the iron bridge from yesterday and near the next grove Isidro pulled alongside a truck and waved to a teenage boy hanging on to the wooden slats that rose from the bed. A second later the boy tossed an orange down and the driver caught it, then tapped his horn as he drove off. Farther along the road he handed the orange back to his passenger. "For when you see your lady friend again, a little souvenir from Linares," he said. "Maybe it will help her to make up her mind about you."

40

She might not have noticed if not for the wisp of white hair she thought she saw coming from the back window of the taxi. If it was him, he would have to catch up to her in Ciudad Victoria. And if it wasn't him, so be it. She had waited a full half hour at the bus station before going up to the ticket counter.

The driver was pulling over onto the shoulder of the road for another passenger, and he took the opportunity to turn and smile at Socorro. He had been smiling at her since she boarded the bus alone, the only woman to do so. On the road, he would glance at her in the mirror from time to time, hoping to catch her looking back. Of all the things she needed right now. To have pulled herself away from one man who couldn't see a future with her and now to be pursued by a man whose job it was to be somewhere else every day.

After lying in bed most of the night, she decided that even if he did wake up, there was little for them to say that wasn't by now obvious. So maybe he had done her a great favor by not pretending to feel something that he wouldn't be able to continue as time went on. But the bigger favor was helping her decide to collect her things and leave. Because this right now was the first time she could say that she had been on her own, without Rogelio or her mother or Celestino. And really, when the bus arrived in Ciudad Victoria, she didn't have to buy a ticket for the next one headed to Matamoros. She could travel south to San Luis Potosí or farther to Querétaro or, if she wanted, go along the coast to Tampico. She could go anywhere she wanted, she didn't have to be looking back to see if some man was coming for her, she didn't have to.

41

The old man swished his mug about until the coffee turned to a muddy brown color. He was used to adding cream and Sweet'N Low, but here they had only evaporated milk and sugar. He supposed it was something he could get used to with time. Certainly there were more difficult things in this life that a person might have to endure; nobody had to explain this to him. Earlier the granddaughter had made him some huevos a la mexicana with just enough chiles and spices that he realized he had forgotten what a real breakfast was supposed to taste like. She wasn't his granddaughter, he realized, but her name had gotten away from him again, and in any case, she treated him like he imagined a granddaughter might treat a grandfather. Just yesterday evening when they had already left the store, it had occurred to her to turn the truck around and go back so she could buy him a pack of cigarettes, just in case he ran out in the middle of the night. And this morning after his breakfast, she had brought the coffee to where he was sitting outside, smoking. A few feet away the chickens walked inside their small fenced-in yard, pecking at the feed she had scattered for them.

Dew still hung from the lowest branches, making it seem as if the tree were as crouched over as the old man who sat beneath it. This was the first chance Don Fidencio had had to examine the tree without someone talking to him or asking that he make up stories. The trunk itself was wider than the house it loomed over. It was no wonder they had built it several feet away and left room for the long horizontal roots that stretched far beyond the base of the tree. He strained to look up past the first forty feet of the trunk, as the branches became more dense and entangled, eventually blocking out most of the rising sun and leaving only a narrow passageway to see where the sky opened up.

He looked down when he heard barking coming from somewhere off in the distance. The dogs had met the taxi at the end of the road and were now growling and yapping at the grille. Carmen finally yelled at them to back away from the doors.

"I hope this isn't too early," Don Celestino said over the last of the yelps.

She opened the gate to let them pass. "We were waiting for you since earlier. I made some food, if you would like to come in."

"I came only to get my brother and say good-bye," he told her.

She nodded as she led him to where the old man was sitting on a metal chair with his cane hooked on the armrest. Her grandmother had opened the side door of the house and was waiting for some help getting into the yard.

"You had a good visit?"

"We talked for a long time, until late in the day," his brother said.

"You remembered more of the story?"

"Some, but later we discussed other things."

"Then we have something to talk about in the taxi." Don Celestino handed him the cane, but his brother only held it between his legs without moving.

"And the girl?" Don Fidencio asked.

"She left earlier this morning."

"Without you?"

"Because of her family," Don Celestino said. "Her brother came home and she wanted to see him. He was only going to be there a few days."

"And you let her go, just like that, by herself on the bus?"

"She wanted to," he said, trying to avoid his brother's gaze. "It was her idea."

The old woman and her granddaughter were now standing near them.

Don Celestino reached down to help him get to his feet. "We should get going, eh?"

"You have to go alone."

"Why, you feel bad?" His brother wasn't moving from the chair.

"Not because of that," the old woman said.

"And then?"

"They invited me to stay, to live here in the house." Don Fidencio poked at the ground with his cane.

Don Celestino tried to smile at the two women before he looked at his brother. "But we have to go back, remember?"

"What I remember is where I have to go if I let you take me back."

"Maybe Amalia will change her mind, after she sees you were strong enough to make the trip."

"That's what I was thinking when we started talking about coming here," Don Fidencio said. "Then last night they took me into town so I could use the phone to call her."

"Knowing that she was just going to blame me?"

"She never mentioned you. All she cared about was that nothing had happened to me. I told her it was my idea to leave, and now this, what I told you."

"And she believed you?"

"What else was she going to do? She argued with me like her mother used to, but I told her I had made up my mind. Then she told me that if I came back I could live with her and her family, that she would talk to you know who." The old man laughed to himself. "Suddenly I have so many places to live — everybody wants me for themselves."

"That's what you wanted, no? To go live somewhere else?"

"It was, but I can see now it wouldn't last and they would send me back and this time for good. No, it would be better for me to just stay here."

"You talk like this is already decided," Don Celestino said, then reached for his brother's arm. "It was nice that they offered this to you, but the decision isn't for them to make."

"If the man wants to stay, tell me who else needs to decide?" the old woman said.

"I only want to do what is best for him, to make sure he's taken care of."

"And you know better than he does?"

Don Celestino looked back at his brother, hoping to put an end to this discussion. They would have been halfway to the bus station by now if he had simply gotten into the taxi. "Can I talk to you over here?"

Then he helped him to stand up from his chair, and together they walked toward the shade. The sun was filtering through the branches, causing the delicate light to shift from one brother to the other.

"Why are you doing this, Fidencio?"

"Just to live in peace."

"You can do that back on the other side," he said. "We need to go now."

"Then go."

"Not without you."

"What you need to do is go find the girl and stop worrying about an old man."

"This wasn't how we planned it."

"And tell me, what is it that happens exactly as we plan it? Do you think I planned to be so old, with my body failing me in so many ways? Who plans such things?"

"They can take care of you better over there, when you need to go to the doctor's office or if you have to go to the hospital."

"Ya, I have seen all I want to of those places," Don Fidencio said. "And anyway, if God is good to me, it won't matter."

"These poor women are going to get tired if you keep talking that way, always about being sick or dying."

"Whether I open my mouth or not will not change things."

"We never said anything about this, only about the trip to see the ranchito, nothing more."

Don Fidencio placed his hand on his younger brother's shoulder. "You were good to offer that. But you also promised me that I would never have to go back."

"I only promised to take you on the trip."

"So you took me, now I want to stay." He smiled and patted his brother's shoulder.

"You were never going to go back with us, were you? You planned this, knowing that you would find a way not to go back."

"What does it matter?"

"You could have at least told me."

"How many times did I say I wanted out of that place?" he said. "And how many times did you listen to me?"

"I wanted to help you."

"You did," he said. "Now you should worry about you and the girl."

Don Celestino wanted to argue with him but wasn't sure what to say anymore or if there was anything left to say. They headed back to where the women were standing and together walked toward the taxi. When they arrived at the fence, Don Celestino turned aside and leaned on one of the posts until his brother was standing alongside him. He felt his arms wanting to tremble in the moment and was calmed only when he finally held his brother's frame.

"Take care of yourself," Don Celestino said.

"You do the same."

"Maybe me and Socorro could come see you later?" he said as he pulled away. "Now that we know how to find the place."

The old man began to say something, but then stopped and only nodded. "Yes, maybe you will."

Isidro had come around to open the taxi door, and without turning Don Celestino stepped in, forcing himself to not look back at the others waving from under the tree.

"Go on," he said.

"To the station?"

"Tell me something," he said, leaning forward. "How long would it take if you were to drive me to Ciudad Victoria?"

Isidro turned to look back. "That's a long way, maybe an hour and a half, maybe a little more."

"But still faster than the bus?"

"Much faster."

The taxi began to coast away, moving slowly in order to make room for the dogs that were barking at the tires. They had traveled only to the end of the road when Don Celestino noticed his brother's plastic shopping bag on the floor, and he said, "Wait, stop the car."

Isidro slammed on the brakes in the middle of the road, sending up a haze of gravel and dust. But when Don Celestino looked inside the bag, the pill dispenser was still packed and the extra vials hadn't been opened. Everything was the same as it was when they left the pharmacy five days earlier.

"Then what?" the driver turned to ask. "I go back or not?"

Don Fidencio and the two women were standing beneath the tree, gazing at the idling car. "Maybe he forgot something," the granddaughter said.

"Who forgot?" The old woman tugged on her granddaughter's shoulder. "Tell me what you see, what did he forget?"

But just then the brake lights faded and the taxi continued down the road.

"Nobody," Don Fidencio said, and then he waved. "Nobody forgot anything."

Acknowledgments

I am grateful to so many of you. To Becky, for making room in our lives for this novel. To my family, immediate and extended, for always being there for me. To Armando Leal Ríos, José Skinner, Dr. Victor M. Gonzalez Jr., Dr. Carlos Pestana, Mando Hinojos, and John "TJ" Gonzales, as well as the staffs of the Hays Nursing Center, Spanish Meadows Nursing and Rehab, and Ebony Lake Healthcare Center, for all their expertise, and graciousness in sharing it. To Tony Zavaleta, Jim Priest, and Shawn Isbell, for providing shelter and a place to write. To José Limón, Jim Garrison, and Richard Flores, for their support at a crucial time. To Richard Abate, for his vigilance and friendship. To Reagan Arthur, for her patience and wisdom. And to tío Nico, for remembering.

About the Author

Oscar Casares was born in the border town of Brownsville, Texas, the setting of his critically acclaimed story collection, *Brownsville.* He has been the recipient of a National Endowment for the Arts Literature Fellowship, and he is a graduate of the Iowa Writers' Workshop. He now teaches creative writing at the University of Texas in Austin, where he lives with his wife and children. *Amigoland* is his first novel.

BACK BAY · READERS' PICK

Reading Group Guide

AMIGOLAND

A novel by

OSCAR CASARES

Crossing the Border Without Losing Your Past

by Oscar Casares

This essay originally appeared on the op-ed page of the New York Times *on September 16, 2003.*

Along with it being diez y seis de septiembre, Mexican Independence Day, today is my father's eighty-ninth birthday. Everardo Issasi Casares was born in 1914, a little more than a hundred years after Miguel Hidalgo y Costilla rang the church bells of Dolores, summoning his parishioners to rise up against the Spaniards.

This connection has always been important in my family. Though my father was born in the United States, he considers himself a Mexicano. To him, ancestry is what determines your identity. If you have Mexican blood, you are Mexican, whether you were born in Mexico City or New York City. This is not to say he denies his American citizenship — he votes, pays taxes, and served in the army. But his identity is tied to the past. His family came from Mexico, so like them he is Mexicano, punto, end of discussion.

In my hometown, Brownsville, Texas, almost everyone I

know is Mexicano: neighbors, teachers, principals, dropouts, doctors, lawyers, drug dealers, priests. Rich and poor, short and tall, fat and skinny, dark- and light-skinned. Every year our Mexican heritage is celebrated in a four-day festival called Charro Days. Men grow beards; mothers draw mustaches on their little boys and dress their little girls like Mexican peasants; the brave compete in a jalapeño-eating contest. But the celebration also commemorates the connection between two neighboring countries, opening with an exchange of gritos (traditional cowboy calls you might hear in a Mexican movie) between a representative from Matamoros, Mexico, standing on one side of the International Bridge and a Brownsville representative standing on the other.

Like many Americans whose families came to this country from somewhere else, many children of Mexican immigrants struggle with their identity, as our push to fully assimilate is met with an even greater pull to remain anchored to our family's country of origin. This is especially true when that country is less than a quarter of a mile away — the width of the Rio Grande — from the new one. We learn both cultures as effortlessly as we do two languages. We learn quickly that we can exist simultaneously in both worlds, and that our home exists neither here nor there but in the migration between these two forces.

But for Mexican-Americans and other immigrants from Spanish-speaking countries who have been lumped into categories like Latino or Hispanic, this struggle has become even more pronounced over the last few years as we have grown into the largest minority group in the United States. Our culture has been both embraced and exploited by advertisers, politicians, and the media. And as we move, individually, from our small communities, where our identity is clear, we enter a world that wants to assign us a label of its choosing.

When I left Brownsville in 1985 to start school at the University of Texas at Austin, one of the first things I was asked was, "What are you?" "I'm Mexican," I told the guy, who was thrown off by my height and light skin. "Really, what part of Mexico are you from?" he asked, which led me to explain I was really from Brownsville, but my parents were Mexican. "Really, what part of Mexico?" Here again I had to admit they weren't really born in Mexico and neither were my grandparents or great-grandparents. "Oh," he said, "you're Mexican-American, is what you are."

Mexican-American. I imagined a 300-mile-long hyphen that connected Brownsville to Austin, a bridge between my old and new world. Not that I hadn't seen this word combination, Mexican-American, on school applications, but I couldn't remember the words being spoken to me directly. In Brownsville, I always thought of myself as being equally Mexican and American.

When I graduated that label was again redefined. One of my first job interviews was at an advertising agency, where I was taken on a tour: the media department, the creative department, the account-services department, the Hispanic department. This last department specialized in marketing products to Spanish-speaking consumers. In the group were men and women from Mexico, Puerto Rico, and California, but together they were Hispanic. I was hired to work in another department, but suddenly everyone was referring to me as Hispanic.

Hispanic? Where was the Mexican in me? Where was the hyphen? I didn't want to be Hispanic. The word reminded me of those Mexican-Americans who preferred to say their families came from Spain, which they felt somehow increased their social status. Just hearing the word *Hispanic* reminded me, too, of people who used the word *Spanish* to refer to Mexicans. "The Spanish like to get wild at their fiestas," they would say, or, "You Spanish people sure do have a lot of babies."

In this same way, the word *Hispanic* seemed to want to be more user-friendly, especially when someone didn't want to say the *M* word: *Mexican*. Except it did slip out occasionally. I remember standing in my supervisor's office as he described calling the police after he saw a car full of "Mexicans" drive through his suburban neighborhood.

Away from the border, the word *Mexican* had come to mean dirty, shiftless, drunken, lustful, criminal. I still cringe whenever I think someone might say the word. But usually it happens unexpectedly, as though the person has pulled a knife on me. I feel the sharp words up against my gut. Because of my appearance, people often say things in front of me they wouldn't say if they knew my real ethnicity — not Hispanic, Latino, or even Mexican-American. I am, like my father, Mexican, and on this day of independence, I say this with particular pride.

A conversation with Oscar Casares

Tell us about the experience of writing your first novel. In what ways was it challenging, and how did it differ from writing a story collection like Brownsville*?*

The challenge for me was finding a story that I felt could sustain a reader's attention throughout the length of a novel. Though most of the novels I read are interesting on some level and certainly well written, they also tend to drag after a while, which is something that happens much less with short stories. The length of the average novel obviously has a lot to do with how difficult it is to keep the reader engaged. But having first written a story collection, I knew there was also an urgency to the short form that I wanted to maintain.

In Amigoland, *you write about old age with humor, depressing reality, and poignancy. What is it like writing older characters as a younger man? How were you able to put yourself in that mind-set?*

I remember a reviewer pointed out all the older characters in my first book, which at the time totally caught me off guard, since I wasn't aware of how many there really were. My parents had me late in life, my father being fifty, and my mother forty-two. They had just celebrated their twenty-fifth wedding anniversary. This was back in the 1960s, before so many people were having children at that age. My father used to tell me people were always confusing him for my grandfather. Because of the experience of growing up with older parents, I guess I always had a slightly different perspective and maybe understood something about what they were going through as they aged. Halfway through my writing the novel, my father, who had just turned ninety, fell and broke his hip, which led to his spending the last three years of his life in a nursing home. This experience, which was possibly one of the most difficult for our family, also brought me closer to my father in ways I would never have imagined.

This is a novel about brothers and what it means to be family. What is your relationship like with your siblings and your family?

Because my siblings are so much older than I am, I sort of grew up as an only child. By the time I was born, my oldest brother, Noel, was already married with two kids; my brother Idoluis was a student at the University of Texas and would soon be in Vietnam; and my sister Sylvia, who was still at home, would later move away to college when I was in the first grade. Though there was this huge gap in our ages, my parents always stressed that we needed to get along, watch out for each other. It stayed with us all these years; enough that in a pinch we each know someone will be there for us.

Amigoland *is based in part on your own family's history. Tell us about the autobiographical details that influenced your book. Were you able to uncover any of the truth behind your family stories?*

I'm not sure if I have ever written anything that wasn't to some degree based on my family's history. In the case of the novel, the story within the story — that of the grandfather being kidnapped in Mexico by Indians and brought across the border to the United States — is based on the story of my own great-great-grandfather's kidnapping in northern Mexico in 1850. This was perhaps the first story I ever heard my Tío Nico, my father's youngest brother, tell me when I was growing up. The only problem was that my father thought the story was all made up, as does Don Celestino in the novel.

I grew up not sure whom to believe, so when I started writing about my family in Mexico I wanted at least to know that the story was plausible, that something like this had in fact occurred at this place and time. In 2002, I traveled to Monterrey, Mexico, and met with the archivist of Nuevo León, the northern state where the incident took place. We met only long enough for him to hand me four books he had written about the Indian raids of the mid-1800s. I stopped my research at this point and started writing.

Discuss how storytelling in your family laid the seeds for your eventual development as a writer. What initially inspired you, and what did you first write about?

It always surprises people when I tell them I never read as a kid and had no literary background before I started writing in 1996. But the truth is my literary experience came in the form of a strong oral tradition. Two of my uncles, Tío Hector and Tío Nico, would come over to the house and tell these incredible tales about our family's history along the border. Hearing their stories was the only thing that brought me inside the house or made me want to turn off the TV.

When I first moved away from Brownsville, and then later Texas, telling these stories was part of what kept me connected to my home. When I first started writing, I basically transcribed these early stories, which was great practice because I obviously already knew the beginning, middle, and end of each one. Now all I had to do was learn how to tell these same stories on paper and then eventually find my own.

The dividing line between Mexico and America is both real and fluid in your writing. In what ways did you try to draw out both the similarities and differences between life on either side of the border?

I think one of the major misconceptions is that there is a clear and distinct line, particularly along the border region. The reality is that the cultures and values of each country have spilled over this supposed line, at times making it difficult to know which country might have influenced the other. Some of this blurring occurs in the novel when we see how the brothers' immediate families are fractured in different but similar ways as those of their distant relatives in Mexico. In each case, we have situations where people have left their families behind in order to find a better way of life. And, of course, neither side of the border has a monopoly on this particular desire.

Questions and topics for discussion

1. Don Fidencio and Don Celestino constantly bicker with each other, but they have more in common than they would admit. What traits do the two men share? How do these similarities influence their relationship?

2. *Amigoland* explores the way family stories survive over time. What stories have been passed down in your family? Have they been reinterpreted, embellished, or debated? How so?

3. What do you think of Amalia's decision to put Don Fidencio in a nursing home? Do you think her father could ever forgive her — or understand her decision?

4. Why do you think Don Fidencio gives everyone in the nursing home a nickname? Do you feel there's a reason for this beyond his failing memory? What does this show about his relationship with his fellow residents? And how might this lend irony to the name of the nursing home — and the title of the novel?

5. Discuss the borders that exist between Socorro and Don Celestino — both geographic and social. How do those borders affect their relationship?

6. The novel's narrative point of view shifts among the three main characters, allowing readers to come to know and understand each of them. Which of the three characters did you empathize with the most, and why?

7. When describing Don Fidencio's realization about old age on the road trip, the author writes that "he had escaped one prison only to discover that there was no way of escaping his own failing body." Did *Amigoland* change your perception of the elderly or the aging process? How so?

8. In the course of the novel we are made privy to several of Don Fidencio's dream sequences, which are moments when time, memory, and reality collapse. What meaning did you find in these passages? Do they symbolize anything about the frustrations and futility of old age?

9. Why do you think Don Celestino was so hesitant to acknowledge his relationship with Socorro?

10. Oscar Casares makes it clear that sexism and certain stereotypes still persist. How does Socorro conform to and break these stereotypes in her roles as a wife, widow, and mistress?

11. What do you think drives Socorro to push Don Celestino so strongly to reconnect with his brother? Do you think it is partly out of her desire to connect with Don Celestino on a deeper level?

12. How does Oscar Casares convey the different flavor of life in Mexico compared to Texas once the trio crosses the border on their road trip? How do the people the trio encounters along the way illuminate the character of the country?

13. Do you believe Don Celestino will be able to give more to his relationship with Socorro after they return from the trip? If so, what do you think changes his outlook on their relationship?

14. Don Fidencio and Don Celestino are both older men in need of reawakenings, and their road trip is something like a quest to reclaim their dignity in old age. Do you think they succeed in accomplishing this goal by the end of the journey?

15. Why do you think Don Fidencio was content to stay in Mexico with Carmen and Mamá Nene? What did he find there, and how was what he discovered meaningful to him at the end of his life?

16. In the end, it is the journey embarked upon by the three main characters that teaches them the most about themselves. Discuss why the journey itself is more important to the story of *Amigoland* than learning the truth about the Rosaleses' grandfather.

Oscar Casares's suggested reading list

Notes of a Native Son by James Baldwin

Women in Their Beds by Gina Berriault

The Family of Pascual Duarte by Camilo José Cela

Slouching Towards Bethlehem by Joan Didion

Lost in the City by Edward P. Jones

The Labyrinth of Solitude by Octavio Paz

Days of Obligation: An Argument with My Mexican Father by Richard Rodriguez

Pedro Páramo by Juan Rulfo

A Sport and a Pastime by James Salter

The Collected Stories of Eudora Welty

Also by Oscar Casares

BROWNSVILLE

"A loving, rueful book. . . . Casares has a lively eye for human comedy. . . . Although the stories aren't linked by shared characters, they all so vividly evoke Casares's hometown that they seem to suggest a single narrative, similar in vein to James Joyce's *Dubliners*."

— Michael Upchurch, *Seattle Times*

"Just about perfect. . . . Casares's characters are border-town castaways with one foot in Texas and the other in Mexico. Their stories, likewise, are Tex-Mex dramedies, sad and yet very funny." — Gregory Kirschling, *Entertainment Weekly*

"This is the real thing, the real life of South Texas Mexicanos, without the mumbo jumbo. . . . Mr. Casares's prose style is clear and straightforward, occasionally and naturally mixing in Spanish, and he can also turn a phrase."

— Ed Garcia, *Dallas Morning News*

"Marvelous . . . resembling early Steinbeck work more than anything else." — Carolyn See, *Washington Post*

"Casares's readers will be tempted to draw a parallel with Flannery O'Connor, whose stories are also populated by wisecrackers and their foils."

— Roger Gathman, *Austin Chronicle*

"What Casares has achieved is rare: a kind of choral view of a culture that is at the same time remarkable for the individuality of the people portrayed and the variety of the stories. . . . This author loves his characters and their home, and readers will, too." — Sandra Scofield, *Chicago Tribune*